The Sanctuary
of Apollo Hylates

EXCAVATIONS AT KOURION, CYPRUS

Editor
David Soren

The Sanctuary
of Apollo Hylates at
Kourion, Cyprus

Edited by
David Soren

The University of Arizona Press
Tucson

About the Editor

DAVID SOREN received his B.A. from Dartmouth College in 1968 and his Ph.D. from Harvard University in 1972. The originator and director of the continuing American excavations at the city of Kourion, Cyprus, he is head of the Classics Department at the University of Arizona and a guest curator and lecturer at the American Museum of Natural History in New York.

THE UNIVERSITY OF ARIZONA PRESS

Copyright © 1987
The Arizona Board of Regents
All Rights Reserved
Manufactured in the U.S.A.

Library of Congress Cataloging-in-Publication Data

The Sanctuary of Apollo Hylates at Kourion, Cyprus.

(Excavations at Kourion, Cyprus)
Bibliography: p.
Includes index.   88-10862
1. Sanctuary of Apollo Hylates (Kourion) 2. Excavations (archaeology)—Cyprus. 3. Cyprus—Antiquities.
I. Soren, David. II. Series.
DS54.95.K68S26 1987   939′.37   87-5917
ISBN 0-8165-1041-5 (alk. paper)

British Library Cataloguing in Publication data are available.

This volume is dedicated to
Dr. Vassos Karageorghis
for his unfailing support of our work.

Contents

Preface
David Soren

The present volume is the first in a series designed to present the results of archaeological excavations conducted by the author at the Sanctuary of Apollo Hylates in southwestern Cyprus.

Volume I deals with the Kourion area in general and with the Sanctuary of Apollo in particular, focusing on the excavation and subsequent partial reconstruction of the Roman Temple of Apollo, the main focus for visitors to the Sanctuary. Volume II will present the seal stones from the site, and Volume III will examine the subject of ring dancing (figures dancing ritually in a group) and its relation to terra cotta figural groups discovered in the Sanctuary. Volume IV will present the Round Building, a large open-air structure found within an enclosed park at the Sanctuary. Volume V, still in the planning stages, will focus on the new excavations of a house destroyed in 365 A.D. by an earthquake in the city of Kourion two miles southeast of the Sanctuary. Additional volumes also are planned.

The present American excavations began in 1978 and were directed by the author and Diana Buitron; the work, now divided into separate projects, continues. The reader will find a detailed history of earlier excavations at the site in Chapter 2, along with a summary of the major accomplishments of the new excavations conducted by the author.

Sponsors of the current project have included the University of Missouri and the Walters Art Gallery (1978-1981), the University of Arizona (1982 to present), Dartmouth College (1978-1980), the National Endowment for the Humanities (1979), the University of Maryland--Baltimore County (1978-1980), Johns Hopkins University (1981), and the Institute for Laboratory Science in Ventura, California (1984). Patrons of the project included Dr. Giraud Foster and Mr. Richard Royall (in honor of his late brother, a Dartmouth alumnus).

The author would like to acknowledge those whose names follow, for without their assistance the present volume would not be. First and above all, I wish to thank Dr. Vassos Karageorghis, Director of Antiquities of Cyprus, for granting me permission to begin the new excavations in 1977 and for continuing to support our work.

Noelle Soren, my wife, first suggested the possibility of excavating on Cyprus during her own work there; she, together with Drs. Lawrence Stager, Jane Waldbaum, Anita Walker, and Ellen Herscher, helped me to obtain a permit.

Particular thanks for financial aid must be given to the University of Missouri Alumni Development Fund and the Research Council, as well as to the Missouri Arts Council and the Archaeological Institute of America, the latter for supporting an international symposium that grew out of the project and was held in conjunction with an exhibition of Cypriote antiquities at the University of Missouri in 1979. The papers given at the symposium were edited by myself and Jane Biers, and were published in the U.C.L.A. Archaeological Monograph Series in 1981. Numerous articles have already appeared about the work at the Sanctuary, and Dr. Diana Buitron currently is preparing a detailed work on her own contributions and discoveries.

A number of scholars and institutions have contributed to the success of our endeavors. Warrant Officer Harry Heywood of the British Forces on Cyprus and his wife, Audrey, have provided uncountable services in helping us to run the excavations smoothly and to make our film documentary *Search for Apollo*. Dr. Stuart Swiny (Director of the Cyprus American Research Institute) and Helena Swiny have provided valuable assistance and support over the years. Roger Edwards of the University of Pennsylvania Museum has supplied otherwise inaccessible notes and photos. David Grose has examined the glass, David Reese the bones and shells, Rebecca Mersereau the seals, and Lucinda Neuru, Ines Vaz Pinto and Luisa Ferrer Dias the pottery.

I wish also to thank Dr. J. P. Neophytou of the Cyprus Geological Service for consultation on earthquakes, Ino and Kyriakos Nicolaou for kind assistance in the Cyprus Museum and at Paphos, Demos Christou and M. Loulloupis for information on the city site of Kourion, Christofis Polykarpou for excellent food and assistance in the museum, Socrates Savva for cultural parallels. Special thanks must also be given to the villagers of Episkopi for their kindness and cooperation throughout the project.

Other individuals who have helped to make this volume possible include Vice-President Melvin George and Chancellor Barbara Uehling of the University of Missouri, Jane and William Biers of the same university, Norma Kershaw and Bea Riemschneider of *Archaeology* magazine, and of course the team members of the first four seasons at the Sanctuary of Apollo. They are too numerous to thank individually here, but special and significant contributions have been made by John Rutherford (four years), Terry Weisser, Sian Jones, John Huffstot, Eugene Lane and Joseph Greene (three years), Reuben Bullard, Frank Koucky, and Giraud Foster (two years), and Robert Scranton, Darice Birge, Carol Snow, John MacIsaac, Margaret Craft, Brian McConnell, Guy and Jan Sanders, Hillary Browne, Rebecca Mersereau and Stephen Glover.

I am especially grateful to George McFadden, Robert Scranton and Joseph Last for laying the groundwork that made our work possible, and to Eleni and Chrystalla of Episkopi for keeping us all so well fed throughout our efforts.

Part One
Introduction to the Sanctuary
of Apollo and Environs

Chapter 1
Methods of Excavation and Recording
Joseph Greene

This account of methods of excavation and field recording is not intended as a general handbook of excavation, but rather as a guide to understanding the results achieved in one project. It describes how one system of excavation and documentation was applied to a particular set of archaeological circumstances encountered over four seasons of digging at the Sanctuary of Apollo. Those circumstances (shallow occupational deposits, numerous multi-phased architectural remains, prior deep disturbances) and the ultimate goal of the excavation (a unified archaeological and cultural history of the site) all affected the working out in detail of an initially formalized system of excavation. The techniques described were not original with the Kourion Excavations, in general or in every detail, but were the product of the accumulated experience of earlier archaeological excavations in the Near East, on Cyprus and elsewhere in the Mediterranean. The heavy debt owed these many predecessors is here gratefully acknowledged.[1]

BALK-DEBRIS METHOD

Excavations at the Sanctuary of Apollo proceeded by the consistent application of a uniform set of techniques in separating and removing discrete depositional units within the site. That uniform set of techniques was the balk-debris method of excavation[2]. The balk-debris method involved the systematic removal of archaeological debris--soil, stones, occupational accumulations, cultural artifacts--from within restricted areas of rectilinear shape and arbitrary size, while allowing vertical earth walls (balks) to remain at the edges of these areas. The balks presented a view, in section, of the debris removed. The layers of debris, excavated in order opposite to their deposition, yielded artifacts that provided clues to the nature and dating of human activity associated with the debris.

To maximize data recovery, all cultural artifacts discovered in the course of digging were saved for later analysis. What constituted "cultural artifacts" was conceived in the broadest sense; the term included not only items of deliberate manufacture (pottery, coins, figurines, inscriptions, architectural elements, etc.), but also the incidental by-products of human cultural activity (animal bone, slag, charcoal, etc.). To prevent loss of smaller artifacts, all excavated earth was sieved in a one-quarter-inch (0.64 cm) wire mesh screen. In surface layers or in obviously disturbed loci, the sample ratio was reduced to 1:10 (i.e., every tenth bucket of excavated soil was sieved), or sieving was omitted altogether. Soil from layers likely to yield floral or faunal remains too small to be recovered even by dry sieving were sampled by flotation at a 1:10 ratio; exceedingly rich loci were sampled at a higher rate (1:5 or 1:2). While sieving was done throughout the digging season, flotation samples were set aside for processing in the closing weeks of each season.

Site Grid

The site constituted the largest unit of analysis to which the method was applied; for logistical and archaeological reasons, much smaller units actually were dug. Those smaller units were defined by the site grid.

The original plan for the Sanctuary of Apollo (Fig. 1) was prepared by Joseph Last and has been extensively revised and added to by John Rutherford and John Huffstot; it was prepared for publication by Noelle Soren. Robert Scranton used the Last plan and superimposed grid in 1967 in synthesizing his own observations and McFadden's unpublished results. Even then the grid existed only on paper. McFadden had used separate local grids (Fig. 2) of different orientation and designation for each of the various portions of the site he investigated. Not until the opening of the new excavations in 1978 was the original grid actually laid out on the surface of the site.

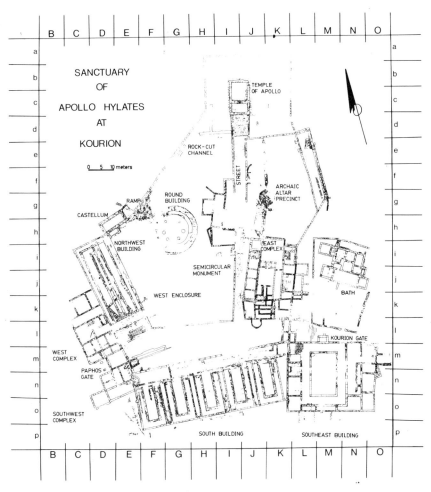

Figure 1. Plan of the Apollo Sanctuary.

The sides of the grid were 170 m long and oriented to the major points of the compass. The grid itself was composed of modules measuring 10 m, [2] each designated by a pair of letters. Divisions along the north-south sides were lettered a-q; those along the east-west side A-P. Aa was the northwesternmost square, Pq the southeasternmost. Individual modules were subdivided into quadrants measuring 5 m on a side. Quadrant 1 of Square Aa was Aa1 (Fig. 3), Quadrant 2 was Aa2, and so forth.

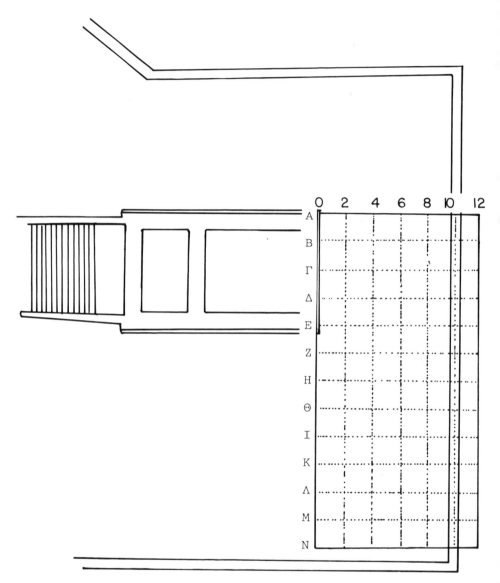

Figure 2. Local grid by George McFadden for excavating the Temple of Apollo.

Area, Locus and Pottery Bucket

The actual work of excavation was done by the area supervisors, who were immediately responsible for digging and recording a restricted portion of the site called an area.

The limits of an area normally coincided with the subdivisions of the grid, but in certain cases areas were defined in relation to the specific architectural features under investigation. For example, the rooms of the Apollo Temple--naos and pronaos--were excavated and recorded without reference to the various grid squares in which they lay, but rather in rectangular quadrants labeled 1, 2, 3 and 4 within the rooms themselves. While the area was a more or less arbitrary unit of investigation, within each area lay natural units of analysis termed loci. A locus was an element of archaeological debris with depositional or construction coherence. (In theory, the entire site was composed of loci, which, also in theory, could be excavated successively and completely from surface to bedrock; as noted, however, for practical reasons and to maintain vertical stratigraphic control, digging was confined to small areas.) In the course of excavation, each locus was separated into its component parts: soil, stone, and occupational debris and the artifacts sealed within them. After sieving and selection of samples for geological analysis and flotation, soil, stone, and debris were discarded and the separated artifacts saved in a pottery bucket.

The pottery bucket, or pottery basket, (PB) was simultaneously (1) a literal container, (2) a unit of collection, and (3) the material collected in that unit. For every operation in which soil was removed, the artifacts recovered were assigned to a pottery bucket. As a unit of collection, the PB represented a discrete

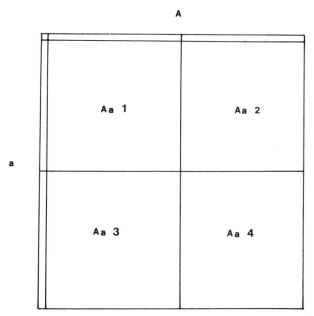

Figure 3. Ten meter grid square and quadrant subdivisions.

quantity of raw data for dating a locus and for interpreting the ancient cultural activity that created it. The material in the PB consisted not only of the pottery (vessels and sherds), but also of other artifacts of material cultural (MC). To preserve the integrity of the data gathered in a PB, each was carefully labelled (Fig. 4). For different reasons, several PBs might pertain to a single locus, but *in no case* was material from more than one locus included in one PB. Mixing of material from different loci in the same PB was termed contamination and was to be avoided. The chronological information from a contaminated PB was unreliable and had, perforce, to be discounted.

Locus Sheets

The area, locus and PB, then, were key concepts in the recording system used at the Sanctuary of Apollo. That recording system was the means by which a complete and continuous account of the steady destruction-by-excavation of the Sanctuary was preserved on paper and film for later study and interpretation. The core of the recording system was the locus sheet (Fig. 5-7), a three-page form designed to contain the essential physical, relational, and artifactual data about a given locus. The particular locus sheet format used at Kourion was similar to that developed for the American Schools of Oriental Research Excavations at Idalion, Cyprus (1970 to present), and used subsequently by the ASOR Punic Project at Carthage, Tunisia (1975-1980).[3]

For each locus recognized, the area supervisor completed a three-page locus sheet. The locus sheet presented a uniform set of questions about the compositional and stratigraphic situation of each locus and its contents. This permitted the supervisor to organize observations and speculations about each locus in a consistent manner, thus facilitating later retrieval of data and interpretation of results. It also diminished the possibility of occasional oversights in recording factual data and encouraged controlled speculation about the locus and its significance.

The information entered on the locus sheets was of two types: observed data and interpretations. The items to be completed were as follows:

PAGE 1: General Data

General ID: A brief, non-technical description identifying the locus (e.g., "top soil," "pit," "stony layer"). In the upper right hand corner of page 1, it was customary to include the area designation (grid coordinates, quadrant number), the excavation code and year (Apollo 19___), and the supervisor's initials.

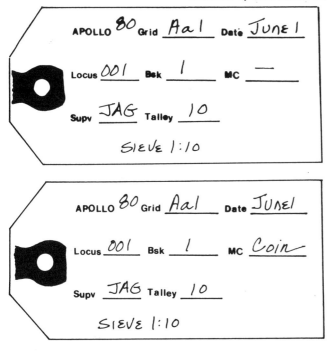

Figure 4. Pottery Bucket and Material Culture Tags.

Locus Number: Locus numbers were assigned to each separate locus, consecutively from 001 within an area. These numbers were maintained from year to year.

Date(s): Calendar dates on which work (removal of soil or artifacts, photography or drawing, etc.) was performed in the locus.

Top Level/Top Plan: Absolute elevation(s) of the uppermost part of the locus and the reference number of the top plan on which it appeared (see Top Plans).

Bottom Level/Top Plan: As above, for the lowermost part of the locus.

Section: Reference number or letters of the section drawing on which a sectional view of the locus appeared (see Section Drawings).

Drawn By Architect: When applicable, reference number of architect's plan or elevation drawing on which the locus appeared.

GENERAL IDENTIFICATION

Locus No. _____
Date(s) _____

Top levels _____ Top plan _____ ; Bottom levels _____ Top plan _____

Sections _____ Drawn by architect _____ Photo No. _____

PHYSICAL DATA

What is it made of?:

What size particles? _____ Color _____

Features	Soil Layers
Compass orientation _____	Direction & Degree of slope:
__ *courses* high; __ *rows* wide	
Overall dimensions _____	Degree of compaction:
How was it built?:	Distribution of particles (e.g., random, laminated, graded bedding:

STRATIGRAPHIC DATA

This Locus is *below* Loc. _____ & is *above* Loc. _____

Lateral extent _____ Max. thickness _____ Touches balk(s) _____

How does this Locus relate to all other loci it touches?:

This Locus is contemporary with which loci mentioned above?:

How was this Locus formed?:

Figure 5. Locus Sheet, page 1.

POTTERY

Tally Total	Basket No.	Date Dug	Level	Field Reading	Reg. Sherds

SPECIALIST SAMPLES

Gen. Reg. Number	Assoc. Pottery Basket Number	Ratio	Identification

Figure 6. Locus Sheet, page 2.

MATERIAL CULTURE and OBJECTS

page 3

Gen. Reg. Number	Object Reg. No.	Bone Reg. No.	Associated Pottery Basket #	Identification

PROGRESS of EXCAVATION (Dates dug, strategy and procedures, etc.)

Figure 7. Locus Sheet, page 3.

Physical Data

Composition: A technical and detailed description of the substance of the locus, its natural and cultural inclusions, insofar as possible without interpretation of the agency of its formation.

Particle Size: Per the Wentworth Scale,[4] which is graduated from smallest (silt = 0.002 mm dia.) to largest (boulder = 7250 mm dia.)

Color: Per the Munsell Soil Color Chart (Munsell 1954). Properly completed, this entry included both a Munsell soil color number and a Munsell soil color description (e.g., 7.5YR 6/4 Light Brown).

Features and Soil Layers

Broadly divided, loci fell into two categories: soil layers and features. Soil Layers were simply that: accumulated layers of soil and/or stones of any depth. A feature was somewhat more difficult to define. It was generally a constructional element, like a wall, drain, hearth or floor, although these features existed in and often were made of soil or stone. Structures were complexes of features--walls, floor, drains, etc. and soil layers--and were not, as such, recorded as loci but as complexes of loci.

Information recorded for features included:

Compass Orientation: Major compass direction of a feature. This was of significance for the isolated, rectilinear feature (e.g., wall or drain), but of less importance for floors or non-rectilinear features, such as pits or hearths. The major axes of these circular or ovoid features could, however, be oriented to compass direction.

Courses High: If coursed, the number of the highest preserved course, numbering from the bottom course (which, of course, was not known until the feature was completely exposed in the area).

Rows Wide: Maximum number of extant rows in a feature.

Overall Dimensions: Gross measurements of height, width, and depth, to give an impression of the scale of the feature.

How Built: Both qualitative and technical information about the nature of the feature's construction.

Information recorded for soil layers included:

Slope Direction and Degree: Compass orientation of the upward or downward slope of a soil layer. The degree of slope is noted not in numerical degrees, but in qualitative gradations: nil, slight, moderate, steep, vertical.

Compaction: The hardness of the soil layer--soft, medium, hard, or some degree in between.

Distribution of Particles: Usually random in the case of dumped fill, water-sorted in the case of water-laid sediments, gravity-sorted in tipped fill, etc. A complex depositional history often produced a complex particle distribution in a single locus.

Stratigraphic Data

This section was designed to elucidate the relationship of a locus to other loci surrounding it. That relationship was in part observed during excavation and in part interpreted on the basis of its stratigraphic position in relation to other loci; the information recorded was drawn both from observation and from archaeological judgment.

Below: The number of the locus (or loci) under which the locus in question lay.

Above: The number of the locus (or loci) beneath the locus in question.

Lateral Extent: Essentially the same information called for under Overall Dimensions; gave some clue to the scale of the locus.

Max Thickness: The maximum thickness of the locus at its widest point, top to bottom; not necessarily the difference between the maximum and minimum elevations, which, in the case of a sloping locus, would not accurately reflect maximum thickness of the locus.

Touches Balk: Literally, which of the earth walls surrounding the area does this locus touch?

Relations with Other Loci: A description of how the locus relates to other loci it touches: lies above, below, cuts or is cut by, abuts or bonds to (in the case of walls), seals or is sealed by; properly, it explained the nature, as well as the fact, of contact between loci.

Contemporaneity: The answer was in part a stratigraphic judgment based on relations with other loci, and in part was keyed to the datable artifacts in the loci.

Formation: Again, this was a matter of a supervisor's archaeological judgment, on the advice of a specialist. A geologist, for example, might give some clue to the formation of a soil layer.

PAGE 2: Pottery

This portion of the locus sheet recorded the PBs removed from the locus along with the reading of the sherds recovered.

Basket No.: Consecutive running number of the PB.

Date Dug: Date PB was removed from Locus. No PB was ever used for more than one day, even if excavation continued in a locus for several days.

Level: Top *and* bottom level of the PB's absolute level.

Field Reading: Date and description of sherds in the PB; comprised as detailed or as exact an entry as the pottery reader could or wished to make (see Pottery Registration).

Registered Sherds: Registry numbers of the sherds, assigned by the registrar.

PAGE 3: Material Culture and Objects

Each item of material culture (MC) from the locus was cross-referenced to its MC registry number, its object number (if any), and its associated PB, and was briefly described. Ceramics were separated from other artifacts (MC), which included all worked bone, metal, glass, coins, terra cotta figurines and fragments, architectural elements, and specialist samples (bone, charcoal, etc.). These items were registered separately by material type and consecutive number (see MC Registration). Intrinsically important or valuable objects were given an additional designation, an object number.

PAGE 3: Progress of Excavation

This was the least structured and most important part of the locus sheet. It consisted of diary-like entries describing the problems encountered, the strategies employed to solve those problems, and the interpretations made and revised in the successive days of excavation in the locus. The entries were completed daily as digging progressed. The diary format afforded the supervisor a forum for speculation about the nature of the locus and its relationship to other loci, about the agents of its formation and destruction, and a place for including observations pertinent to the locus offered by directors, specialists, and other supervisors.

Area Notebook

The locus sheets were printed on 8-1/2 x 11-inch plain paper and punched for insertion in a three-ring loose-leaf binder. This binder became the area notebook for an excavated area. The area notebook held, in addition to the completed locus sheets, index lists of pottery buckets dug in the area, of loci assigned, and of photographs taken (and, when available, prints of those photographs), along with scale plan and section drawings of the area, the annual final reports, and the sequence diagrams for the area.

POTTERY BUCKET LIST

The pottery bucket (PB) list was a running list of all pottery bucket numbers assigned in an area. Numbering began with 1 and continued consecutively throughout the season and from season to season. This list served as an index of pottery buckets used and as a summary diary of work in an area. With each PB number were recorded the date that the PB was used (no PB was ever used for more than one day), the number of the locus from which the material in the PB came, the top level and bottom level of the PB (not of the associated locus), and a brief list of the material cultural artifacts (MC) recovered from the locus along with the pottery. The last entry served as a check against MC being lost or mislabeled in later registration processing. Also entered was the talley total (T), which was the total number of buckets of earth removed from a locus in the course of the digging that produced the pottery collected in the PB. This enabled supervisors to keep track of the number of buckets of earth removed from a locus for sieving or flotation sampling. It also permitted crude calculation of the soil-to-pottery ratios in loci, which in turn provided clues to the type of ancient cultural activity associated with the locus.

LOCUS LIST

The locus list was a consecutive listing of all the loci assigned in an area. Locus numbers were assigned consecutively from 001 and were continued from season to season. The list served as an index to loci in an area and as convenient summary of all layers identified in the course of excavation. Entered on the list with the locus number was the date that the locus and a new locus sheet were begun, its top and bottom levels (as entered on page 1 of the locus sheet), PBs associated with it (as on page 2), and the dates on which the locus was worked (identical with the "Dates" entry on page 1 of the locus sheet).

PHOTOGRAPH LIST

The photograph list catalogued all field photographs taken in an area. Photograph numbers were assigned by the photographer, not by the supervisor (see Photography). All other data relevant to a particular field photograph were worked up by the photographer and supervisor in consultation: direction of view, locus (or loci) shown, date taken, lighting conditions, and a brief description of what the photograph was supposed to depict. This information was recorded by both the area supervisor (for the area photograph list) and by the photographer (for the photograph registration card and the field photograph master list). These data were later collated with prints of the photographs returned to the supervisor for inclusion in the area notebook.

TOP PLANS AND SECTION DRAWINGS

In addition to written documentation, supervisors produced measured scale drawings of their respective areas. These drawings, executed on graph paper divided into 1-mm squares, recorded each area in plan and sectional view through successive stages of excavation.

Plan views (top plans) were drawn at scales of 1:25 (1 cm = 25 cm) or 1:50 (1 cm = 50 cm), depending on the size of the area under excavation, its stratigraphic complexity, and the need to show detail. Top plans were not conceived as miniature architect's plans (showing only structures), but as excavator's plans (showing soil layers, features, and the locations of PBs and finds). Top plans were revised as necessary during a season as deeper excavation or wider exposure revealed successive soil layers of different features in an area. Depending on the size and stratigraphic complexity of an area, as well as on the pace of archaeological activity in it, such changes occurred as frequently as once a day or as seldom as once a week. In illustrating the day-by-day and week-by-week progress of excavation in an area, the top plans supplemented the excavation diary included in the locus sheets.

Section drawings added depth to the two-dimensional top plans. Where the top plans recorded the layers of archaeological debris in successive plan views, the section drawings recorded the cross-sectional view of the superimposed layers visible in the vertical earth walls (balks) surrounding the area. Section drawings were, in fact, scale drawings of those earth walls, and sometimes were referred to as "balk drawings." Unlike top plans, section drawings usually were done at 1:25 scale (to emphasize details) and were done only once, at the close of excavation in an area, usually upon reaching bedrock.

Section drawings were as unlike architectural elevations as top plans were unlike architectural plans. Section drawings showed actual soil layers and their inter-relations, not simply sectional views of walls, floors, and other built features. These drawings fell on a stylistic scale somewhere between the vividly realistic and the starkly schematic, since they were intended, above all, as interpretive documents. As records of the actual stratigraphy, the section drawings were realistic drawings; as interpretations of that stratigraphy, the drawings were schematic in their emphasis on what were adjudged the important differences among layers. They were drawn to show a particular interpretation of stratigraphy already agreed upon by the supervisor and the director. The interpretation agreed upon was based on stratigraphy actually observed in the balk, of course, but photography was unequal to the task of depicting it. Even if photographic film were sufficiently sensitive to record all the nuances visible to the human eye, there is no substitute for firsthand examination of the stratigraphy in the field and its interpretation on paper in a scale drawing.

Since the Sanctuary of Apollo had no deeply stratified deposits of occupational debris, but was rather an architectural ruin already heavily disturbed by previous digging, no master section through the site was contemplated or even possible. Section drawings were of primary use in solving local stratigraphic problems relevant to individual structures or groups of structures. Likewise, a drawn section of the intersecting balks of the West Enclosure demonstrated the relationships among the various parts of the "Round Building" excavated there.

FINAL REPORT AND SEQUENCE DIAGRAM

At the close of each season, each area supervisor prepared a final report, summarizing the work done in the area in the course of the digging season, and a sequence diagram, illustrating schematically the stratigraphic inter-relationships among the loci found within the area. Both the final report and sequence diagram were at once descriptive and interpretive documents. A brief connected prose account, the final report, recounted the progress of excavation in an area, while at the same time offering chronological and stratigraphic interpretations of layers and groups of layers based on the sum of data collected in that area. The sequence diagram was a schematic conflation of the stratigraphic inter-relationships described in the locus sheets and depicted in the top plans and section drawings. The diagram was not a substitute for these primary records or for the final report, but a visual aid to understanding the written accounts.[5]

Registration

Catalogs of the artifacts excavated at the Sanctuary of Apollo were compiled into ordered lists called registries (Fig. 8). These

APOLLO

University of Arizona Cyprus Project
Apollo Sanctuary

Official Registry

Number	Locus	Date	Description	P	D	Comments

Figure 8. Registry Sheet.

were a means of systematizing the excavation results for later retrieval and restudy. There were two main types: the pottery registry for ceramic vessels and sherds, and the material culture (MC) registry for all artifacts other than sherds and vessels. The registries were overseen by the registrar, who maintained the ordered lists and cared for the stored materials during the digging season. The two registries were separated for purely practical reasons. The overwhelming bulk of finds from the Sanctuary of Apollo consisted of pottery vessels and sherds. The pottery registry, therefore, held a comparatively greater number of entries. Moreover, vessels and sherds, once excavated, were processed in a slightly different way than were the other MC artifacts, and the results of that processing were entered differently in the registry.

The registries cataloged both pottery and MC artifacts with information about provenience (area, locus, PB as originally recorded in the locus sheets) and subsequent identifications. The registries were, in fact, abstracts of artifact data from the area notebooks. Such abstracts were essential to specialist studies of

pottery, sculpture, inscriptions, coins, metal, terra cotta
artifacts, etc., as well as of lithic, botanical, and faunal
samples. Thus abstracted, the data could be reshuffled and studied
under different categories (all material of the same type, of a
certain date, or from a given locus, for example) without losing
track of the original excavated context.

POTTERY REGISTRATION

Pottery registration was an essential part of the pottery
reading process. Pottery reading (i.e., the identification of the
form, ware, and date of sherds) was done in the field by the
director, with the assistance of area supervisors; the registrar
attended as recorder. Sherds were washed, read, and registered in
the field to minimize the handling and possible confusion of
unread, unregistered sherds.

Pottery reading proceeded in this manner: the pottery buckets
(the units in which the sherds were collected) were prepared for
reading by the area supervisor or by an assistant, who washed,
dried, and sorted the sherds onto wooden trays. This gave the
excavators preliminary familiarity with the ceramics from their own
areas. It also eliminated chances of inadvertent confusion of
pottery bucket labels by non-English-speaking local laborers hired
to wash pottery. From each PB thus prepared, the reader selected
sherds in turn and described their form and ware, relating them to
known and dated materials from the site and elsewhere. The
supervisor recorded these readings on page 2 of the appropriate
locus sheet, while the registrar copied the same readings into the
pottery registry. The reader indicated which sherds or vessels were
to be drawn and/or photographed and counted the different classes
of indicators--rims, bases, handles, decorated sherds--and, if
possible, read the diameters of the rims and bases from a diameter
wheel. The registrar assigned registration numbers to each piece as
it was read. The numbering scheme was consecutive from 1 for the
first sherd of the first season and continuous from season to
season. The registrar immediately inked the registration number
onto the sherd, along with the name and year of the excavation and
the area and locus of the sherd's provenience (Fig. 9). The
registration number was entered along with the reading in a
separate reading book by the reader, and in the area notebook by
the supervisor.

Thus, the pottery readings were recorded in triplicate: in the
pottery registry (by consecutive registration number), in the
director's reading books (by dates on which the readings were
done), and in the area notebooks (by locus). The sherds, once read,
were stored in the excavation storeroom, where they could be later
retrieved for restudy or comparison with subsequently excavated
materials.

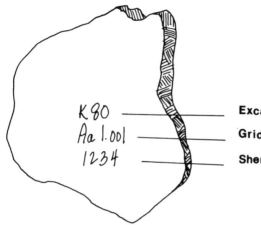

Excavation Code & Year

Grid Square, Area & Locus

Sherd Registration Number

Figure 9. Sherd Registration Data.

MATERIAL CULTURE REGISTRATION

The material culture (MC) registry was organized differently and the artifacts were handled in a slightly different way. The MC registry was divided into categories based on material type:

T - Terra Cotta: all ceramic artifacts (figurines, tools, toys, etc.) that were not vessels or vessel sherds

M - Metal: metal artifacts and fragments (but not slags--see below)

S - Stone: worked architectural, sculptural, or inscriptional stone (but not lithic samples for geological analysis--see below)

C - Coins

Q - Miscellaneous: all materials not fitting into one of these other categories

Samples for specialists' analyses were assigned to one of four subcategories:

GS - Geological Samples: all materials for geological analysis--stone, soil, slag (metallic and vitreous)

ZS - Zoological Samples: primarily bone and bone fragments and teeth (worked bone or ivory, however, was entered under category "Q")

BS - Botanical Sample: macrobotanical samples recovered by means other than flotation (larger pieces of charcoal, carbonized seeds, etc.)

FS - Flotation Samples: the light and heavy fraction recovered by flotation.

Material cultural artifacts individually bagged and tagged were removed to the excavation house at the close of each day's digging. There the registrar sorted, cleaned, cataloged, and labeled each artifact. Artifacts were labeled in the same manner as the sherds (with excavation code and date, area and locus number) and numbered with a prefixed letter (designating the MC category) and a consecutive number (beginning with 1 in each category). For example, the first terra cotta figurine fragment of the first season was number T 1, the first geological sample GS 1. After registration, the artifacts were routed to the appropriate specialist (geologist, numismatist, epigrapher, etc.) for further study. Those artifacts needing conservation treatment were sent to the conservator; artifacts of significant importance were selected for photography and drawing. After the MC artifacts had been registered, the supervisors entered these registry numbers and descriptions in page 3 of the locus sheets.

THE OBJECT REGISTRY

From the artifacts cataloged in the pottery and MC registries the registrar, in consultation with the directors, selected certain whole pieces and significant fragments notable for their chronological, aesthetic, or intrinsic worth for inclusion in a supplemental list, the object registry. The items in this list were numbered consecutively from 1 starting with the first object of the first season. The object registry was, in effect, a list of the artifacts worthy of museum display discovered by the excavation. These pieces were documented in comparatively greater detail than were the other artifacts in the pottery and MC registries.

Photography

Photography formed an essential part of the excavation recording system. Photographs of various excavated areas taken in the course of a season's digging augmented the written notebooks prepared by supervisors, and artifact photographs supplemented the descriptions entered in the registration lists. In both cases, a written record of the photographs was maintained to facilitate retrieval of the visual information for later study and publication.

All photographs were taken in 35 mm format, in black-and-white print (Kodak Plus-X) and color slide (Kodachrome 64), by the excavation photographer or by another staff member acting in that capacity. All black-and-white film was developed and proof sheets were printed during the season in a makeshift darkroom at excavation quarters. Color slide film was returned to the United States at the end of the season to be processed commercially.

Photographs were of two types: field photographs and artifact photographs. Field photographs were done, as the name suggests, in the field. There, lighting conditions usually were less than ideal. In order to avoid deep shadow that obscured detail, field photographs were taken early in the morning, late in the afternoon, or, in rare cases, at mid-day with the sun directly overhead. The subject occasionally could be shaded artificially by a shade cloth (a pair of bed sheets sewn together and stretched between two poles). Subjects for field photographs included excavated areas and the loci therein, along with large objects (usually architectural fragments) that could not be removed to the excavation house. Field photographs were always taken with a scale, usually a 1-m rod divided into 20-cm segments painted alternately black and white. No people or extraneous objects appear in the photographs, as all were taken with a view to eventual publication. Artifact photographs were made of all significant small finds after their registration and, if necessary, cleaning and conservation. Artifact photography was done in the excavation photo studio (a darkened corner of an empty storeroom) under controlled light. All artifacts were photographed with appropriate scale and a card bearing the artifact's registration number and excavation data. This permitted the printing of study photographs with complete information about the artifact's provenience appearing in the photograph. The card, however, was positioned to permit later cropping of the print, should the photograph be published. Photographs of artifacts were referenced only by registration number, even if several views of the same item were taken. Field photographs, on the other hand, were recorded by a different system.

In a method similar to that described for the Tell el-Hesi (Israel) excavations, field photographs were numbered consecutively from 1.[6] A unique number was assigned to each field photograph, even to different views of the same area or large objects. This eliminated the cumbersome and confusing method of referencing photographs by roll and frame number. For each photograph, a photograph registration card was completed by the photographer. The registration card was identical to the pottery bucket tag, though slightly different information was entered in certain blanks. The completed card was photographed in the frame immediately before or after that in which the subject to which it referred was exposed. Thus, when the contact sheet was printed each field photograph appeared beside a facsimile of the registration card bearing the data pertinent to it. To conserve color slide film, this procedure was omitted for color photographs of the identical view. After processing, the slide was matched to the black and white print and labeled with the appropriate photograph number. A duplicate record of the information recorded on photograph registration cards was maintained in a separate, bound notebook. Its expanded format permitted the recording of supplemental data about each field photograph (time of day, exposure data, details of the subject photographed). This became the master list of field photographs for the entire excavation and was continued from year to year. All photograph information was given back to the area supervisor for inclusion in the photograph list for each area maintained in the various notebooks.

Chapter 2
The Excavation and
Its Significance
David Soren

The Sanctuary of Apollo Hylates is located about 1.5 km west of
ancient Kourion on the southwest coast of Cyprus (Fig. 10),
overlooking the Bay of Episkopi (Fig. 11). This cult center has
been excavated extensively over the past 120 years, producing many
and varied objects of art and exposing many of the buildings.
Surprisingly little has been published; the rituals, architectural
development, and destruction of this major cult center remain only
partially and, in many cases, incorrectly understood.

The first published excavations were conducted by General Luigi
Palma di Cesnola during his tenure as American Consul to Cyprus
from 1865 to 1875. Cesnola was not so much concerned with
scientific investigation and planning of the area as he was with
rivaling the contemporary discoveries of Heinrich Schliemann at
Troy. His hunt for Kourion treasure is illustrated in a letter to
his friend Hiram Hitchcock:

". . . your friend Cesnola has just made the discovery of many *gold*
things, beneath a temple here, the quantity and quality of which
throws into shade Schliemann's so-called Treasure of Priam."[1]

Determining the location of the temple cited by Cesnola in this
passage has proved impossible thus far, and many doubt the veracity
of the passage. It is clear, however, that he did excavate another
temple, the Temple of Apollo, to which a good portion of this
volume is devoted.[2] Excavations at the site ceased for many years
after those of Cesnola. The site became a haven for· looters and
slowly reverted to scrub growth, rain washed mounds, and valleys of
soft earth.

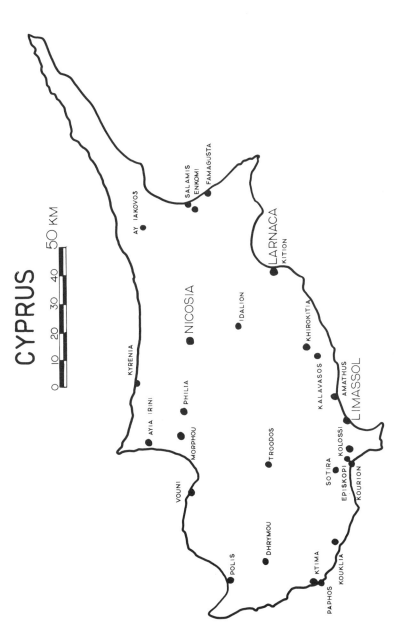

Figure 10. Map of Cyprus.

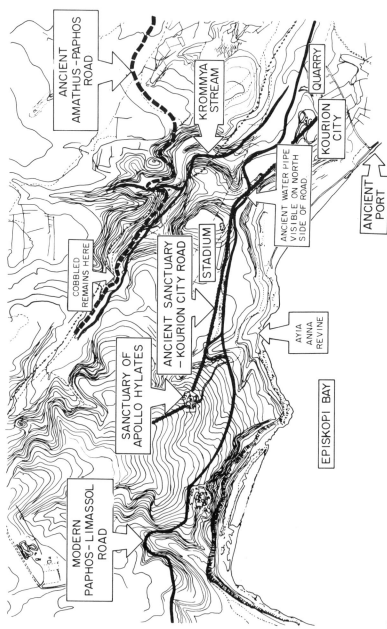

Figure 11. Map of Episkopi/Kourion area courtesy of Dr. Giraud Foster.

It was not until 1935 that the first serious work at the sanctuary occurred under the direction of George H. McFadden, a Princeton graduate with the financial resources to excavate; he did so in collaboration with B. H. Hill of the American School of Classical studies in Athens. Unfortunately, McFadden drowned in a boating accident in the Bay of Episkopi in 1953, without publishing a more detailed account of the site than those which appeared in the *University Museum Bulletin* of The University of Pennsylvania, the *American Journal of Archaeology*, and the *Illustrated London News.*[3]

Hill labored for years to reconstruct a large part of the site, which remained essentially destroyed after an earthquake in the fourth century A.D. The present restorations in the South Building, East Complex, and Southeast Building (to be discussed below) are his work, but unfortunately none of the detail of this work was published.

The most important contribution to the understanding of the Sanctuary was made by Robert Scranton, professor emeritus, University of Chicago.[4] In 1962, working with a grant from the American Philosophical Society, Scranton studied the excavation diary of McFadden and the plans of his architect, Joseph Last, before making his own plans and observations about details of the Sanctuary. The result, published in 1967, was the first major synthesis of all buildings then known on the site.

In 1979 Scranton returned to Cyprus as an adviser to the present project and became an invaluable member of a small group of architectural specialists (including John Rutherford, John Huffstot, and Alexandra Corn) whose work would lead to a restoration on paper of the Temple of Apollo and to the beginning of the partial rebuilding of the temple now being supervised by Professor Stefanos Sinos of the Athens Polytechnical Institute. Not all of Scranton's hypotheses would be confirmed. Differences between his conclusions and ours have occurred in the interpretation of the temple, the West Enclosure and the final earthquake, but his work is a milestone that constantly provided a measuring standard for our own efforts.

Other contributions to the site include a study of the water supply system by Joseph Last, published posthumously.[5] John and Suzanne Young contributed an important study of clays and the thousands of terra cotta statuettes and associated objects dedicated by worshippers at the Sanctuary.[6] Another major publication was the account by Terence Mitford of the Kourion inscriptions.[7] The latter work offered not only a catalog of all known references dealing with the site and Kourion City, but also provided valuable observations on periods of building activity and the nature of the cult.

Coins from the McFadden excavations were published by Dorothy Cox, but no find spots were given for any coins cited and the book is useful only for giving an idea of coins in use and periods of particular activity at the Sanctuary.[8]

Finally, the work of Roger Edwards must be cited; in addition to safeguarding the excavation diaries and exported objects, he typed McFadden's handwritten notes and maintained the photo catalog of the excavation. His cooperation has enormously aided our understanding of McFadden's unpublished work.

The present excavations have run from 1978 to 1985, and despite the discovery of the Round Building, additional rock-cut channels, pipes, and pits, the plan of the site is close to that described by Scranton in detail and features primarily buildings and streets of the Roman period, although the Sanctuary itself dates back to at least the seventh century B.C.

Diana Buitron, working on the altar and Archaic Precinct at the Sanctuary since 1978, has shown that the sacred heart of the site would seem to have been well established for animal sacrifices by some time not long after 600 B.C., with traces of an even earlier wall beneath the altar.

When the Sanctuary was in use in antiquity, visitors brought clay votives to be placed in the Archaic Precinct, and many even brought goats and/or sheep for sacrifice. Or they might have come to participate in the veneration of sacred trees, much as many villagers do today on Cyprus. In any case, a worshipper of the second century A.D. would have entered the site through the Kourion Gate to the southeast, or the Paphos Gate to the southwest (see Fig. 1). The large South Building (Fig. 12) was perhaps for lodging or a series of cult *exedrae*. Scranton (1967: 67) suggests that it was used for "essentially dormitories," and Terence Mitford (1971: 207) has shown that it was built in its final form in the Trajanic period.

Scranton's detailed account of the various buildings of the Sanctuary (Fig. 13-15) makes superfluous a similar recounting here, but a brief review of the major monuments would not be out of place. East of the South Building is the Southeast Building, which may be a Palaestra and which had a series of rooms around a sizable central court, in the north corner of which was a large jar supplied with water (Fig. 16). On the west side, in a niche in the west wall of the second room from the north was found an athlete/ballplayer sculpture discussed by Scranton and published by Richard Jensen in the 1984 *Report of the Department of Antiquities of Cyprus.*

The date of the Palaestra is a problem, although it is well in place by the mid-second century A.D. and probably does not predate the first century A.D. A major building of the fourth century B.C. (Fig. 17) preceded the building and was obliterated by it, as our excavations of 1979 and 1980 showed. After the earthquake of circa 365 A.D., an addition was made to the northeast of it, using the ruins of the Palaestra. The date of this squatter structure was not before the fifth century A.D., long after the Sanctuary had ceased to function as such.

Figure 12. View through "Priest's House" of East Complex to South Building.

Continuing north from the South Building, a street leads past the East Complex--with its stoa on the street, "Priest's House" behind the stoa, and treasury with barred windows (just east of a narrow corridor)--and proceeds to a large Central Court. Just east of the street and north of the stoa is the Archaic Altar (Fig. 18) discovered by Scranton within a precinct enclosed by temenos walls. It was, perhaps, the monument which, according to Strabo, could not be touched on penalty of death.[9] Violators were flung from the edge of a nearby cliff into the Mediterranean.[10] Scranton located a large ashlar stone, with a roughly rectangular hole in its upper part, next to the altar (Fig. 19). He believed it to be a stone fence post, and so set it on end just north of the altar in 1979. The stone remains an enigma, with suggestions ranging from a dedicated anchor to a *baetyl*, or sacred stone, for which parallels might be cited on Cyprus.[11] Southeast of the altar precinct were baths of the Trajanic period. Immediately east of the precinct was a stoa, or storage area, affixed to the east temenos wall; it had replaced a smaller stoa of the first century, which was only partly excavated.

Figure 13. Aerial view of the Sanctuary of Apollo Hylates, Kourion, courtesy of Warrant Officer Harry Heywood, RAF Episkopi Garrison, Cyprus.

Figure 14. Aerial view of the Sanctuary of Apollo Hylates, Kourion, courtesy of Warrant Officer Harry Heywood, RAF Episkopi Garrison, Cyprus.

Figure 15. Aerial view to the north of the Sanctuary by Warrant Officer Harry Heywood.

Fig. 16. View to northwest of the Palaestra showing large jar *in situ.*

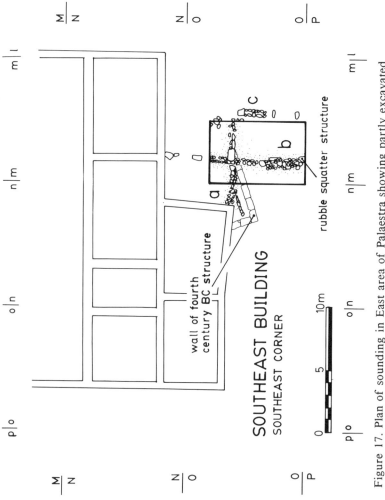

Figure 17. Plan of sounding in East area of Palaestra showing partly excavated squatter walls A through C and pre–Palaestra wall D of the fourth century B.C.

Continuing northeast on the main street, the pilgrim arrived at the focal point of the Sanctuary, the Temple of Apollo, originally with an altar before it. West of the Central Court was the West Enclosure and its dominating feature, the recently discovered (1979) Round Building (Fig. 20), which, with its hypaethral center and pits cut into bedrock for plantings, may have been a center of the tree cult of Apollo of the Woodlands. The building featured a roughly circular interior floor of mortar and river pebbles bordered by foundations for some sort of ring wall around the outside of the structure. The West Enclosure (Fig. 21) was a kind of park, bordered to the southwest by what was called by McFadden Temple A or the Northwest Building. The purpose of the latter structure is unknown; it may have lodged visitors waiting to make offerings and receive the favor of Apollo.

Adjoining the West Enclosure and the Northwest Building are two cisterns and a *castellum* (Fig. 22), or water distribution system (Locus 003), with clay pipes servicing the Sanctuary and the baths adjoining the southeastern limit of the Archaic Precinct (Fig. 23). Clay water pipes from the castellum branch out under and across the street. Some constructions and a possible quarry just northwest of the cistern have not been excavated since McFadden worked there in 1935.

Figure 18. View from bipod camera over Archaic Altar. The single ring of stones in the foreground was added by Diana Buitron.

At the eastern limit of the West Enclosure is the Semicircular Monument (Fig. 24), which John Rutherford has convincingly assigned to the Hellenistic period as a statue base.[12] Worshippers also would have passed a kitchen just below the stoa of the East Complex at the corner of the Temple Street.

Figure 19. Stone "fence post," anchor or sacred stone from the Archaic Precinct.

If the visitor left the site by the Paphos Gate, he passed by the West Complex, a series of rooms which were full of quake debris when McFadden excavated there in 1948. A visitor could also leave through the Kourion Gate, passing by the Palaestra, or Southeast Building.

The new excavations at Kourion have been devoted primarily to problem-solving archaeology, which meant working in specially chosen areas of the previously excavated site in order to test hypotheses about how the site developed over the centuries, rather than digging large trenches. Because the rest of this volume deals in detail with the monuments, artifacts and chronological

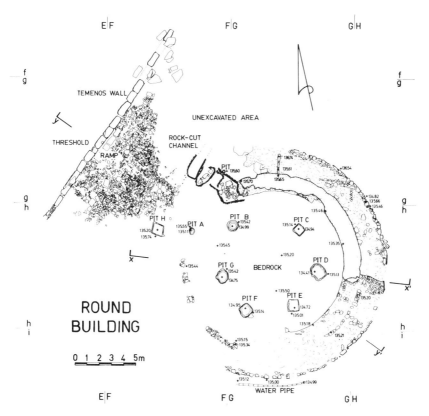

Fig. 20. Plan of the Round Building and West Enclosure.

development of the site, I summarize here the new ideas that have come forth as a result of the current excavations.

The 1984 University of Arizona campaign has made it possible to understand better the expansion and development of the northwestern area of the Sanctuary in pre-Roman times, and to understand for the first time the sophisticated refinements carried out at the site in the Julio-Claudian period.

Figure 21. Aerial view of Round Building, South Building, Palaestra, Baths, East Complex, and Temple Street, proceeding counterclockwise. Courtesy of Dr. Giraud Foster.

The following conclusions have been reached concerning the development of the site:

1. The Sanctuary developed over time from a simple open-air site, with altar in place by the sixth century B.C. in the Archaic Precinct.[13]

2. It expanded in the sixth century B.C. to include the main street, a simple first "temple" (or at least a sacred structure right beneath the later Temple of Apollo), a West Enclosure with Round Building, and probably rock-cut channels for planting and bordering of the West Enclosure, along with other structures not yet discovered.

3. A large concentration of coins and pottery of the late fourth century B.C. suggests that this was clearly a period of major activity here, accounting for a building of ashlar masonry in the area of the Palaestra and perhaps the first stoa of the East Complex. Fifty percent of the Greek coins recovered are of this period, or in the first fifteen years of the third century.

4. The site underwent some alterations in the Hellenistic period, including a series of predecessors of the South Building (discussed by Scranton), perhaps a predecessor of the Northwest Building, and the Semicircular Monument, but there was little major change.

5. It is now possible to understand the Roman contribution to the Sanctuary, which was embodied in the modernizing and refining of existing areas. The Romans did not change the ritually fixed division of this space, as was previously believed.[14]

6. The Augustan period saw intensive development, culminating in major works of the Neronian period. This probably includes the rusticated, stately second Temple of Apollo and the aqueduct to supply the castellum and Kourion City to the east. The final phase of the Round Building, its initial northwest ramp, the paved street, the filling in of one cistern (No. 3) at the southeast limit of the East Complex (this may be as late as the Flavian period), and probably the rebuilding of the Northwest Building belong here, as does the building of the temenos wall around the West Enclosure and possibly of the first eastward extension of the Archaic Precinct to add a stoa, or storage magazine. The rock-cut channels were filled and the Palaestra may have been built at this time.

7. The final major Roman phase included the Baths, the Kourion Gate, and changes in the castellum and the present South Building. The present stoa area east of the Archaic Precinct probably dates to the time of Trajan. The final cobbled northwest approach to the Round Building may also date to this period.

8. The only pre-earthquake constructions that can be assigned thus far to post-Trajanic times are the stepped area in the northwest corner of the Southeast Building (at least Antonine) and the fourth-century simple reflooring in the West Complex.

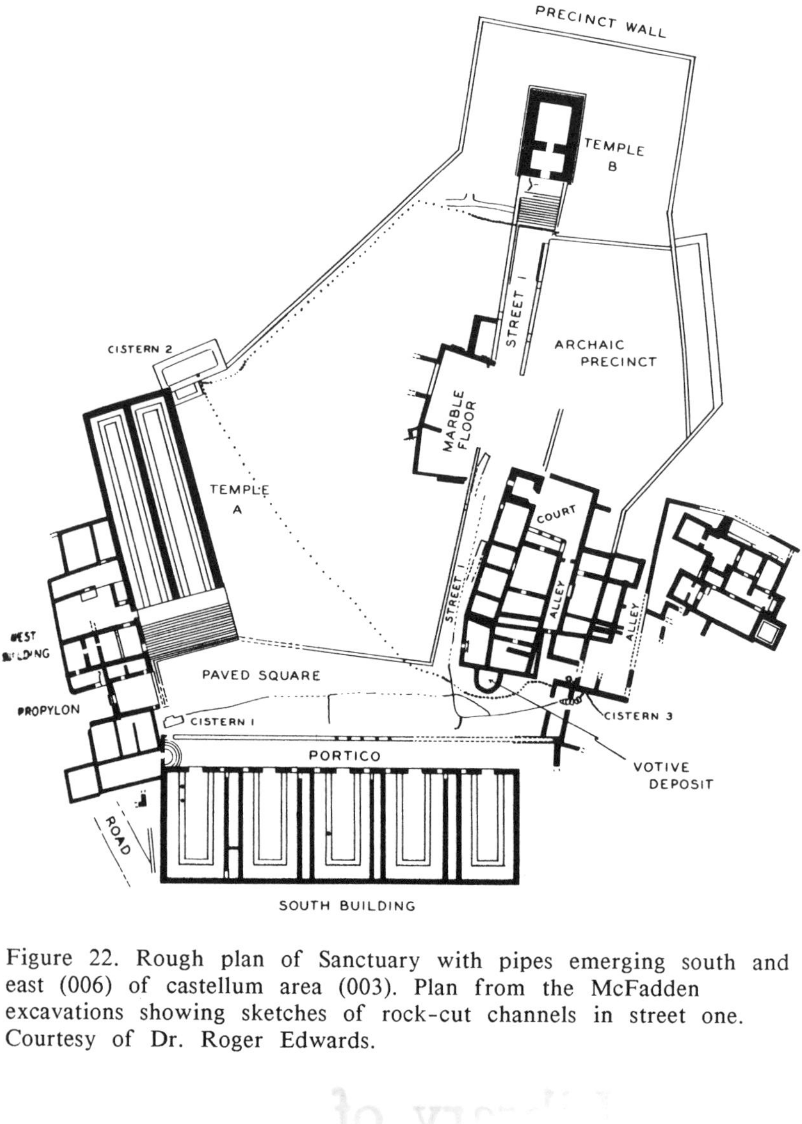

Figure 22. Rough plan of Sanctuary with pipes emerging south and east (006) of castellum area (003). Plan from the McFadden excavations showing sketches of rock-cut channels in street one. Courtesy of Dr. Roger Edwards.

9. Although quite a few buildings cannot be assigned to phases, enough have been understood to reveal the sanctuary's patterns of growth and decline. The site began in a simple, rustic vein, and was monumentalized by the Archaic period. The Classical period hosted a further boom and a cult change to Apollo. The Hellenistic period added monuments and renovations, but few drastic changes were made, while the Romans respected the site, modernized it architecturally, and brought flowing water and a tighter organization of buildings and spaces.

10. There was little post-Trajanic building activity and the latest evidence suggests that the site was destroyed by earthquake on July 21, 365 A.D., at about 5:30 A.M., by which time it may already have been in diminished use and ill repair, judging from the poor quality of the West Complex flooring at this time and recent discoveries by the author at Kourion City.

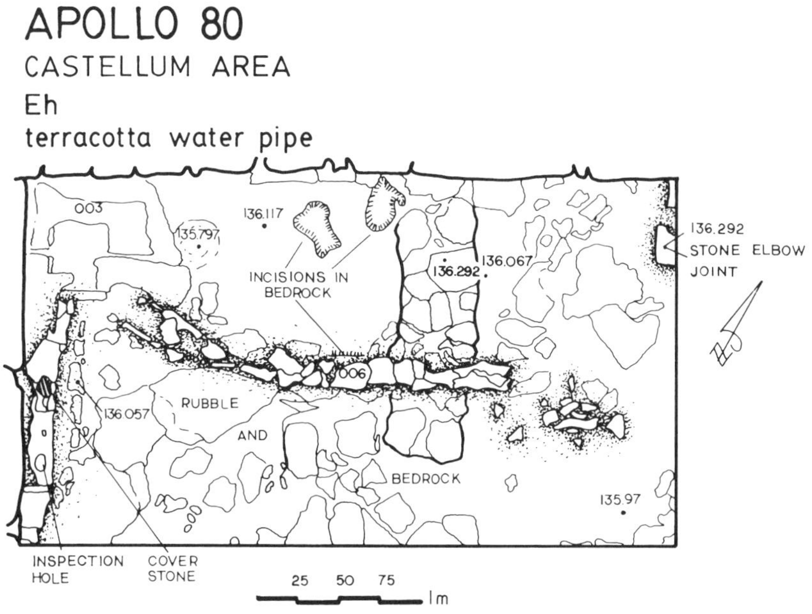

APOLLO 80
CASTELLUM AREA
Eh
terracotta water pipe

Figure 23. Plan of the Castellum area showing distribution of water: late pipe (006) running east from *castellum* 003, early pipe with inspection hole running to the south.

11. This earthquake destroyed much of southwest Cyprus; the previous dating of the final quakes as ca. 325 to 350 A.D. over *all* of Cyprus cannot be substantiated. Kourion City and Paphos apparently ended at the same time, since the epicenter was located about thirty miles southwest of Kourion.

12. The Sanctuary was not rebuilt, but squatters did settle and do some building in reused materials, especially in the eastern area of the Palaestra. A Christian community grew up at Kourion City in the late fourth or early fifth century, but not before 383 A.D., when coins reappear with some frequency.

In addition to the urban studies that produced the above conclusions, other new ideas were formulated:

1. The Round Building, the only structure discovered in the new excavations, apparently is unique in Mediterranean archaeology: it is a cult building, perhaps for ring dancing, planted with sacred trees.

2. The *alsos*, or sacred grove area, cited in Aelian (*De Nat. Anim.* 11,7) may include the park area of the West Enclosure and might have functioned as a sort of zoo or sacred animal preserve.

Figure 24. Bipod overhead photograph of the Semicircular Monument.

3. The religion practiced at Kourion involved strong Near Eastern connections, including the worship of sacred trees, baetyls and bulls, sheep or goat sacrifices, and ring dancing; these practices apparently remained, like the site, little changed over many centuries, perhaps as long as one thousand years.

4. The second Temple of Apollo not only can be dated fairly precisely, but can be partly reconstructed in detail up to and including the roof tiles; it is now being rebuilt by the Cypriote Department of Antiquities and Professor Sinos. The first temple may also be fairly well dated.

5. The Semicircular Monument most likely can be dated to 200-193 B.C., and apparently was a statue base for Demetrios of Thessaly, Commandant of Kourion, his wife, and their children (Inscription I 158).

6. The coins and architecture of the Roman period suggest connections with Syria more than with the western Roman world, and the pottery is a mixture of western and eastern imports and local material, especially in the Early Imperial period.

7. Excellent examples of Archaic Cypriote pottery, of Gjerstad Type IV, Greek mainland pottery, and terra cottas were recovered from the first temple and the Round Building. The Cypriote pottery is difficult to date, with various scholars suggesting a range from 800 B.C. to the mid-sixth century B.C., but the accompanying Greek pottery suggests the late date is closer to the date of these buildings.

8. The earthquake that devastated the area was assigned, on the basis of the coin evidence, to the July 21, 365, quake cited in Ammianus as occurring at about 5:30 A.M.[16]

Although these conclusions will be elaborated upon in this and subsequent volumes, a few explanatory observations are useful. One of the focal points for the study of the development of the site must, of course, be the Temple of Apollo. The fill of the cella floor of the first temple, along with the foundations of the temple walls, yielded only Archaic pottery, of which the latest identifiable piece dates to about the middle to end of the sixth century B.C. If this fill contains material from about the time of the construction of the first temple, then one could imagine a simple, Archaic building with, presumably, an adequate street leading up to it even at this early period.

Apparently associated with the first temple to the southwest is a T-shaped rock-cut channel. This channel would have marked out the *temenos*, or sacred area, here and separated it from the temenos of the West Enclosure. But the rock-cut channel was filled in during the creation of the second temple, as shown by pottery found in the channel fill and in fills placed against the second temple. A number of pits to the east of the temple, dug in grid areas Jc3 and Jd1 and 2 (see Chapter 1), also would seem to have functioned as planting pits for bushes or trees in a grove associated with the first temple, and then to have been filled in when the second temple was built. The same planting idea appears to have been used for two other areas: (1) the rock-channel discovered by McFadden (but no longer visible) before the East Stoa along the temple street, and (2) the channel along the northwestern temenos wall of the West Enclosure.

This is important, because now it is possible to suggest that the rock-cut channel west of the temple was installed to frame the first temple with landscaping. It cannot be proved that the cuttings were not added some time after the construction of the first temple, but the careful relationship of the channels to the main sacred areas of the Sanctuary allows us to believe that it may all have been done as part of an original, quite inventive, and attractive scheme of demarcation.

The East Stoa, which has its own channel before it, has been tentatively dated by Robert Scranton to the fourth century B.C. Certainly the two rock-cut channels found by McFadden along the main street predate the Roman rebuilding of the street in the Julio-Claudian period; despite an apparently slightly angled orientation (unverified because these channels are not visible today), they could have provided a landscaped border to the sacred way.[17]

A sacred temenos (the West Enclosure) appears to have been enclosed by the following areas: the rock-cut channel running along under the temple steps, the original main street to the east of the West Enclosure, the rock-cut channel of the northwest temenos wall already cited, and, we believe, some rock-cut channel or predecessor of the Northwest Building (the so-called Temple A) to the southwest. A southern limit may have been the street area just east of the Paphos Gate and, of course, this precinct could have been further subdivided.

The site developed rapidly from a simple open core in the Archaic Precinct to larger, well-defined sacred enclosures and a "temple." In 1984 it was discovered that the area of the West Enclosure was in use as a sacred precinct from at least the later sixth century B.C. Finds from fills just over bedrock, as well as from within the ring wall of the Round Building itself, are exclusively of this date or earlier, even though the paving within the Round Building did not predate the first century A.D. It is not inconceivable, based on our finds, that the temple, rock-cut channels, and the initial phase of the Round Building went closely together as part of an expansion of the site from the Archaic Precinct. How much earlier the Archaic Precinct actually is will be determined when Buitron completes her study of these finds. Certainly the expansion of the site in the sixth century B.C. helped to bring the Sanctuary more into line with parallel sanctuaries of Cyprus such as Ayia Irini, which may have developed and expanded somewhat earlier (seventh century) and Meniko (largely sixth century).

Because of the difficulties in dating Cypriote pottery of the Archaic period, it is hard to give a precise date to this expansion and development of the site, but a date in the later sixth century is suggested by the Greek pottery found in the Temple and under the Round Building, as studied by Luisa Ferrer Dias and Ines Vaz Pinto. Further excavation and pottery studies will, it is hoped, determine more precise dates for the expansion and will settle the question of whether it happened at one time or more gradually.

Whatever the details turn out to be, it seems clear that the first temple (without crosswall) and the initial Round Building were built, and that a good deal of landscaping, construction, and ritual demarcation went on, around the middle to late sixth century B.C. There was also considerable activity in the Sanctuary between the end of the fifth century B.C. and the end of the fourth, as the coin evidence shows. It is also significant that, unlike the Archaic Altar, there is no evidence of any structure *preceding* the first temple or the Round Building, a fact which further supports the idea that the Sanctuary expanded for the first time in the sixth century.

There is thus far only one example of construction from the period between the later fifth and later fourth centuries B.C. In the Southeast Building, or Palaestra, an L-shaped course of ashlar blocks can still be seen jutting out from the eastern end of the structure. This wall is all that remains of a sizable and possibly elegant building that predated the Southeast Building and rests on nothing but a uniform fill placed over bedrock. The pottery from the fill in which the wall rests was studied by Diana Buitron in 1978 and will be published by her. But it is significant to note that the date assigned to the imported material in the fill was approximately mid-fourth century B.C.[18] This is one indication of what may have been another master plan falling within the Classical period, rather than the Archaic, but the precise nature of the predecessor of the Southeast Building is unknown.

It is beyond the scope of this chapter to establish the reasons for so much cult activity and expansion in the mid to late sixth century B.C., but a few tentative, preliminary observations might be offered. Certainly the Round Building occurs in Greek architecture, and there are at least some examples of Greek (Corinthian and Athenian) pottery at the Sanctuary in the sixth century.[19] Euelthon, ruler of the period in the great city of Salamis, is known to have dedicated an altar at Delphi, home of many *tholoi*, including a sixth-century example found in the ruins of the Sikyonian treasury.[20]

Whether the tholos form moved from mainland Greece to influence Cyprus (a land with a strong underpinning of Greek culture from Bronze Age times), or whether the round form reached Greece from Cyprus, cannot be settled here.[21] We can but re-emphasize that the two cultures were in contact. The use of the round form to enclose what may be an hypaethral tree shrine appears to be unique in Mediterranean archaeology.

After the late Archaic and Classical periods of development at the Sanctuary, the identification of architectural growth or change there becomes difficult. The West Enclosure probably was a park or an unpaved ritual area, whose function might have been to facilitate access to the Round Building and to promote the open-air veneration of sacred trees. A brief discussion of the chronology of this area from the sixth century B.C. to the Roman Imperial period will show how these are developed.

The excavation of the fill in the West Enclosure in the area of the Round Building shows that artificial terracing over bedrock begins with material of the sixth century B.C., then progresses upward to a mix of Hellenistic and Julio-Claudian material, itself mixed with earlier finds. Occasional Roman sherds were carried down toward bedrock through root action, burrowing, pitting, and even some plowing, and the soil is always loose and lacking in distinct floor levels. In short, it reflects the typical progression of a park area over centuries, during which the floor level would rise slightly from period to period, reterracing would occur, and material would occasionally intermix. But within the wall of the Round Building itself, the finds were absolutely uniform and sealed.

Access to the terrace of the Round Building, a large landscaped precinct of artificial fill and high undulating bedrock, probably came through the southwesternmost room of the Central Court; a low-lying wall has been located running under and at an angle to the present northwest wall of the room. Within this wall is a threshold block at about terrace level; this would appear to lead to the Round Building and its terrace (see Fig. 1: the room just above the Semicircular Monument). The wall had no foundation trench and the fill packed up against it contained no Roman material, but precise dating of the wall has not yet been achieved.

The Round Building would have sat on its relatively flat, artificially elevated terrace, framed originally by rock-cut channels apparently planted with trees and bushes. There was originally no entry to the terrace from the northwest. The Round Building, with its wide but poorly made sixth-century B.C. ring wall, could have supported an exterior colonnade, but no trace of this survives. Indeed, its poor state of preservation makes any attempt at reconstruction purely conjectural.

At this point it is instructive to pause and admire this popular Sanctuary as it looked in the second century B.C., before the Romans redeveloped it. One can imagine what it was like to walk down the main temple street noting the predecessor of the Roman East Stoa and its planted frontal area, the Central Court (central organizational point), and the lovely view of rounded forms (the Semicircular Monument and the Round Building on the terrace above it), the whole surrounded by an orderly, attractive row of bushes and/or trees.

From the Central Court, the Round Building was reached by going west. The Archaic Altar, untouchable under penalty of death, was in its precinct to the east, and the adyton, or temple box, was straight ahead. Some predecessor of the South Building added a framing touch to the south part of the street. The boundaries of the central and western parts of the site seem similar to those respected later by the Romans, who would simply further monumentalize, focus, and enclose the structures of the Apollo Sanctuary.

In light of our work at the Sanctuary, the Roman alterations now seem to be more in the nature of aesthetic and functional refinements of previously existing structures than of dramatic development. The main Roman building took place, so far as we know, in two major phases: the Julio-Claudian period (culminating in massive changes under Nero), and the Trajanic period. By the time of Nero the temple street was repaved and its rock-cut channels filled in. Buildings along the street were renovated, perhaps including the East Stoa and the southwest room of the Central Court, which would have been straightened out to provide better access to the terrace of the Round Building. Ground level in this room, as it leads up to the terrace, varies from 5 to 15 cm higher than ground level in the rest of the Central Court.

The simple pre-Roman temple was rebuilt on the same foundations and then dedicated between 50 and 75 A.D., according to the fragment of the dedicatory inscription found by John Rutherford in 1980 and interpreted by Eugene Lane. The Temple of Apollo was reconstructed in Syrian style with Roman rusticated wall blocks, which were only slightly behind the times. The vogue for rustication began with the Roman Emperor Claudius and can be seen in such main-line Roman monuments as the Claudeanum and the Porta Maggiore. The large number of Julio-Claudian coins found around the site, and tallied by John MacIsaac of Johns Hopkins University, attests to major urban growth in this period, as well as to strong eastern connections in the mint marks.

In order to emphasize the new temple, the rock-cut channels west of the temple were filled in and the pits to the east were also apparently put out of use. The temple was then beautifully surrounded, as if it were in a large exedra; this was accomplished through the construction of a fine ashlar temenos wall at least six courses high.

The pits were replaced by a surface level of, perhaps, grass. At any rate, collapsed wall blocks from the earthquake of circa 365 A.D. covering the fill in the rock-cut channel in grid area Hc covered *only* earth; there was no trace of a floor ever having existed in that spot in Neronian times or later. This desire to leave much of the Sanctuary unfloored, of course, renders excavation of the site very difficult.

The rock-cut channel inside the northwest temenos wall was filled in at this time and replaced by the continuation of the temenos wall, but there were even more important changes in this area of the site. The large cistern and castellum complex that bonds into the temenos wall was put in place at this time, bringing the site into the path of the aqueduct for fresh water supply. Many sites on Cyprus received their first Roman water supply systems under Claudius or Nero, so it is especially appropriate that the

Sanctuary of Apollo should be able to be placed among this group. At the Sanctuary itself, a Julio-Claudian inscription commemorates a pavement before a fountain area.[22]

It seems reasonable that the nearby city of Kourion would also have fit into this scheme, and Joseph Last has shown that the city and Sanctuary were supplied from the same source, through a common pipe for most of the distance. Thus the dating of the water supply at the Sanctuary has important corollaries for dating the first aqueduct supply in the city, for which there previously had been no evidence.

The high level of the cistern, castellum, and pipes is evidence that the ground level was high to the west of the temenos wall in this area. As the revived Sanctuary was being lavishly redeveloped during the Julio-Claudian period, the street entry to the previously existing Round Building was redone, but this work apparently was insufficient to provide access to that structure. A monumental entry was installed, therefore, in the temenos wall near the castellum (Fig. 25). This new entry, one presumes, could accommodate processions into the West Enclosure, but one problem remained: the disparity between the high ground level west of the temenos wall and the lower, flatter level of the terrace of the West Enclosure had now to be linked. This was done by building a sort of stepped platform and ramped viewing area leading from the new entry down to the Round Building through an eight to ten per cent slope beginning in grid Gg. These changes may reflect a revival in popularity for the cult during the Imperial period, following more limited activity in the late Hellenistic period.

The relationship of the water supply system to the remodeled Round Building also is worth noting. One pipe from the castellum area ran under the ramp and headed off to points still unknown (the stone elbow joint of it is just visible in Fig. 22). It may have linked up with a pipe embedded in the wall in the northeast area of the Round Building. No doubt the Round Building itself was revamped and provided with an appropriately monumental northwest entry, but future seasons will have to enlighten us further on this badly preserved but fascinating monument.

A second original pipe left the castellum and ran southeast, curving around the previously existing Round Building and continuing around the second-century-B.C. Semicircular Monument. It ended in front of that structure, feeding water under the newly re-laid street into a conduit. Thus street, temple, ramp, temenos wall, pipes, castellum complex, and the entry from the street to the Round Building were all bound up in a lavish development program associated with the bringing of water by aqueduct to the Sanctuary.

A word of caution: despite the unified look of the building program, one must be careful not to ascribe all of it to circa 50 or 75 A.D. The large amount of Julio-Claudian material all over the site shows much activity here over the entire first two-thirds of the first century. But Nero and his representatives, in particular,

Figure 25. View from northwest over Round Building and its Northwest Entry, the Castellum and the Northwest Building.

were quite active in our area and elsewhere on Cyprus, perhaps even overspending in the Kourion area: a limited rebuilding of the theater of Kourion took place in 64 or 65 A.D.[23] It would seem, too, that the Sanctuary was in need of updating and rejuvenation, since we seem to lack structures or evidence for any elaborate building schemes in the Hellenistic period.

As the water pipe from the castellum emerges from the southern end of the temple street, it jogs eastward and enters a large well house, not yet fully studied, in the East Complex. Next to this area was a cistern, which contained a good amount of late Hellenistic material in its bottommost layers but was filled up to the top with pottery and lamps datable between the Julio-Claudian and the early Flavian period. Perhaps with the introduction of the aqueduct and water supply system this cistern was no longer needed. The Hellenistic material from the cistern floor would date from the natural accumulation in it over time and may suggest that it was virtually out of use for quite some time before it was filled in.[24]

A few additional remarks on the Julio-Claudian phase of the site are in order. The temenos wall is set further from the second temple on the east side than on the west, perhaps in deference to the area originally marked out for a sacred grove, or perhaps indicating that some monument is still waiting to be discovered in that area. In 1978 the temenos wall was traced south from grid Ld to Lg; a small wall parallel to and just east of the temenos wall, forming a small room, was discovered. Such a room might be a much needed storage area/magazine for excess dedications, or perhaps a mini-stoa. In any case, it should not be earlier than the Julio-Claudian period in date.[25]

A late pipe (Locus 006) was found cut into the castellum above the level of the original pipes and running northeast. McFadden followed this pipe for some considerable distance and noted several changes in direction, which we shall discuss momentarily. There now appears to be much evidence that this particular pipe is Trajanic. The evidence is: (1) the next post-Neronian major building period at the Sanctuary occurred under Trajan and included at least the South Building, Baths, and Kourion Gate; (2) such a building period must have put new demands on the forty-year-old castellum and forced some changes in it; (3) the bath, dated by inscription to 101 or 102 A.D., would have had to have been linked up with the aqueduct in order to insure a satisfactory water supply.

Some cosmetic surgery on the cobble ramp leading to the Round Building must have been required so that this late pipe could be installed. As yet, however, the ramp has not been excavated enough to determine for certain that this pipe was installed as an after-thought. In any case, the pipe continues along the temenos wall, then turns sharply eastward in grid Hd. The pipe then rather awkwardly crosses the street in front of the temple, presumably because the Trajanic pipe needed to cross an already existing Julio-Claudian paved street.

The pipe ran just north of the north wall of the Archaic Precinct (Fig. 26) and around and perhaps partly through the double wall of a large and long stoa-like structure existing from grids Le to Mg. This larger "stoa" replaced the simpler stoa already cited. The pipe emerges from the south end of the final version of the stoa and heads directly for the water supply area of the Trajanic baths.

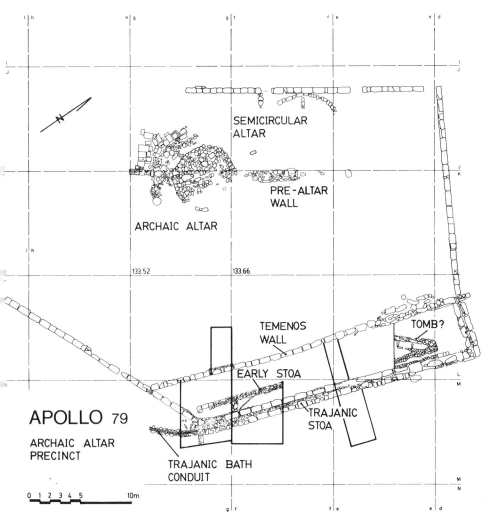

Figure 26. Plan of eastern limit of Archaic Altar Precinct showing only area excavated and cleaned in 1978.

Just how the Southeast Building, West Complex, East Complex, and some buildings of the Central Court fit into the two main periods of building is still in need of clarification, but it seems that little building activity can be dated to the period between Hadrian and the earthquake of circa 365 A.D., save for some new steps leading up from the Southeast Building. Essentially, by the middle of the reign of Trajan the site was complete and very much resembled what is now visible.

Some reflooring was done in the West Complex during the 330s, but the Sanctuary may have fallen on evil days even before the final quake. Floor slabs were missing from the West Complex under the quake debris. However, the major monuments were still standing at the time of the quake. Wall blocks from the South Building, the Temple of Apollo, the principal street and the West Enclosure tended to fall to the north and east, the earthquake's epicenter having been to the southwest.

Simple squatter additions to the Southeast Building, and perhaps to the Baths, seem to have closely followed the devastation, but the most extensive squatter occupation did not predate 500 A.D. in the Southeast Building, where quake debris has been mounded up under a dirt floor and a window-sill from the earlier building has become a crude threshold.

It is fascinating to observe the growth and death of a great Sanctuary over some one thousand years, from its rustic open-air origins through gradual expansions and refurbishings to final Roman focus and monumentality. The unusual combination of cult space (open air altar precinct), a ring dancing space, a sacred grove, formal landscaping and planning, and Greek forms (temple, tholos form), finally infused with Roman flowing water, more monumental buildings, and more formally enclosed spaces, gives the Sanctuary unique appeal for students of the evolution of architectural and spatial design in an area where eastern ritual met the Hellenic *koiné* and syncretized. It must be noted that the suggestions offered here are merely hypotheses based on the facts, and that the conclusions are subject to alteration as we come to understand more about the development of this most extraordinary cult site.

Finally, it is impossible not to observe that the continuity of the pagan way of life can still be seen on Cyprus (as in most agrarian societies) in the continued veneration of stones and trees, and in the faith in the healing powers of Christianized saints, to whom votives not much different from the clay offerings at the Sanctuary are brought. This continuity through time of religious thought and ritual space in this region has been repeatedly emphasized by Karageorghis and is brought out by our work at the Sanctuary.

Chapter 3
Environmental Geology
Reuben Bullard

Kourion is situated in an area underlain by the Pakhna Formation, a
rock unit composed of beds and lenses of bioclastic limestone (a
calcarenite with layers of shell fragments, locally well-cemented,
but in some occurrences friable) and argillaceous biomicrite. This
formation is everywhere blanketed with a solution-generated deposit
known as caliche. It is not the soil zone hard-pan of the American
Southwest, but a sub-solum, less soluble residue capping on the
partially dissolved parent rock. The fossil forms and bedding
fabric usually are lost in this weathering process, as the
identifying morphology of both is completely altered. This
weathering process yields a red/brown terra-rossa type soil, from
which the flora and fauna of the area draw their vital sustenance.

Historically, during the Miocene Epoch, this area of Cyprus
constituted a continental shelf depositional environment with
abundant shallow water marine organisms, such as reef colonies,
with ecologically related forms, such as pecten up to 10 cm in
size. Subsequently, this region has undergone at least two major
phases of uplift: a gradual one in the Late Pliocene and Early
Pleistocene, as is evident from outcrops in the valley on the
eastern side of the British military base two miles west of
Kourion, and another in Roman times, yielding headlands with
characteristic sea cliffs enhanced by the rapid erosion of wave and
breaker activity (Fig. 27-29).

The decision to locate the Sanctuary of Apollo where it is may
have been influenced by the commanding topographic relief that is
so abruptly punctuated by the geologically recent and relatively

53

54   *Environmental Geology*

unstable vertical cliff faces bordering the area on the south. The remote location of this facility from the city-site of Kourion may be most logically viewed from this perspective.

A stone quarry (Fig. 30-33) on the north and east flanks of the bluff on which Kourion City was situated exploited the lithic commodity so much in evidence in the Sanctuary and city structures. Here the Khalassa Member of the Pakhna Formation seems to have attracted the interest of Roman architects. This calcarenite facies (Fig. 34) exhibits considerable variation in texture and fabric, ranging from silt- and sand-sized bioclasts to adult wave-worn mollusk shells and shell fragments, usually well bonded by calcite cement. They occur in massive units locally over a meter in thickness or in lenses that are poorly cemented and friable. The weakly bonded particles of any size in this unit are eroded in pockets and lenses by mass wasting, by rain-drop impact, and by wind, both in the quarry faces and in certain architectural remnants on the archaeological sites.

Figure 27. View from south of Kourion cliffs overlooking harbor due south of the Apollo Sanctuary.

The character of the lithic material available in this and other quarry sites of similar composition was suitably resistant for such uses as threshold blocks, door jambs, and lintels. Wedges and lenses of quality stone were quarried and worked with a minimum of loss in the fabrication process. It is important to consider the effects of stone selection: one threshold in the South Building (Fig. 35) was cut from a poor quality rock layer, and one-third of its thickness of weakly cemented fabric eroded from the Roman traffic over it.

There appears to have been a great interest in ledges of thin-bedded fissile rock (Fig. 36) in the area. Those occurring in the upper part of the Kourion quarry consisted of a very fine-grained calcarenite and provided a convenient thickness suitable for paving blocks. The sides of these blocks were not always trimmed, because joint faces (trending mainly north to north 4° east) were in no need of cutting by those masons responsible for

Figure 28. View to west of Figure 1.

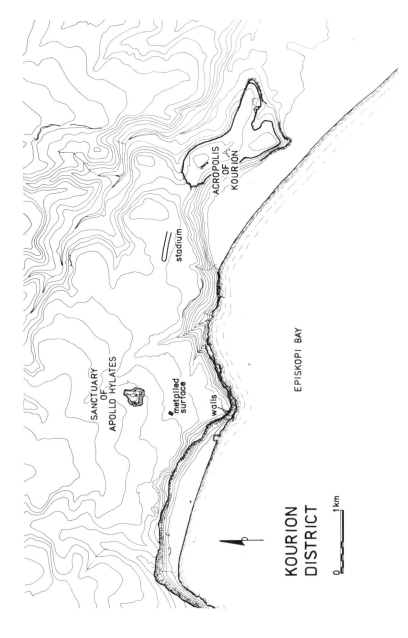

Figure 29. Map of Episkopi Bay area. Drawing by Noelle Soren and John Rutherford.

Figure 30. View of Calcarenite quarry northeast of Kourion City.

Figure 31. Ancient quarrying area of calcarenite showing Roman step-ledge quarry technique and ancient weathering on the surface.

the paving of floors, terraces, and streets in antiquity. The flag-stones employed at the Sanctuary have a marked fissility: bedding planes with microlaminations. Some examples appear on the floors of Rooms 2 and 3 of the South Building, with a few blocks showing a relatively coarse-grained texture. Thousands of cubic meters of building stone have been quarried from this source. Evidence of masons working the quarry is visible on most of the worked faces, the exception being the joint faces, which, of course, need no effort on the part of quarrymen.

Recent examination of the quarry provided evidence for the antiquity of the workings. The eastern shelves of the quarry site show advanced calicheation, to the extent that all tool marks have vanished in the surface solution process. Yet the shelving and ledges have the tell-tale troughing that reflects ashlar-block or ashlar cutting techniques. One especially massive unit was noted in the quarry. It is 90 cm thick and quite suitable for small and medium diameter column drums (e.g., the ones used in the Apollo Sanctuary area).

Ashlars fabricated from the Kourion quarry often have textures grading from fine to coarse within the same block. Quarrymen always cut such lithics parallel to the original bedding planes in the rock faces, with respect to the long and intermediate dimensions of the finished block. In these cut lithics (Fig. 37 and 38) and in the quarry faces one can easily observe the evidence of storm conditions existing in the shallow marine shelf-type sea floor environment in which pod and nodular fragments of that bottom area are torn up and carried to local depositional sites. Locally, the quarry facade shows convoluted bedding planes indicative of submarine slump. Such fragments in the instances noted are composed of granule- to pebble-size pellets of calcareous silts and clays. Many of the larger ones are weathered differentially to form pits and cavities in the surfaces of the worked architectural members, including columns throughout the Sanctuary site and several ashlars in the western foundation of the Temple of Apollo. Another popular lithic used in this site consists of tabulate blocks fashioned from soft chalky limestone, used not in traffic-bearing surfaces, of course, but in wall aggregate make-up.

Several fault lines running through the center of the quarry are oriented north 4° east and 00 north, respectively, and there is a 3-cm drop visible in the fault areas of the quarry. Thirty-centimeter displacements exist in the area of the Achilles Mosaic in the northwest area of the city site. This is reminiscent of the natural north-south fault line in the pools of Qumran on the west side of the Dead Sea.

Caliche was used in the building, terrace, and free-standing walls of the site. This stone is formed by weathering processes operating in a semi-arid environment on porous to semi-porous fine-grained calcareous lithics, especially chalks and chalky gypsiferous marls. It occurs under soils of the Mediterranean type as a solution-deposited, brittle, brecciated $CaCO_3$ crust to about

2 m in thickness on the unaltered parent rock. Small, local, ancient quarry sites, shallow and perhaps without clearly delineated rock faces, seem to have wasted rapidly and are not as clearly evident as the city-site source. Since seventy to eighty percent of the Sanctuary site is constructed of this material, it would not be surprising to consider the ledge capping the eastward-trending valley, south-southeast of the site (just south of the modern entrance off the Limassol-Paphos highway) as one of the principal sources. Another series of cutting disturbances is evident along the side of the upper valley immediately northeast of the Sanctuary. Other sources may abound and certainly existed.

Specific use of this lithic occurs in all internal courses of the temple cella and pronaos. The whole south wall of the South Building and most of its other foundation courses are composed of it. The caliche foundation courses on the north facade of this building are interrupted by thresholds of the bioclastic calcarenite; the interspersed caliche is arranged by design into patterns. The calcarenite constituted a more expensive architectural commodity, since it was quarried and trimmed with more care and its source is more remote from the Sanctuary site.

It is not surprising to discover that the Archaic Altar is composed entirely of caliche. These blocks have a variant fabric and seem to have originated from quarry sites other than those used by the Roman builders, a confirming note for an earlier construction of this feature.

A terra-rossa soil cover produced by the solution weathering of the carbonate bedrock overlies the caliche crust in areas where it is held in place by plant growth. The crust-soil interface is typical of a solution-depositional surface exhibiting an irregular undulating appearance quite characteristic of the solution/precipitation-generated material.

The caliche provides an architectural commodity that varies from a hard, brittle, and crusty fabric to a friable, sometimes powdery fabric. Other than the solution surface, its trimmed sides are rough and raspy, never very smooth. The softer components of the rock consisted of nodules and lenses of chalk (sometimes gypsiferous), clayey to powdery white, cream to yellow-tan in color, and occasionally fine-sand to granular-sized loose carbonate fossil Protista shell fragments (note that calcareous or chalky clay may be termed marl). A redeposited late floor in grid area Om 3/4 (palestra annex) is of this nature and is derived from a subcrystal caliche bedrock source.

The term havara, employed frequently by George McFadden and by the present excavators of Phaneromeni (James Carpenter and Field Director Stuart Swiny), refers to a concentration of calcium carbonate within the soil clays above the rock crust. The term relates to caliche conditions (such as exist in the semi-arid American Southwest), but must be used with caution, as it refers to a soil hard pan and not to the recrystallized rock itself.

Evidence of caliche wasting can be seen in the ashlar blocks in grid area Hg3 exposed in section in the west area of the Central Court. Such caliche disaggregation still goes on (Fig. 39) as tourists climb the soft temple walls (which excavators and exhibitors should cap and point with appropriately pigmented portland cement).

A gypsum-rich mortar matrix with selenite crystals was used in temple construction (Fig. 40). A potential source for this is the Pissouri area about ten miles west of the Sanctuary. Modern tuck-pointing accounts for mortar about two-thirds of the way down the pronaos and cella wall. A white, pure calcined lime plaster with pebble aggregate was used for the floor of the Round Building.

Traces of a roadway were detected running south-southwest from the Sanctuary to the vertical sea cliff (see Fig. 29). Traces of metalling on an incipiently troughed caliche bedrock surface seem to have arisen from abrasion movement along this route. It follows a direct alignment between the cliff and the site. There is a local and ancient tradition of such a road. Vestiges of an ancient structure are present on the edge of the cliff surface. There are also some cuttings and shelvings in the caliche west and northwest of the site, which may represent localized quarry activities and house foundation excavation. Weathering precludes the assignment of recent activity here.

Finally, the castellum in the northwest limit of the site was examined and found to have cracked in antiquity (Fig. 41), perhaps from seismic settling activity. The cracks were sealed by a mortaring-in of ceramic and tile fragments, as well as by placement of elongated limestone stream-rounded pebbles. The original mortar surfacing of the cistern is composed of a dispersion of hematitic terra-rossa fragments, which imparts to the layer its pinkish hue. Crushed ceramics and tiles were employed at other Roman sites as mortar aggregate.

An understanding of the relationship of the Apollo Sanctuary to its geological environment is essential for an understanding of its historical geography. The topographic setting of this area, operating together with the floral (forest) environment of the site, undoubtedly influenced its location. The aesthetic sensitivities of the Greek and Roman occupants of the island of Cyprus are seen in the lithic repertoire selected from both local and occasionally distant sources for the architectural statements they made with their structures.

Figure 32. Quarry site overview illustrating volume of area removed between top of cliff and calcarenite ledge to the extreme right.

Figure 33. Calcarenite quarry cliff face showing chisel techniques.

Figure 34. Quarry face showing mollusk shell deposition pellets and pods of calcareous muds, and nodular chert in a fabric illustrating storm conditions.

Figure 35. Weathered calcarenite threshold in the South Building.

Figure 36. Flagstones from the temple street showing marked fissility.

Figure 37. Blocks from north wall of the South Building showing fossiliferous limestone with megascopic mollusks and pecten in a biopelsparite.

Figure 38. Western foundation of the Temple of Apollo showing depositional environment storm conditions.

Figure 39. Evidence of caliche abrasion from traffic on the southeast corner of the podium of the Temple of Apollo.

Figure 40. Recrystallized gypsum mortar (selenite) from the northern interior wall of the Temple of Apollo.

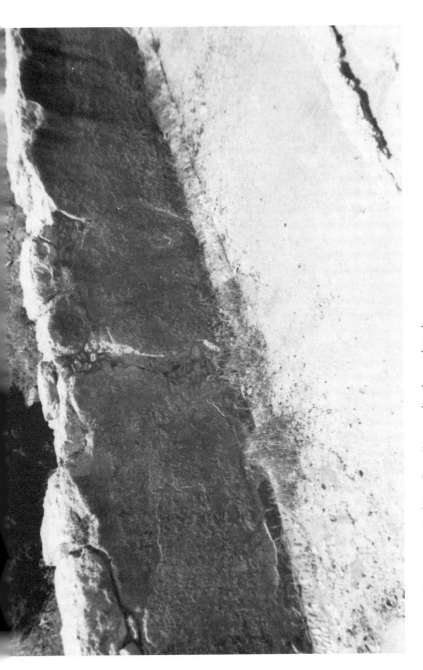

Figure 41. Cracked wall of the Castellum main cistern interior.

Chapter 4
Recent and Fossil Shells
David S. Reese

The excavations conducted at the Sanctuary of Apollo Hylates at
Kourion from 1978 to 1980 produced fifty-six recent marine shells
from forty-seven individuals, twenty land snails, and five fossil
bivalves. Table 1 catalogs the shells recovered, giving the
scientific name, English and Greek common names, and the number of
specimens preserved.

The twenty land snails are of three species found living at the
site today. The small number does not indicate that any were
consumed and they probably are fortuitous. In fact, eleven of the
thirteen *Rumina* and all of the *Eubania* (one still preserving some
of the natural coloring) come from one superficial locus (Jg 001).

Because of the nature of the site, the archaeological contexts
were filled with earlier intrusive materials, so that dates must be
taken as a *terminus ante quem* for all shells. One *Arcularia*, with
an irregular hole on the side of the body, one *Donax* and one *Helix*
(Gh4 017), and one *Patella* (Gh4 021) from the fill beside the Round
Building of the Western Enclosure may be sixth century B.C. or
earlier. A vermetid and sponge-bored *Charonia* columella (gastropod
central "stem") fragment from the cella of the first Temple of
Apollo (Jb 003) is from a sealed context of the sixth century B.C.
or earlier, and one *Murex* fragment is from a context of the
mid-first century A.D. (Eh 002) in the castellum area, but the
layer has much earlier material.

Deposits dating to about the middle of the first century A.D.,
including much earlier material, in the West Enclosure (Gi1/Gh3
001, Gi2 001, Gi2-Gg4 034) produced one worn *Murex* fragment, one
Patella, and four *Donax* fragments from four individuals, one of
which is charred grey. A similar locus in the same area (Ii 002)
contained a 24-mm-long *Erosaria* cowrie with a 4 x 2 mm hole at the
small end, a *Rumina*, and a small fossil oyster fragment.

72

TABLE 1

Recent and Fossil Shells from the Sanctuary
of Apollo Hylates, Kourion, Cyprus

Grid Area	*Locus*	*No.*		
1978	Hg3	003	SH6	1 *Donax*(right)
	004			1 *Helix* land snail
				4 *Donax* (all r)
	007		SH5	1 *Arcularia* with nice circular hole
	007		SH7,SH8	1 *Rumina* land snail
				2 *Donax* (both r)
	008			1 *Donax* (left)
	012		SH9	1 *Patella*
	013		SH10	1 *Patella*
	Mg1	001	SH3	14 *Donax* individuals (23 valves)
1979	Cl	002	ZS.46	1 *Dolium* fragment (large shell)
	Glhl	008	ZS.51	1 *Cerastoderma* fragment - worm
	Jb	003	ZS.52	1 *Charonia* columella fragment
	Mf3	005	ZS.49a	1 *Donax* (left)
		005	ZS.49B	1 *Helix* land snail fragment
	Om4	008	ZS.47a	1 fossil *Glycymeria*
		008	ZS.57b	1 fossil *Cerastoderma*
		008	ZS.47c	1 *Patella*
		010	ZS.48	1 *Donax* (left)
		010	ZS.50a	1 *Patella*
		010	ZS.50b	1 *Donax* (right)
		010	ZS.50c	1 *Pecten* fragment
1980	Eh	002	ZS.54	1 *Murex* fragment
	Gh3	001	ZS.60	1 *Murex* brandaris fragment
		013	ZS.63	1 *Donax* (left)
	Gh4	001	ZS.53	1 *Helix* land snail fragment
		017	ZS.65	1 *Helix* land snail fragment
		017	ZS.65a	1 *Donax* (left)
		017	ZS.65b	1 *Arcularia* with irregular hole
	Gh4	021	ZS.64	1 *Patella*
	Gil/ Gh3	001	ZS.57	1 *Patella*
	Gi2	001	ZS.56	1 *Murex* fragment - worn

Table 1 (con't)

Grid							
Area	*Locus*		*No.*				
G12-							
Gg4	034 7/28 152 ZS.68a				1 *Donax* (right)		
				b	1 *Donax* (left)		
				c	1 *Donax* (left),		
					?charred		
				d	1 *Helix* land		
					snail fragment		
	Id	008	ZS.55		1 *Helix* land snail fragment		
		013	ZS.59		1 fossil oyster fragment		
		013	ZS.61		1 *Cassis* lip fragment		
		022	ZS.62		1 fossil oyster fragment		
	Ii	002	ZS.66a		1 *Cypraea* holed at smaller end		
		002	ZS.66b		1 fossil oyster - small		
1980	Ii	002	ZS.67		1 *Rumina* land snail		
	Jg	001	6/20	13	ZS.58 JAG, HWL 2 *Eobania* land		
					snails and 11		
					Rumina land snails		

The rock-cut channel filled in the mid-first century west of the Temple (Id 008, 013, 022) produced one *Semicassis* lip fragment, one *Helix* fragment, and two fossil oyster fragments. A locus east of the Southeast Building (Om4 008) dated to circa 365 A.D. contained one *Patella* and the fossil *Cerastoderma* (31 x 32 mm) and *Glycymeris* (39 x 37 mm). Both the Id and Om areas contained earlier material mixed in.

Some of the other undated shells also are worthy of description. The second *Arcularia* (Hg3 007), dating from the Archaic period to the first century, has a well-made circular hole on the body whorl. The largest shell sample (Mg1 001) contained 41 percent of all the marine shells, with twenty-three *Donax* valves from fourteen individuals. Probable fourth-century B.C. fill from Om4 010, east of the Southeast Building, contained two *Donax* shells from two individuals, one *Patella*, and one *Pecten* fragment (maximum length 55 mm). One *Tonna* fragment (Cl 002) from a large individual comes from mixed fill in the Temple cella.

Donax, Patella, Murex, Cerastoderma and *Pecten* are all edible species, but all *Murex* and *Cerastoderma* were worn and were collected dead on the beach. *Donax* is today eaten in the Mediterranean Basin, often in soup, but is not particularly common from Mediterranean archaeological sites. The large number of valves from Late Neolithic Franchthi cave in the southern Argolid of Greece "may have been collected for decorative reasons."[1] The Bronze Age and Frankish site of Ayios Stephanos in southern Laconia in Greece produced large numbers of *Donax*, more than 10,800 valves, which make up seventy-five percent of that shell collection (my analysis). The thirty-seven unworn food inviduals at the Kourion Sanctuary cannot be considered a significant food source, and would yield less than one-quarter pound of meat. All of the recent marine and fossil shells might, instead, be considered votives associated with the Sanctuary. With this suggestion in mind, it is worth examining other votive shell collections from Cyprus and Greece.

In southern Cyprus, one tomb in the Kition-Bamboula necropolis produced seventeen holed *Arcularia*.[2] The Hellenistic (first century) Tomb 8 at the Ayios Ermoyenis necropolis at Kourion produced one *Pinctada margaritifera* L. valve, imported from the Red Sea, with two rows of holes punched on the inside of the valve around the outer edge.[3] It is interesting to note that the contemporary Apollo Sanctuary has no imported Red Sea shells, although these are found at the Phoenician Kition sanctuary and in CAII and CCI tombs at Salamis (see below).

The Kition sanctuary complex in southern Cyprus produced eighteen holed *Arcularia*, seventeen from the LCIIIA/B and one from the Cypro-Geometric (CG) I. Holed *Arcularia* are the most frequent shell at Phoenician levels (800-450 B.C.) there. The LCIIB-IIIA/B at Kition yielded seven Mediterranean cowries, three of them holed. The Phoenician Bothros 1 (600-450 B.C.) produced one holed Mediterranean cowrie and twenty-five holed Red Sea *Cypraea annulus* (L.), as well as three other Red Sea shells of two species.

The Kition sanctuary complex also produced nine *Murex*: one LCIIB, four (with two holes) LCIIIA/B, three Sub-Mycenaean to CGI, and one CGI. There are also seven *Cerastoderma*: one LCIIB, five LCIIB-IIIB (one holed), and one Sub-Mycenaean.[4]

The CAII sanctuary at Meniko-"Litharkes" produced a large *Murex* and a fossil *Ostrea*.[5] The late CAII Tomb 3 at Amathus in southern Cyprus produced one *Murex*.[6] The CCII tomb at Ayia Marina (Skyllouras) produced one holed Mediterranean cowrie.[7]

Ten funerary pyres at Salamis in eastern Cyprus produced *Donax* valves dated to the CCI (three pyres with five, nine, and fifty shells), CCI-CCII (four shells), CCII (c150), late fourth century B.C. (one, thirty, thirty-five, one hundred), and one undated.[8] *Arcularia*, frequently holed and sometimes burnt, are also very common: CAII (nine shells in three deposits), CAII-CCI (twenty-three shells in two deposits), CCII (fourteen shells in eight deposits), and late fourth century (eight shells in three deposits).

The late eighth to early seventh-century B.C. Tomb 79 at Salamis produced ninety-four *Murex*; seven *Charonia*[9] and *Murex* also were found in one CCII and two late fourth century pyres.[10] There are also seventeen holed cowries, including some from the Red Sea, from three CAII and one CCI tombs, and *Cerastoderma* remains from one CCI and three late fourth century pyres.

The Temple of Astarte-Aphrodite at Tamassos in central Cyprus, more than 15 miles from the coast, has produced a shell collection very similar to that from the Kourion Sanctuary. That excavation produced seventy-three *Donax* cf. *semistratus rostratus* valves[11] from about forty-two individuals. There are twenty-seven individuals from the southeast corner of the temple in "TA I," eight from the faunal dump in trench E8, and nine from the southeast corner of "TA III," in or near the temple. *Donax* is the only recent shell from the site; *D. semistratus* is smaller, more pointed, and rarer in the Mediterranean than is *D. trunculus*, but is very similar in shape.

The Tamassos temple also produced five fossils, including one *Strombus bubonius* gastropod, one *Cerastoderma* or *Cardium* cf. *echinatum*, one *Ostrea* sp., and two *Gryphaea* cf. *vesicularis* bivalves. The last two shells come from inside the temple in the southwestern section of "TA III."

The superimposed Greek sanctuaries at Kommos in southern Crete produced many of the same species found at the Kourion Sanctuary, as well as numerous other species. Temple B (Geometric to Orientalizing, circa 800-600 B.C.) yielded 130 *Donax* from seventy individuals, 10,300 *Patella*, eight *Murex trunculus*, nineteen *Arcularia* (eight of those holed), sixteen *Tonna*, three *Semicassis* (including two lip fragments), thirteen cowries, about twenty *Cerastoderma* valves and six fossil oysters, one fossil scallop, and one fossil echinoid fragment. Temple C (Classical to Early Roman, circa 400 B.C.-150 A.D.) produced fifty-one *Donax* valves from at least thirty individuals, twenty-six of them collected dead. Fifty-two *Patella*, eight *Murex*, seven *Arcularia* (four of them holed), twenty-three *Tonna* (including five from under a reused Minoan stone lamp),[12] three *Charonia*, one *Semicassis*, two cowries, numerous *Cerastoderma* fragments, one *Pecten*, fourteen fossil oysters, and one fossil asteroid (personal analysis). The temple C *Donax*, unlike those from B and Kourion, were, for the most part, collected dead.

Numerous *Donax* were found in the Roman fill of a cistern at the Sanctuary of Demeter at Knossos on Crete,[13] while the Archaic to Late Roman Sanctuary of Demeter and Kore at Corinth on the Greek mainland produced mainly the Spiny or Thorny Oyster (seventy-six valves), *Spondylus gaederopus* L., but also thirty-five *Murex*, nineteen *Cerastoderma* valves, two *Pecten*, and one *Patella*.[14]

The common votive use of *Donax* at Kourion, Salamis, and Tamassos on Cyprus is of special interest; the other recent shells probably also were votives, although the holed *Arcularia* and *Erosaria* might have been personal ornaments or sanctuary hangings.

The presence of fossils at the sanctuaries at Kourion, Meniko, Tamassos, and Kommos also is of significance. To these votive uses of fossils we can add fossil deer remains from a Minoan shrine at Knossos,[15] fossil molluscs from the Minoan peak sanctuary on Mt. Juktas near Knossos (personal analysis), fossil molluscs and echinoids from the Temple of Hathor at Timna in southern Israel and the Iron Age sanctuary at Buseirah in Jordan (personal analysis), and a fossil elephant molar from the Asklepieion on Cos.[16]

CATALOG OF SHELLS

Marine Shells

39   *Donax trunculus* Linnaeus, 1758
30 individuals from 9 loci; 1 charred
(Abrupt) Wedge-shell, Bean clam, Butterfly
shell, Coquina; Greek: *kochíli*

6   *Patella caerulea* Linnaeus, 1758
6 loci Limpet; *petalida*

3   *Murex* cf. (=*Trunculariopsis*, =*Hexaplex*)
trunculus (Linnaeus, 1758)
3 loci; all fragmentary
(Rock) Murex; *porphýra*

2   *Arcularia* (=*Nassarius*, =*Nassa*) *gibbosulus*
(Linnaeus, 1758) 2 loci; both holed on body whorl
Basket shell, Nassa shell, Dog-whelk

1   *Tonna* (=*Dolium*) *galea* (Linnaeus, 1758)
body fragment from large individual
Giant tun, Tun shell, Dolium shell, Cask shell

1   *Charonia sequenziae* (Aradus and Benoit, 1876)
columella fragment
Triton, Trumpet shell

1   *Semicassis undulata* (Gmelin, 1790)
lip fragment Helmet shell

1   *Erosaris* (=*Cypraea*) *spurca* (Linnaeus, 1758)
man-made hole at one end Cowrie

1   *Cerastoderma edule glaucum* (Bruguiére, 1789)
distal fragment, abraded and worn
(Common) Cockle; *kydoni*, *methýstra*

1   *Pecten maximus* (Linnaeus, 1758)
fragment Scallop, Pecten; *kteñi*

Land Snails

12 *Rumina decollata* (Linnaeus, 1758)
3 loci

5 *Helix* cf. *aspersa* Muller, 1774
5 loci, all fragments
Common garden snail, Helix; *bourboures*

2 *Eobania vermiculata* (Muller, 1774)
1 locus

Fossils

3 *Ostrea* sp. (3 loci; all fragments) Oyster

1 *Cerastoderma/Cardium* sp. Cockle

1 *Glycymeris* sp. Dog-cockle

Chapter 5
A Brief Survey
Albert Leonard Jr.

During the month of August, 1980, an eight-day program of archaeological survey was conducted in the immediate environs of ancient Kourion.[1] This program of field-walking, carried out in association with the University of Missouri-Walters Art Gallery excavations at the Sanctuary of Apollo, focused its attention primarily on the slopes below (south and east of) the ancient city of Kourion, eastward from a line south of the stadium to the road that runs from the Limassol-Paphos road to the beach (Fig. 42). Secondary attention was given to the area called the "Yerokarka" between the city site and the modern village of Kourion.

For purposes of control, the southern and eastern slopes of the city were divided into 24 sections, A through X (Fig. 43); each was sampled by members of the survey team spaced at three-meter intervals. Material from each area was collected and bagged separately. When a specific architectural feature (Fig. 44) or artifact scatter was found it was assigned a consecutive number; all associated artifactual material was processed separately and related to that particular feature.[2]

THE SOUTHERN SLOPES OF THE CITY

The complete catalog of the individual survey areas follows in outline form, but several noteworthy features deserve fuller discussion in the context of the topography of the survey area as a whole.

The southwestern slopes, which drop to the sea more sharply than do those on the southeastern side of the city, exhibit several sections of walling that appear to be relatively modern retaining

walls. Some of these walls, however, were in association with
fairly intensive scatters of pottery and roof tiles, possibly
indicating that the southern slopes of Kourion may have been
occupied in antiquity. Because of the steepness of the land and the
attendant problem of material washing down from above (fragments of
pipe from the water supply of the ancient city were especially
frequent in this area), this is a question that can be clarified
only by excavation. One especially promising area (Area F, feature
16) was noted high on the slope below the Basilica, where, in
connection with roughly hewn blocks and ancient mortar, a small
section of mosaic floor with white and grey *tesserae* is visible
(Fig. 45). Unlike other bits and pieces of mosaic noted during the
survey, this floor appears to be *in situ.* Lower down the slope,
just before it levels off to form the plain north of the beach, is
another area (Area F, feature 13) that warrants future
investigation. Here, for about 30 m along the contour and 15 m up
the slope, can be seen a scree of dressed building blocks and roof
tile fragments. Two (40 cm diameter) column drums also were noted,
as was an unusual architectural element (capital?) with double
dowelling (Fig. 46).

   The flatland between the beach and the cliffs produced much less
surface material than did the slopes.

Figure 42. View from Kourion City towards the western portion of
the survey area.

Whole sections, especially in the western portion of this area, were devoid of artifactual material. With the exception of a Roman cippus in local stone at the northeastern corner of the small house behind the beach (Area M, feature 17), no architectural fragments were detected until the extreme eastern edge of this area was reached. Here (Area R, feature 25), about ten ancient basins (or ancient blocks cut to function as basins), were being used to water sheep. Just to the north of these basins (Area R, feature 26) is a single block of local stone bearing an inscribed "broke bar" *alpha* (Fig. 47), possibly a mason's mark. It is difficult to tell whether the other stones in close proximity to the inscribed one are ancient or modern.

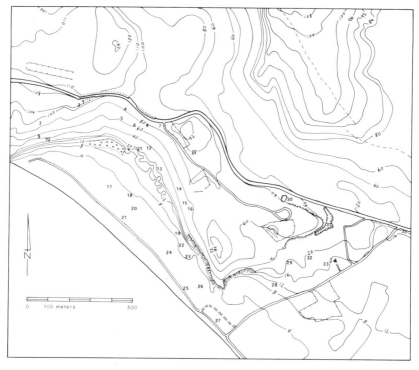

Figure 43. Map of Kourion showing the survey areas of the slopes of the city and the Yerokarka hill.

The southeastern side of the city slopes gently down to the fertile coastal plain. The eastern limit of our survey was formed by the small road that leads from the Limassol-Paphos road to the beach, between Kourion and Kaloriziki. Considerable archaeological work has been done in this area, with Cesnola, Walters, and McFadden all excavating tombs between the chapel of Ayios Ermoyenis and the sea.[3] Almost thirty years ago McFadden pointed out the ancient approach way to the city,[4] and since the (artificially?) raised "roadway" is still a rather distinct topographical feature we will discuss the survey material in relation to it.

South of the ancient entryway, near the beach, the 1:5000 map references three "ruins" (Area S, feature 27). On closer inspection, however, we could find nothing but relatively modern

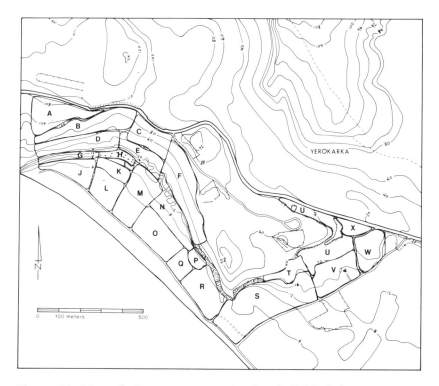

Figure 44. Map of the survey area showing individual features.

concrete work, perhaps a relic of World War II defenses. North of these features the sherd material is quite even, if rather slight, with neither an increase nor a decrease as one approaches the area of Walters's Site B cemetery.[5] The most prominent lithic feature here (Area S, feature 28) is a large stone drum (Fig. 48), measuring 1.50 m in diameter, the central portion of which has been cut down (ca. 19 cm) to form a shallow basin or grinding surface. Whether this stone originally served an architectural function or was put to some domestic use is unclear, as is the question of whether the cutting of the upper surface is original. In the quarries on the southern tip of the Akrotiri Peninsula, within the confines of the British Base, is a partially quarried, cylindrical stone of exactly the same diameter.[6] If this quarry was the source of the present piece, it seems a great distance to transport such a large stone if it was meant only to serve a domestic function.

Figure 45. Section of mosaic from Area F, feature 16.

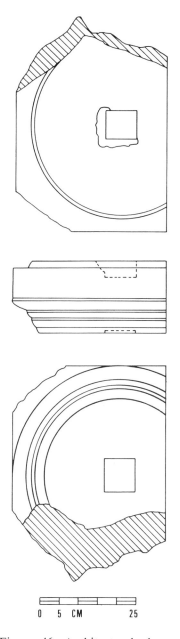

Figure 46. Architectural element with double dowelling, Area F, feature 13.

As noted above, the eastern entrance to the ancient city of Kourion was approached by what appears to be an earthen ramp, artificially constructed to facilitate the climb between the plain and the ravine that passes into the city just to the south of the theater (Fig 49). Above this approachway are circa 10 m of cuttings in the bedrock (some now fallen down the slope) for a stairway (Area T, features 29a). The steps are circa 3.50 m wide; although now quite eroded, the risers originally would have been low enough to provide easy access for pedestrian traffic.

Immediately below the stairway cuttings we discovered the most surprising find of our short season. A relatively recent clandestine digging operation had produced a large hole with cut blocks thrown up on all sides (Area T, feature 29b). In the northern and southern faces of this excavation can be seen sections of architecture built of large rectangular blocks of local stone (Fig. 50). They appear to have been built up against an almost vertically cut face of bedrock. At first it was suggested that the blocks might have formed part of a tower or other outwork connected with the east gate of the city,an attractive hypothesis because the eastern side of the city would be the most difficult to defend.

Figure 47. Block with broken-bar *alpha* from Area R, feature 26.

Figure 48. Stone cylinder with recessed upper surface from Area S, feature 28.

A second hypothesis would explain this architecture as part of a
large built tomb, such as Tomb B dug by McFadden at Ayios Ermoyenis
a short distance to the northeast.[7] In attempting to decide between
these two hypotheses, we sherded the entire area intensely. This
operation produced about a dozen early Iron Age sherds (Fig. 51),
both from immediately below and within the hole. With but a single
exception from the southern slopes, this was the only early Iron
Age material found during the survey. Whether a defensive tower or
early tomb, this area definitely warrants further investigation.

About midway between the eastern entryway and Ayios Ermoyenis
lies the most interesting of the individual architectural elements
discovered during the survey (Area V, feature 32). It is a large
(ca. 54 x 66 cm) *voussoir* with mouldings and a single row of
dentils (Fig. 52). One side of the stone bears a broken-bar
alpha of dimensions similar to those on the inscribed block from
Area R (feature 26). Identical cuttings can be seen at the city
site on an *ex situ* block southeast of the Basilica and on a block
in a low (rebuilt?) wall north of the Basilica.

Figure 49. The eastern approach to Kourion City.

Below the northeastern slopes of the ancient city, in the cuttings made by the early quarry workers, are over a dozen tombs (Area U, features 30, 31). They are of two varieties: a simple rectangular pit cut down into the rock from a horizontal plane, and a more elaborate type cut into the vertical faces of the rock. The latter form includes the sunken, rectangular cist, but adds an *arcosolium* above. The combination of the two types can also be seen near the quarries at the southern tip of the Akrotiri Peninsula. All of the examples recorded during the survey have been open for a very long time and offer no independent dating evidence. The bottoms of plain rectangular sarcophagi are at present being used to water the animals in the sheep pen at the southern end of the larger of the two quarries.

Three Roman cippi in soft local stone (Fig. 53), now standing at the entrance to the chapel of Ayios Ermoyenis (Area V, feature 33), complete the most noteworthy items from the survey area south of the Limassol-Paphos road.[8]

Figure 50. Architecture exposed in southern side of clandestine digging in Area T, feature 29b. (Scale: 1 meter)

Survey Results South of Kourion City

Area A: includes gently sloping area south of the stadium and the Limassol-Paphos road. Area covered by thick scrub and pine trees. Where open, bedrock is visible or covered by only a few centimeters of soil.

Figure 51. Pottery from the Early Iron Age. a–i, k, l from Area T feature 29b, j from Area B.

Figure 52. *Voussoir* with broken-bar alpha from Area V, feature 32.

1.   Architectural feature south of modern bridge, consisting of a straight cutting in the bedrock, oriented NW-SE. Immediately to the south is a circular (diam. .85 m) cutting separated from a rectangular (ca. 1.00 x .70 m) "cistern" ca. 2.50 m deep; 15 m south of the "cistern" are four dressed blocks, aligned and oriented NW-SE. No associated artifactual material.

2.   Cluster of three (or more?) rock-cut tombs. Severely filled with asphalt and construction material from the Limassol-Paphos road directly above. A few sherds, ceramic pipe fragments, and roof-tiles are obviously secondary deposits.

Area B: below Area A and extending further east along the Limassol-Paphos road. Extremely thick covering of thickets, thorn, and grass. See Figures 54:h, i, j, m, p, r; 55:e; 57:h, j, r; 58:e, q; 61:e; 62:c, e,; 63:b, c; 64:m, p, t; 65:b, c, k.

3.   Possible rock-cut tomb (ca. 1.00 x 2.00 m). Very eroded. No associated artifactual material.

Figure 53. Three *cippi* presently in front of the chapel of Agios Ermoyenis, Area V, feature 33.

Area C: east of Area B. Ground surface much more open than B.

4. Two rectangular (.30 x .70 m) blocks embedded (secondarily) in the cliff-side. No associated artifactual material.

5. Large (60 m E–W by 45 m N–S) sherd scatter. Portion of possibly ancient concrete flooring (?), *ex situ.* Figures 54:c 56:a; 57:d, j, k, f; 58:i, n; 62:f; 64:l, q.

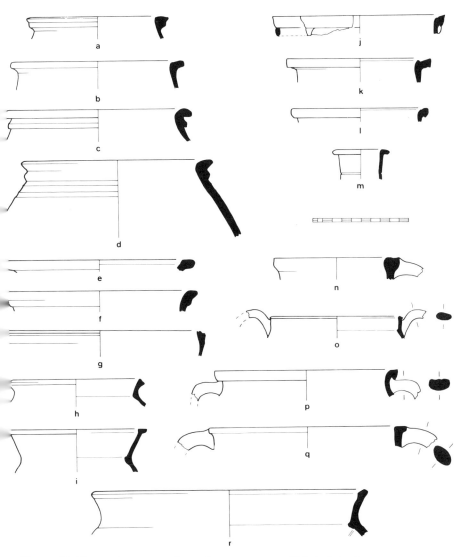

Figure 54. Domestic pottery from the survey area: Fabric I (red).

6.   Eleven-meter wall segment, oriented E-W. Two courses visible. Eastern most block is cut with interior and exterior angles (corner block). Sherds, roof-tiles, and pipe fragments associated. Figures 54:d; 55:a; 57:e; 60:a, h; 63:e, m; 64:i, s; 65:h, n. About 10 m west of this wall lies a column drum (ca. .40 m diam.), which may originally have been part of this "structure."

7.   Eighteen-meter wall segment oriented NW-SE, constructed of a mixture of dressed and non-dressed stone. Western end appears to be an original corner, and suggests a wall width of ca. .55m. Associated roof-tile fragments.

8.   Seventy-five-meter terrace (?) wall oriented E-W. Stone and rubble collapse (?) above. Associated scatter (60 m E-W and 25m N-S) of artifactual material. Figures 54:b; 55:f; 57:m; 58:b; 59:c; 61:a; 62:a; 63:d; 64:e, w.

Area D: from western limits of survey area to road east of present orchard.

9.   Ephemeral traces of (ancient?) retaining wall. No definitely associated artifactual material.

10.   Staircase with several ancient dressed blocks added to uphill footpath. No associated artifactual material.

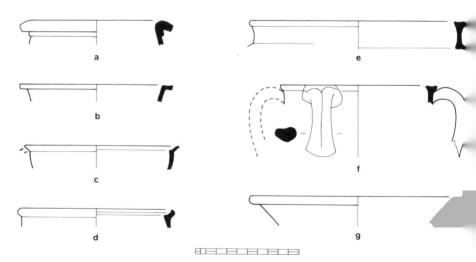

Figure 55. Domestic pottery from the survey area: Fabric I (gray).

Area E: located east of Area D and south of Area C in open ground.

11. Twenty-meter retaining wall following topographical contour for ca. 20 m. Downhill face preserved to four courses. Little associated artifactual material. Figures 57:g; 63:f, j, k; 65:j.

12. Ephemeral traces of (ancient?) retaining wall. No associated artifactual material.

Area F: east of Areas C and E on steep slopes below city site. Open ground. Figures 57:l; 60:f; 63:l; 64:g, j, k, n; 65:f.

13. Thirty meters of (ancient?) wall oriented E-W. Traceable for 15 m up the slope. Built of field stones, reused(?) dressed blocks, and two (.44 m diam.) column drum fragments. A broken capital is situated immediately to the west.

14. Small (ca. .10 x .25 m) section of ancient concrete "pavement" protruding from the side of the cliff. About 1.50 m to the west is a small piece of *ex situ* mosaic with white (.01 x .01 m) tesserae. Possibly to be associated are two rectangular (.60 x .54 x .24 m) dressed blocks lying 2 m down slope.

15. Patchy stretch of walling running ca. 30 m E-W and disappearing into the slope. Large rectangular (.70 x .60 x .35 m) dressed blocks. Preserved to two courses in one small stretch.

16. Small (ca. .70 x .50 m exposed) section of mosaic (see Fig. 45), apparently *in situ*. White tesserae (ca. .02 x .02 m). Possibly associated on the east with small stretch (1.0 m N-S) of walling disappearing into slope.

Area G: unplowed tract of land south of Area D and west of citrus orchard. Very sparse sherd cover.

Area H: citrus orchard east of Area G. No artifactual material on surface.

Area I: small tract of land south of citrus orchard (Area H). Recently cultivated in onions. No artifactual material on surface.

Area J: tract of land between Area G and the beach road. Low scrub mixed with harvested grain. A modern well in the southeast. No artifactual material on surface.

Area K: tract of land between Areas I and L. Harvested grain. Very sparse artifact scatter.
Area L: tract of land between Area K and the beach road, recently plowed. Very sparse artifact scatter.

Area M: tract of land east of Area K. Modern building with water pump at western end, second pump towards southeastern corner. Figures 57:a; 64:f.

17.   Uninscribed cippus next to pump house.

18.   Broken section of column (.43 m diam.). Preserved height .53m.

Area N: tract of land between Areas F and O. Very sparse artifact scatter.

19.   Two (*ex situ*) rectangular (.56 x .52 x .18m) dressed blocks. Little associated artifactual material.

Area O: tract of land between Area N and the beach road. Figures 51:j; 64:r.

20.   Fragment of column (.46 m diam.). Preserved height .40 m. No associated artifactual material.

21.   Depression in ground, overgrown with scrub. Possible cistern. No artifactual material.

Area P: tract of land directly beneath Kourion cliffs. Little surface material, except in scatter 22.

22.   Sherd scatter ca. .80 m E–W by 15 m N–S. Eight pieces of marble veneer within scatter. This material may be associated with a scree of cut, but badly weathered, blocks that extends ca. 35 m west of the pottery scatter. Figures 58:l; 61:h.

Area Q: tract of land between Area P and the beach road. Covered with "sea grass." Sherds infrequent except in scatter 24.

24.   Light scatter of sherds (ca. 15 x 15 m) in center of area. No associated architectural remains. Figures 58:f; 64:v.

Area R: tract of land east of Areas P and Q. Figure 64:u.

25.   Scatter of ten cut (recut?) ancient blocks (1.00 x .75 m) used as troughs by modern shepherd. Small, badly weathered cippus in association.

26.   Low pile of square cut (.50 x .50 m) blocks. One block bears inscribed broken-bar *alpha* (see Fig. 47).

Area S: tract of land below Kourion City, bordered by the beach road on the southeast and southwest. Covered with thick grass and thistles. Figure 58:a.

27. Area marked "Ruins" on map. All are poured and/or reinforced concrete, most probably part of relatively recent (now disused) coastal defenses.

28. Large cylindrical stone (1.50 m diam.), lower portion buried (exposed height 1.75 m). Central part of top surface cut down (.19 m) to form a "basin" (see Fig. 48) with rim (.15 m wide).

Area T: high land below (SSE of) theater, including (artificially?) raised roadway to ancient city. Thick grass and thistles. Because the features here are too close together to stand out on the plan, they are included here as 29a and 29b. Figures 60:g; 63:a, g; 64:c.

29a. Rock-cut stairway at end of raised approachway to the city. Tread width is 3.50 m. Preserved length is 10 m. Very eroded and partially collapsed down the hillside. This stairway is to be associated with the many sections of walling that are traceable in the ravine that passes into the ancient city just below (south of) the theater.

29b. Architectural construction of large dressed blocks built against the vertically cut bedrock just below the steps (29a). Scene of relatively recent clandestine digging, which has scattered many of the blocks down the slope (see Fig. 50). Figures 51:a–i, k, l.

Area U: tract of land northeast of Area T, including the quarried area bounded on the north by the Limassol-Paphos road, on the south by the city cliffs, and on the east by Area X. Very dense covering of thickets, bushes, and trees. Very few sherds. One tile fragment.

30. A minimum of three rock-cut tombs.

31. At least twelve tombs cut in the sides (N, S, E, and W) of the quarried area. Most are completely overgrown by scrub or hidden by trees. More may exist. Tombs in the western side of the quarried depression have been incorporated into the modern sheepfold, where two large (unmeasured) sarcophagi are in use as troughs and where fragments of column drums are used in blocking walls.

Area V: tract of land between Area U and the beach road, containing the small chapel of Ayios Ermoyenis. Sparse artifact cover. Figure 57:f.

32. *Voussoir*, from arch with mouldings and single row of dentils. Broken-bar *alpha* carved on one side (see Fig. 52). Greatest dimensions: width 55 cm (top), 30 cm (bottom); height 54 cm; depth 65 cm.

33.   Three uninscribed *cippi* (see Fig. 53), presently located in front of the chapel of Ayios Ermoyenis.

Area W: triangular tract of land east of Areas U and V. Eastern extent delineated by quarries at the junction of the beach road with the Limassol-Paphos Road. Thick cover of grass, bushes, and trees. Very few sherds.

Area X: area bounded on the north by the Limassol-Paphos Road, on the south by the city cliffs, and on the east by Area X. Very dense covering of thickets, bushes and trees. Very few sherds. One tile fragment.

THE YEROKARKA AREA

After completing work on the southern slopes of the city site, the survey team moved northward across the modern highway to gather some impression of the degree to which the adjacent hillsides had been inhabited or utilized. The gently sloping southern flanks of the Yerokarka were chosen because they seemed to offer the least possible contamination from material washed down from higher levels.

The ancient water system that traversed the upper part of the Yerokarka from north to south has been described by Last. Our work overlapped with his only slightly, along the long runs of water channel in the northernmost part of our area.[9] At several points in the area to the south and east of these channels we noted scatters of potsherds and roof tiles, suggesting that the Yerokarka was "inhabited" during the Hellenistic and Roman periods. The largest of these scatters, marked ("R") on the 1:5000 map, contained--in addition to ceramic fragments--a half-dozen large stone blocks, a pair of column drums, and a weathered column base. The few pieces of marble veneer in this area would suggest that the structure that once stood on this ridge, with its fine view of the city and the sea, had been more than a simple farmhouse.

Below this scatter is a sheep pen incorporating ancient rock-cut tombs. At least three could be positively identified. At the eastern end of the pen is a very weathered tomb that originally had three arcosolia parallel to each other in the rear.

Situated to the west of this scatter, between it and the 115 datum point, is the only rock-cut tomb that was clear enough to be entered (Fig. 67). An 8-m, roughly cut, *dromos* running to the north narrowed at the far end before opening into a 1.5 x 2.0 m rectangular burial chamber. No sherds were visible.

The final group of tombs noted during our work on the Yerokarka lies just to the north and east of the 116 bench mark. At least a dozen tombs were discernible, but all were overgrown and none could be entered. The *dromoi* were consistently 1m wide, but their orientation varied. The noteworthy thing about these tombs is the presence of what appear to be very eroded inscriptions in Cypro-Syllabic (Fig. 68) on the natural rock between them. These were recorded on the last day of our project, and it is quite possible that there are others in this area.[10]

CERAMICS

Early Iron Age Pottery

The survey recorded sixteen pieces of pottery that can be assigned to the early part of the First Millennium B.C. With a single exception (Fig. 51:j), found in Area B on the southwestern slopes of the city, all of these sherds came from the immediate vicinity of the architecture exposed by clandestine digging in Area T just to the west of the Kaloriziki cemetery near the eastern entrance to the ancient city.

The fabric of four of these fragments (Fig. 51:a-d) was described in the field as 10YR 8/2 (white) to 2.5YR 8/4 (pale yellow). The latter color often appeared quite "greenish" to the eye (in comparison with the other fabrics encountered during the survey), which agrees well with Gjerstad's description of the clays utilized for White Painted Wares.[11] Sand-sized to 1 mm white and grey mineral inclusions are frequent in the Kourion survey pieces. The painted decoration ranges from 10YR 4/3 (dark brown) through 2.5YR 3/2 (very dark greyish brown) to black.[12] The specific combination of the wavy line on the rim and the line-group decoration on the neck parallels a White Painted Ware amphora from Tomb 151 at Amathus.[13]

The fabric of three sherds (Fig 51:e-g) is similar in appearance to the White Painted Ware fragments from the survey, but the decoration is embellished with a second color approximating 5YR 5/3-5/4 (reddish brown), similar to Gjerstad's Bichrome Wares.[14] A similarly outsplayed and down-turned rim with a band of painted triangles appears on an Archaic II vessel from Ktima.[15]

The third of the early Iron Age ceramic types (Fig. 51:h-l) is executed in a 2.5YR 6/6 (light red) to 5/6 (red) fabric with extremely frequent, sand-sized to 1 mm white and grey grit temper. The core can be grey. The surface may be either plain or covered with a slip of a color similar to that of the fabric. Decoration is in black paint. From the field description, this should be equated with Black-on-Red Wares,[16] but the polished or lustrous surface characteristic of this ware was not noted during the initial study of the abraded samples from Kourion.

Later Pottery

A. *The Plain Wares.* In addition to the early Iron Age ceramic material, the surface collection from the slopes of Kourion and the Yerokarka produced a large quantity of domestic pottery in a variety of (evidently) local wares. This pottery was divided (in the field) into four basic fabric groups and is so presented here.[17] Unfortunately, published comparative material from occupation sites is extremely limited, and dates mostly to the Hellenistic/Early Roman Period or to the seventh and eighth centuries A.D. Very few *comparanda* are available for the intervening centuries.[18] This material, therefore, is presented primarily according to the fabric groups established in the field, with parallels to excavated material added when possible.

   Fabric I: Red Domestic Ware. Fabric I is a fairly common fabric of well levigated clay with very frequent, sand-sized to one millimeter, white grit temper. Although a few grey centers were noted, the core usually is fired 2.5YR 5/6 (red), as is the surface. A thick, gritless slip often is present, which can range from 10YR 5/6-5/8 (red) to 2.5YR5/8 (red).

   The cooking pots with flaring necks (Fig. 54:h, i, o, r) appear to be early. They can be compared with similar vessels from the pre-kiln, late Hellenistic/Early Roman (Period I) deposits from Catling's salvage excavations at Dhiorios-Meresineri in the north part of the island,[19] as well as with first century B.C. vessels from the Athenian Agora and elsewhere.[20] Other cooking pots in this fabric (Fig. 54:c, d), however, are morphologically closer to Catling's "lipped" cooking pots, which begin in the seventh century A.D. (Period II) deposits at the site;[21] pots illustrated in Figure 54:a, and possibly in Figure 54:f, are examples of his type I "bead-rim" cooking pots of the slightly later Periods III and IV.[22] Three vessels that could possibly be identified as "casseroles" (Fig. 54:j-l) might also find parallels in the Period II material from Dhiorios.[23] More distinctive is a rim fragment (Fig. 54:g) from a casserole-type with double-lug projections and a flange on the lower body, which appears at Dhiorios in Periods II and III[24] and may be related to morphologically less complex rims on cooking vessels from Period VII (fifth-seventh century A.D.) at Ayios Philon.[25] Jugs with incised grooves on the neck, such as that illustrated in Figure 54:m, are not represented at Dhiorios, but are seen in third and fourth century A.D. contexts from the Athenian Agora.[26] The rest of the Fabric I forms are more difficult to document.[27]

   Fabric I: Grey Variant. A few of the Fabric I vessels are mottled to grey. On some pieces this is confined to the lower extremities of the pot and is most probably the result of their use as kitchen wares. On others, however, the mottling appears on the upper parts of handles, suggesting that the color change occurred in the kiln. This allows us to associate, with the red ware, a grey variant identical in fabric and differing only in its color.

Morphologically, the most obvious connection between the red and grey variants of Fabric A is the appearance in both groups of Catling's "lipped" cooking-pot form (Fig. 55:a). Two vessels that may also be identified as cooking pots (Fig. 55:e, f), however, seem to be more closely related to late Hellenistic/Early Roman material at Dhiorios than to seventh or eighth century A.D. forms.[28] The two "casserole" rims (Fig. 55:c, d) are difficult to place chronologically and might appear at either end of the chronological spectrum represented at Dhiorios.[29] Outsplayed and horizontally flattened rims such as that illustrated in Figure 55:g (and possibly Figure 55:b) appear on frying pans, the majority of which are assigned to Period II at Dhiorios.[30]

Fabric IA. Also related to the main (red Fabric I is a similar ware with considerably less mineral tempering, which is here designated as Fabric IA. It can appear either plain or covered with a thick 10R 4/6 (red) slip.

The limited repertoire in which this fabric appears in the surface collection consists of a lid with knobbed handle (Fig. 56:a), a ring base (Fig.56:b), and two rims (Fig. 56:c, d). A flanged rim fragment from a semi-closed vessel (Fig. 56:c) may be related to the more atrophied examples of Periods III and IV cooking pots from Dhiorios;[31] the horizontally flattened rim illustrated in Figure 56:d is reminiscent of the frying pans from that site (cf. Fabric I/grey: Fig. 55:b, g).

Fabric II. Fabric II, with its color variants (II A-C), is the most common of the wares collected during the survey. It is a well levigated fabric with very frequent, sand-sized to one millimeter, white and grey mineral inclusions, which make the fragments feel gritty to the touch. Cores and surfaces range between 10YR 6/8 (light red) and 5/8 (red). That designated here as the basic Fabric II is unslipped.

Although a relatively wide range of vessel types exists in Fabric II, several lack convincing *comparanda*. This is especially true of the series of bowls with outsplayed rims (Fig. 57:j-m). Some of the vessels, however, do find parallels at Dhiorios.

The shallow bowl with sharply inverted rim (Fig. 57:a) appears to survive into Period II at Dhiorios,[32] while the large, relatively open form (Fig. 57:n) is similar to Period III vessels at the site.[33] The pot illustrated in Figure 57:o may be related to Catling's fine bowl "type" 6 from Period IV.[34] Thick, heavily "sculptured" rims such as those illustrated in Figure 57:p, q appear at Dhiorios on short-necked jars of Period II date.[35] Both the profile and size should equate the sherd illustrated in Figure 57:r with Catling's Period III-IV *mortaria*, with squarish rim and wide flange below.[36] The larger sherd shown in Figure 57:s does not find ready parallels in vessels of comparable size from the Dhiorios corpus, but the shape of its rim is not dissimilar to some of the smaller "casseroles" that mark the final development of the type at that site.[37]

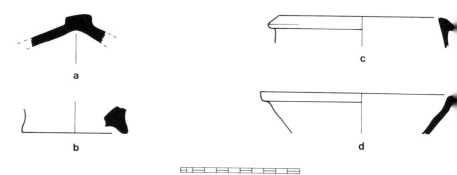

Figure 56. Domestic pottery from the survey area: Fabric IA (red).

Amphora toes are frequent in this group and present a variety of profiles that can be paralleled at other Cypriote sites.[38] It will be seen below that the large, open form with "pie-crust" rim (Fig. 57:d) morphologically helps to relate the main Fabric II to variant IIA, as well as to Fabric IV.

Fabric IIA. Based on the frequency and types of inclusions, as well as on the texture of its surface, Fabric IIA is merely a color variation of the basic Fabric II. The core can range from grey (infrequently) through 10YR 5/3 (brown) to 2.5YR 4/6 (red). The basic characteristic of the "A" variant is the presence of a rather fugitive slip, which most commonly ranges from 10YR 8/3 to 7/4 (very pale brown). Values closer to 7.5YR 7/4 (pink) are not uncommon and, in fact, link this with the "B" variant of Fabric II described below.

Supporting the hypothesis that Fabric IIA is essentially a slipped variant of the main Fabric II is the presence in this group of the "sculptured" jar rim (Fig. 58:f) and the "pie-crust" rim on a large, shallow, open form (Fig. 58:h). Smaller, open forms include the Dhiorios-type frying pan (Fig. 58:b) described above under the grey variant of Fabric I, to which the vessels depicted in Figure 58:j and k, with greater diameter and shorter rim, may be related. Morphologically, two open forms (Fig. 58:c and d) are similar to a type of vessel that is produced in several variants of "Roman" red wares, including examples of Catling's "Cypriote Late Roman Ware" from Dhiorios, where at least some of these vessels also appear in a "sandy buff" ware suggestive of our Fabric IIA. The sherd seen in Figure 58:o could be associated with the cooking pots of Chiorios II, which have horizontally flattened rims,[40] while that illustrated in Figure 58:e appears to represent the last

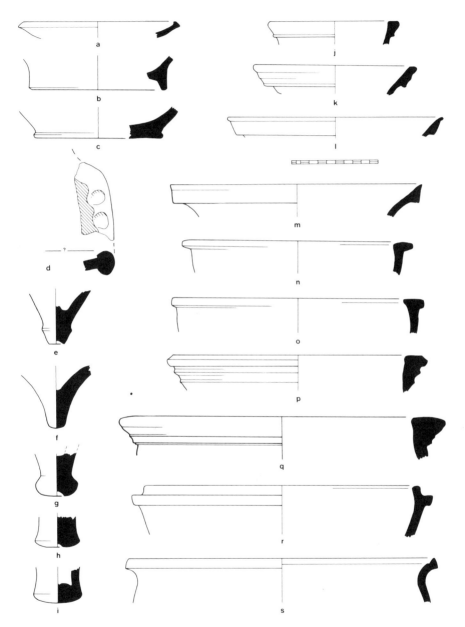

Figure 57. Domestic pottery from the survey area: Fabric II (red).

stage of atrophy of the casserole rim in the Period IV kiln at
Dhiorios.[41] The size and rim profiles of the sherds shown in Figure
58:f and i associate these vessels with a group of "flange-rim
bowls or basins" with a limited presence at Dhiorios from Period II
through IV,[42] and in Late Roman contexts at Ayios Philon.[43]

A jug with neck and rim similar to that illustrated in Figure
58:l appears in a "pinkish buff clay" from the seventh-century A.D.
Kornos Cave deposit, although in the Kornos example the upper
portion of the handle joins the vessel at the rim rather than at
the neck as it does on the Kourion piece.[44] Articulated rims, such
as that in Figure 58:p, have a wide chronological range at
Dhiorios.[45] The sherd shown in Figure 58:q shares the squared rim
and body flange of the Dhiorios *mortaria* (see Fig 57:r), but the
present piece is much smaller in diameter and actually appears to
be from a vessel of semi-closed form. Vessels with outsplayed rims
that have been turned back to the point where the neck ceases to
exist as a distinct morphological entity, such as that illustrated
in Figure 58:a, are rare in the domestic assemblage from Dhiorios,
occurring only on vessels of much more open form, but they do
appear in Early Roman occupational contexts in the Athenian Agora
and in the roughly contemporary Level II at Khirbet Qumran.[46]

If the parallels with the corpus from Dhiorios are valid, the
sherd seen in Figure 58:m would seem to belong with the "plain
white amphorae" of the earlier, Period I occupation at the site.[47]

Fabric IIB. Fabric IIB is represented in the survey sample by
only four sherds. In temper and core color, Fabric IIB is the same
as the main Fabric II, but it is covered with a 7.5YR 7/4 (pink)
slip.

In the present collection, forms in this ware are restricted to
an open form with horizontally flattened and slightly bevelled rim
(Fig. 59:d), which occurs at least once in the series of casseroles
from Dhiorios,[48] and to three "sculptured" jar rims (Fig. 59:a-c).
One of these (Fig. 59:b) has been decorated with a horizontal row
of impressed lozenges at the base of the rim.

Fabric IIC. Fabric IIC is a relatively fine variant of Fabric
II. It is a well levigated clay with a core color approximating
2.5YR 5/8 (red). The temper is grey and white, but is much finer
(sand-sized) and much less frequent than that in the main Fabric
II. All examples collected had been covered by a 5YR 7/6 (reddish
yellow) slip.

The sherds shown in Figure 60:b and c both exhibit
a rim profile that appears on at least one cooking pot from
Dhiorios (Period II) in a slightly more outsplayed version.[49]
Figure 60:g represents the lower potion of a solid-stemmed fusiform
unguentarium with slightly concave base, while Figure 60:f is of
the hollow-stemmed type with a convex base.[50] The sherd illustrated
in Figure 60:d is the greater portion of a second to third century
A.D. bell-shaped *unguentarium*, a shape considered by Hayes to be
characteristic of Cyprus.[51] The other forms (Fig. 60:a, e, and h)
are more difficult to parallel.[52]

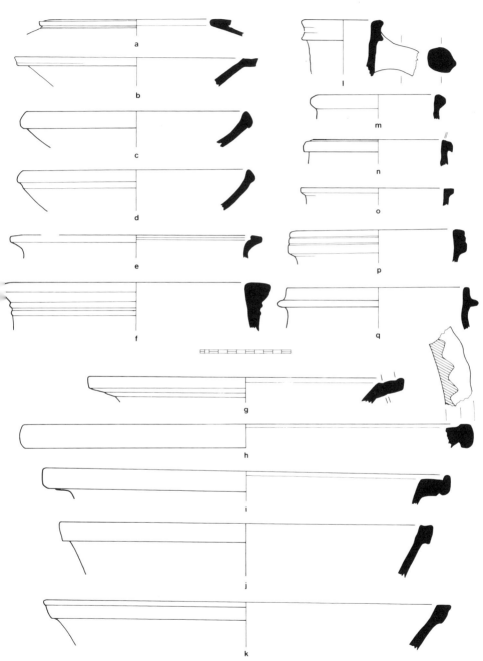

Figure 58. Domestic pottery from the survey area: Fabric IIA.

Fabric III. Fabric III is another ware that is sandy or gritty to the touch. It is a very well levigated fabric, tempered with fine, sand-sized grey and white grit rarely exceeding one millimeter. The core is either 10YR 7/4 (very pale brown) or 5YR 7/6-6/6 (reddish yellow). The surface is covered with a 10YR 8/4 (very pale brown) or 2.5YR 8/2 (white) slip.

Fabric III is the finest of the non-Roman wares collected during the survey and one that exhibits a long chronological range. The ring base (Fig. 61:e) would seem to be more at home in the earlier (late Hellenistic/Early Roman) deposits from Dhiorios,[53] while the vessel here identified as an amphora or jug (Fig. 61:b) is paralleled in the seventh or eighth century A.D. material from the Kornos cave.[54] It is not impossible that we are dealing here with an imported fabric, especially in light of the presence of the double-rolled handle (Fig. 61:c),[55] the bulging neck and rim (Fig. 61:a),[56] and possibly the articulated amphora toe (Fig. 61:d).[57]

Fabric IV. Fabric IV is the last of the "local" wares in the survey material that readily forms a group. It is a well levigated fabric with grey and white grit that averages about one millimeter. The main characteristic of this ware, however, is the presence of a red mineral grit. The color of the core can be either a 5YR 7/6 (reddish yellow) or a 10YR 7/4 (very pale brown); all pieces are covered with a 10YR 8/2 (white) to 7.5YR 8/2 (pinkish white) slip.

In spite of the distinctive tempering agent, Fabric IV must be closely related to the mainstream of plain wares included in the survey collection. This is apparent from the two "sculptured" rims (Fig. 62:d and e) seen in Fabrics II (Fig. 57:p and q), IIA (Fig. 58:f), and IIB (Fig. 59:a-c), and in the large "platter" with pie-crust rim (Fig. 62:f), which appears in this collection in Fabrics II (Fig. 57:d) and IIA (Fig. 58:h).[58] The sherd seen in Figure 62:c is best paralleled in a Period III context at Ayios Philon.[59]

Miscellaneous Fabrics. Several fragments of the (evidently) local pottery from the Kourion survey do not belong to any of the main ceramic "types" isolated here; in fact, they appear in a variety of fabrics.[60] They are, nevertheless, included here in order to give an impression of the total spectrum of forms encountered during the survey.

Basically, the group consists of two kinds of pottery: the large storage vessels (Fig. 63:k-n), which by their size can be expected to have been made in the immediate vicinity of Kourion, and the amphorae (Fig. 63:a-j), which by their nature can be posited to have come from further afield and bear witness to the vigorous commercial activity enjoyed by inhabitants of the ancient city.[61]

B. *The Fine Wares.* In addition to plain wares, the survey produced a small sampling of fragments in a variety of "Roman" red wares.[62] They are presented here in two groups: those considered to have been produced in Cyprus (Fig. 64: Cypriote Sigillata and

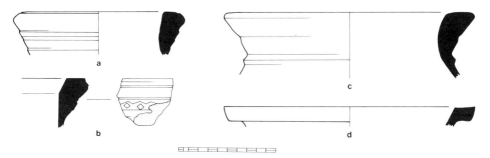

Figure 59. Domestic pottery from the survey area: Fabric IIB.

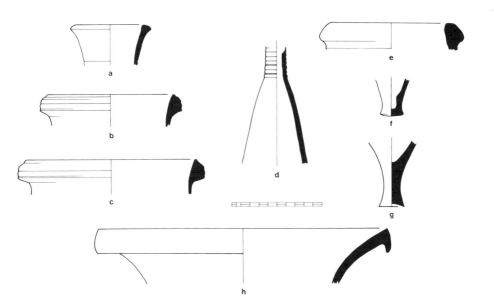

Figure 60. Domestic pottery from the survey area: Fabric IIC.

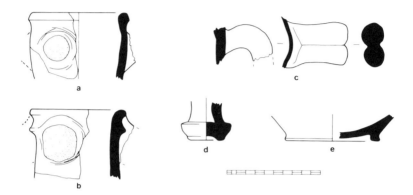

Figure 61. Domestic pottery from the survey area: Fabric III.

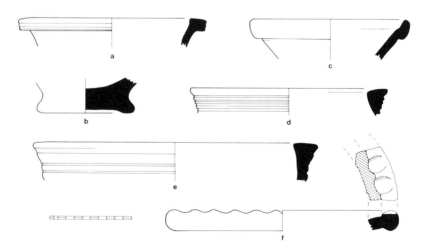

Figure 62. Domestic pottery from the survey area: Fabric IV.

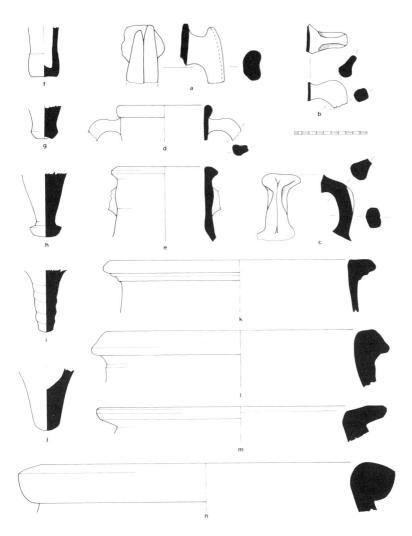

Figure 63. Domestic pottery from the survey area: Miscellaneous amphora and storage jars.

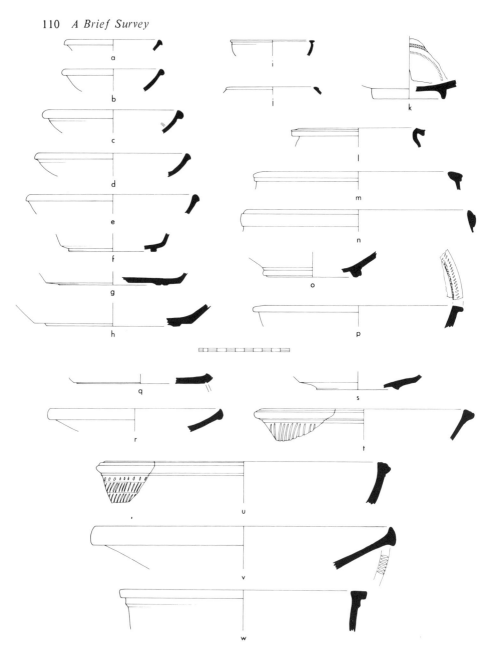

Figure 64. Cypriote sigillata (a-p) and Cypriote Red Slip Ware (q-w).

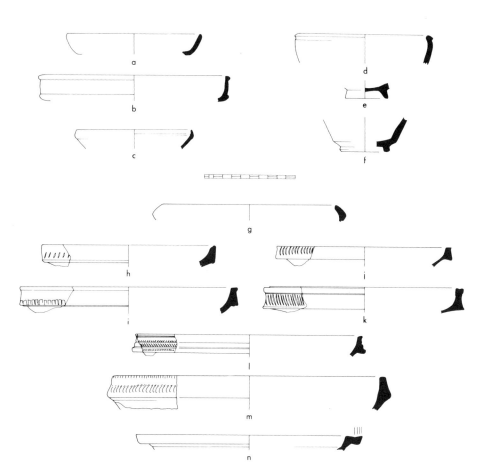

Figure 65. Tschardarli (a, b), Eastern Sigillata A (d-f) and B (c), African Red Slip (g) and Late Roman C/Phocaean Red Slip (h-n) Wares.

Cypriote Red Slip Ware) and those whose production center is assumed to have been further afield (Fig. 65: Tschandarli Ware, Eastern Sigillata A and B, African Red Slip Ware, and Late Roman C/Phocaean Red Slip Ware).

Sixteen fragments of Sigillata Ware, belonging primarily to the first century B.C. through the mid-second century A.D., comprise the commonest group of early fine wares. These pieces, which include both open and semi-closed forms, are discussed below according to Hayes' original isolation of this fabric,[63] as well as his subsequent study of the fabric type from the House of Dionysos at Paphos.[64]

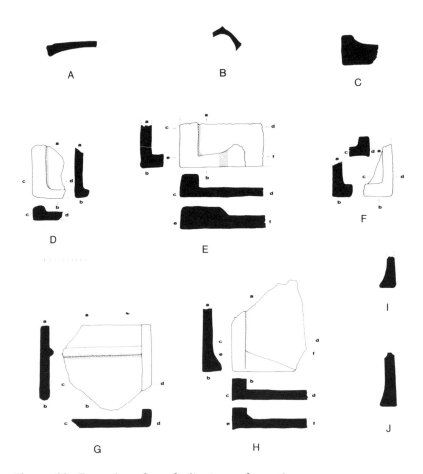

Figure 66. Examples of roof tile types from the survey area.

The Augustan Form 2 (Hayes P.5) or Form 10 (Hayes P.11) is illustrated in Figure 64:f. Cypriote Sigillata Form 2 or 3 (Hayes P.4A-4B, Pl.7) is suggested by the foot with double moulding, (Fig. 64:g), and perhaps the foot with single moulding (Fig. 64:h). The presence of Cypriote Sigillata Form 3 is definitely illustrated in Figure 64:p, Form 9 in Figure 64:a-d, and Form 10 in Figure 64:e. Of the Paphos open forms, Hayes P.21 (or 22 ?) is indicated by Figure 64:i, while Hayes P.22a is illustrated in Figure 64:j. One foot is from an open form, apparently an early bowl or cup, but the exact form is undetermined. A ring of discoloration, the result of

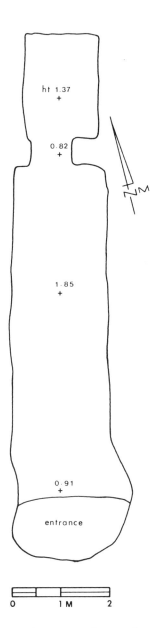

Figure 67. Plan of a rock-cut tomb on the Yerokarka.

stacking in the kiln, appears on the interior of this vessel
outside the rouletting (Fig. 64:k).

Of the semi-closed forms, late first century B.C. Cypriote
Sigillata Form 1a (Hayes P.40) may be related to the sherd seen in
Figure 64:l, while Hayes P.40 is suggested in Figure 64:m and o,
and Hayes P.41 in Figure 64:n, of the first half or middle of the
second century A.D.

Cypriote Red Slip Ware is illustrated in seven fragments that
date, most probably, to the fifth and sixth centuries A.D.[65] Three
different forms can be identified with a fair degree of certainty.
Hayes' Form 1 may be represented by the sherd seen in Figure 64:s,
while Form 2 is seen in the heavily rouletted sherd pictured in
Figure 64:t and u, and Form 9 in Figure 64:r and v, to which the
grooved base seen in Figure 64:q should also be assigned. The
horizontally flattened rim illustrated in Figure 64:w, however, is
not easy to parallel among the forms presented by Hayes, and may,
in fact, find its antecedents in earlier Cypriote domestic wares.[66]

Three early sigillata wares of Augustan or first half of the
first century A.D. date have been identified in the surface
collection. Two fragments of a fabric identified as Tschandarli
Ware of the first half of the first century A.D. appear in forms
that are not exactly paralleled in the literature. However, Figure
65:a might be compared with Loeschcke Form 8,[67] and Figure 65:b
with Loeschcke Form 1.[68] Three sherds of Eastern Sigillata A also
date to the Augustan period, or the first half of the first century
A.D. They include those illustrated in Figure 65:d, equivalent to
Samaria-Sebaste Form 16 with beaded rim, and in Figure 65:e and f,
related to Samaria-Sebaste Form 21 (or 23?). A single fragment of
Eastern Sigillata B (Fig. 65:c) also was found. Its parallels date
to the second quarter of the first century A.D.[69]

Two imported late Roman wares include a single fragment of
African Red Slip Ware (Fig. 65:g), which probably is Hayes Form 61A
of the late fourth century A.D.,[70] and examples of Late Roman
C/Phocaean Red Slip Ware, which appears in approximately the same
quantity as does the contemporary local ware, Cypriote Red Slip.
The forms identified in the survey collection are limited to the
most common shapes: Hayes Form 3 (Fig. 65:h-k and m), Form 5 (Fig.
65:n), and Form 8 (Fig. 65:l) of the fifth and sixth centuries
A.D.[71]

Other Terra Cotta

Fragmentary ceramic roof tiles and water pipes were encountered
frequently during the survey.

Roof tile fragments were cataloged in the field according to any
morphological feature(s) they presented. Eight types (I-VIII)
seemed to be distinct. However, since a larger group of more complete tiles from the Apollo Sanctuary is at present under study,[72]
only a selection from the survey group is offered here. The survey
examples can be correlated with the Sanctuary typology as follows:

Survey Type	Illustrations	Sanctuary Type
I.	Figure 66:a	none
II.	Figure 66:e	Z
II. Small	Figure 66:f	Z
III.	Figure 66:c	Y
IV.	Figure 66:d	Z
V.	Figure 66:l, j	Y (?)
VI.	Figure 66:g	X
VII.	Figure 66:h	X
VIII.	Figure 66:b	"peak"

Fragments of terra cotta water pipe were also common in parts of the survey area. In shape and size they are similar to those published by Last from other parts of the water system on ancient Kourion.[73] Field analysis indicated five major fabric groups in the survey collection.

Fabric 1. Moderately well levigated clay with very frequent white grit to 3 mm. Fabric color ranges from 7.5YR 6/2 (pinkish grey) to 6/4 (light brown). Areas B and C:8.

Fabric 2. Possibly a variant of Fabric 1. Fabric color can range through 7.5YR 7/4 (pink) to 7/6 (reddish yellow). It differs, however, in that the clay is much finer and the white grit temper so frequent in Fabric 1 is almost absent; when present, it usually is smaller than 1 mm. Fine straw casts are also present. Areas C:6 and R.

Fabric 3. Well levigated clay with a moderate use of sand-sized to 1 mm white, and occasionally grey, grit. Surface color ranges from 5YR 7/6 (reddish yellow) to 2.5YR 6/8 (light red), but the common denominator is the solid core, which is a standard 2.5YR 6/8 (light red). A light 7.5YR 7/4 (pink) or dark 2.5YR 5/6 (red) slip can be found on some examples of this fabric. Areas A:2, B, C:6 and 7.

Fabric 4. Very gritty fabric with white mineral temper averaging 1-2 mm. Surface and core colors range from 2.5YR 6/6 (light red) to 5/6 (red). One example exhibits a thin 7.5YR 8/4-7/4 (pink) slip similar to some Fabric 3 pieces. Areas B; C:5 and D.

Fabric 5. The most poorly fired of the fabrics used for pipe manufacture, it is a poorly levigated clay with frequent white and grey grit averaging 1-2 mm. There is a thick grey core with a thin (ca. 2 mm) layer of 2.5YR 5/6-4/8 (red) immediately below a slip which approximates 7/5YR 7/4 (pink). Area A:2.

The distribution of these pipe fabrics in the survey areas can be summarized as follows: Survey Area A--fabrics 3 and 4; B--fabrics 1, 3 and 4; C--fabrics 1, 2, 3, and 4; D--fabric 4; R--fabric 2. All of these areas are located on the slopes of Kourion City. Surprisingly, no pipe fragments were collected on the Yerokarka.

Figure 68. Cypro-Syllabic inscriptions from Yerokarka tomb area.

Part Two
The Temple of Apollo Hylates
at Kourion

Chapter 6
The Temple
David Soren

One of the major attractions at the Sanctuary of Apollo Hylates near Kourion is the Temple of Apollo (Fig. 69), the focus for visitors of the Roman period and for tourists since 1936.

Despite two previous excavations, the building had never been dated securely, and in 1967 Robert Scranton, writing a synthesis of all earlier work, was forced to admit: "As to the date of the building we are unfortunately without any direct evidence."[1] But enough new evidence has emerged during our campaigns of 1978-1981 to merit a complete reexamination of the temple in an attempt to clarify its date of construction, ancient rebuilding, and final destruction by earthquake in circa 365 A.D. In addition, it has been possible to suggest a reconstruction of the entire temple, to offer an account of our finds in the temple area, and to publish for the first time some of the discoveries made by George McFadden.

The first excavations of the temple were conducted by General Louis Palma di Cesnola in 1874 during his tenure as American ambassador to Cyprus. In a newly discovered letter written by Cesnola to a friend, he tells of his discovery of the temple: "I have *undoubtedly* discovered the Temple of Apollo Hylates here and I have already found beautiful Greek objects."[2] In his book *Cyprus: Its Ancient Cities, Tombs and Temples*, he gave a detailed account of his work:[3]

> Following the traces of the aqueduct north of Curium always among very thick bushes from which start flocks of partridges and francolins, I reached the ruins of the temple of Apollo Hylates, this locality being called at the present day by the inhabitants of the neighboring villages Apellon. Its ancient name was Hyle, and it was from this that the epithet Hylates was derived.

119

The mass of stones on the ground shows that the temple had been a magnificent edifice. It probably faced the sea from which it was only a thousand yards distant, and was entirely surrounded by a forest. This temple was seventy-nine feet in length, and thirty-two in width. Its columns, in white marble and bluish granite, are lying scattered in every direction. They are of different dimensions. The largest measure three feet two inches in diameter; the next in size two feet; and the smallest sixteen inches. Portions of the latter stand on their bases. This spot is well worthy of systematic exploration, but that could not be accomplished without ample funds. I dug along the eastern foundations for several weeks, and laid bare a part of the pavement, but met with no sculptural remains, except a few terracotta warriors with helmet and shield and the fragments of a very large earthenware jar inscribed in Greek letters with a dedication of Apollo Hylates. The latter were found beneath the stone pavement of the temple. Within the area of the temple, I found also several mutilated inscriptions, on one of which occurs the name of Ptolemy Philadelphus and Cleopatra . . .

At this point the view from the west is imposing in the extreme.

Figure 69. View of Temple of Apollo Hylates from the southeast in 1979 before restorations.

Whatever one may say about Cesnola's avowed interest in treasure hunting and his lack of interest in method, this passage reveals his sharp eye for detail and is invaluable as an account of the temple before it was again plundered and lost.[4] Cesnola had no difficulty in locating the building, owing to a local tradition associating the area with Apollo. In fact, the term Apellon had been applied as early as 1838 in the writings of American Consul Lorenzo Warriner Pease.[5]

The proportions quoted by Cesnola correspond well enough with the actual dimensions of the temple, and the view from the west towards the Akrotiri peninsula is still as wondrous as he describes. There can be little doubt that he found and excavated the actual Temple of Apollo.

No trace survives of his columns in white marble and bluish granite, nor even of the pavement he laid bare along the eastern foundations, but these attractive items could easily have been prime targets for looters. And one need not quarrel with Cesnola's claim to have unearthed terra cotta warriors with helmet and shield. These could have come from the temple fill, although shields are not common accessories for Kourion warriors.[6] His inscribed jar fragments still exist and were recently sent by the University of Pennsylvania Museum to the University of Missouri for an exhibition commemorating twenty-five years of Missouri in Cyprus. (This jar is discussed below.)

"Since Cesnola," wrote George Jeffery in 1928, "the site has been almost completely devastated by stone-seekers."[7] Jeffery believed that he had located several Doric capitals belonging to the temple, but his description of the temple area does not agree with the actual remains and his idea of a large building with a paved court before it and other buildings around it describes more accurately the Northwest Building (originally referred to by McFadden as Temple A).

So the account of Jeffery, the former Curator of Ancient Monuments for Cyprus, really helps very little, except perhaps indirectly, for it suggests that Cesnola's temple may have been plundered once it was exposed and then forgotten--all within the space of fifty-three years. It disappeared under a mound of earth, which George McFadden, working with the University of Pennsylvania, would rediscover and excavate in his first campaign.

McFadden (1907-1953), a 1930 graduate of Princeton University, undertook the first serious excavations at the site in November of 1935. In his third trench he uncovered a curious and deep rock-cut channel (Fig. 70), along with a large water conduit that apparently originated at the castellum (water distribution center) in the northwest area of the site.[8] As he continued in his third trench to follow the conduit, he inadvertently discovered a small section of the west stairway wall of the Temple of Apollo at the edge of an area he called "the mound."

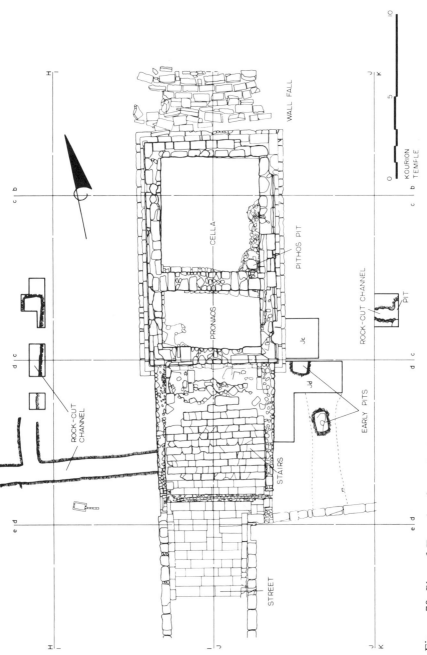

Figure 70. Plan of Temple of Apollo by John Rutherford and John Huffstot including rock-cut channel to west, conduit and settlement basin south of channel, and pre-second-temple pits to east of temple.

His Trench 4 (Fig. 71) exposed the southeast corner of the structure, and once again the elusive Temple of Apollo (or Temple B as it was briefly christened) was discovered: "We soon had two trenches dug across this mound and laid bare a small temple, Temple B, 13.50 m long by 8.35 m wide."[9]

The top of the mound corresponded to the level of the present cross-wall of the cella, 135.90 m, while the surrounding surface soil was considerably lower. As the structure emerged, McFadden noted the disturbed nature of much of the fill, possibly the result of Cesnola's work or even of looters: "Large disturbed area (intrusion) both in center of naos and pronaos reaching down to 1.30-1.80 m below surface."[10]

Encouraged by his promising discovery, he stopped all work around the rest of the site and exposed the temple, employing nineteen workmen and six wheelbarrows.[11] He was the first scholar to note that the temple actually had two phases, the first of which he dated "Hellenistic or Roman," while "the later one is undoubtedly Roman."[12] The first temple proved to be essentially that shown in Figure 69, minus the front staircase and cross-wall.

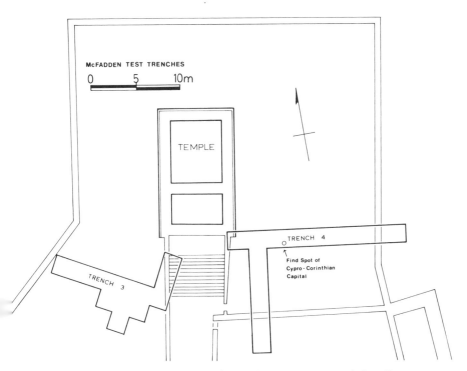

Figure 71. Plan by Joseph Last of temple area excavated by George McFadden in 1935.

The second temple contained the cross-wall and reused the earlier foundations. In subsequent campaigns he cleaned out the surface earth around the temple in order to make it "much clearer to view."[13] In April and May of 1937 he cleared the area between the temple and the western temenos wall of the sanctuary, as well as the area up to 12 m east of the building. He also cleaned as far as the temenos wall to the north.

The notes from these early days of systematic excavation are quite detailed, but McFadden died before presenting his final report and it is not always easy to match up his recording system with actual objects scattered among the University of Pennsylvania Museum, the Cyprus Museum, and the museum and four storerooms at Episkopi. An attempt has been made here to publish not only our own finds from the temple, but also those of McFadden, and these are appended to this article.

The Temple of Apollo as it survived in 1979 was a modest structure consisting of a cella and pronaos reached by a flight of steps facing the street to the south. The first temple (or at least the structure that preceded the Roman Temple) was at a lower level than the present structure and, as Scranton has stated, had no pronaos.[14] The first temple was small but well made of ashlar blocks, and with an attractive base moulding on the sides and front.

Most of the blocks (Fig. 72 and 73) found *in situ* and which composed the first temple are made of a stone called calcarinite, sometimes referred to by the more general term caliche (McFadden refers to it even more generally as limestone).[15]

Although it is not clear why McFadden stated that the blocks were placed without mortar, mortar obviously is present and was generously applied to the joint interstices, serving to smooth out the more poorly prepared blocks.[15] (This is a gypsum-rich mortar with selenite crystal aggregate, according to Bullard).

Close scrutiny of the first temple reveals that for all its apparent beauty it is made in part of either reused or at least poorly fitted material. Its highest preserved course contained blocks of irregular sizes. Some of the blocks in the lower courses are just tiny filler pieces wedged in to help the longer pieces complete the courses making up the building. A number of rough-finished or rusticated blocks may have been installed with the second temple.

As far as can be determined, no trace of an upper podium cornice has been located for either the first or second temple, but it is most unlikely that either temple would have lacked this element. It is possible that this podium crown, which most probably did not fall in the final earthquake, was carried off by stone robbers, along with the column bases and shafts above it. As to the base moulding, McFadden observed that it does not continue around the back of the temple.[15] The back wall of the temple, however, has such perfectly cut unweathered blocks that it appears to have been rebuilt or at least patched up by McFadden's skilled masons, even

Figure 72. View of temple from north in 1980 during reconstruction.

Figure 73. Aerial view of temple from northwest in 1980.

though there is no mention of this in his preserved notes or articles. One indicator that at least some of it may be modern is the terra cotta tinted mortar found within the interstices between several blocks. McFadden even gave his own special formula for the production of this material, which he called his colored cement solution: "1 cup sand, 1 cup cement, 2-1/4 spoons yellow terra cotta. 1 cup equals 25 spoons."[16]

The first temple, a simple rectangular building, was entered by a central opening still preserved slightly above street level. Due largely to the undulating character of the bedrock, the building rests partly on bedrock and partly on a foundation of rubble stones.

Scranton, in his 1962 investigations, was able to offer important observations about the first temple.[17] He noted that the calcarinite base moulding did not continue into the front doorway, thus suggesting that doorjambs were added to each side and that the actual central opening was circa 1.8 m wide.

Although the first temple proved to be less than excellently preserved, abundant remains of the second temple were located, especially in the form of blocks fallen and still preserved in the immediate vicinity.

Whether the second temple was prostyle (more likely and more aesthetically appealing from a distance) or in antis, the cella walls would most likely have been indented slightly (perhaps some 10 cm) from the outer edge of the podium (with its now missing crown).

If the temple were prostyle, this 10 cm can be arrived at by considering the size of the well preserved extant capital (discussed below) and comparing it with bases associated with capitals of similar size, proportion, and type at the Kourion City site. Such bases would have lined up at the corners with the antae of the pronaos of the temple, but would have been slightly wider than the antae. The bases should have required about 10 cm per side more than the width of the pronaos in order to be positioned properly.

In his study of the second temple, Scranton was able to identify a well preserved "Cypro-Corinthian Capital" found by McFadden on April 23, 1937 (Fig. 74), and which gives the appearance of an unfinished Corinthian (Fig. 75-77). This capital was not complete, but in 1980 project senior architect John Rutherford found a "volute" or "ear" piece from it lying in a pile of blocks about 10 m west of the temple. The new corner fitted perfectly (Fig. 78). Rutherford later located yet another possible fragment of capital (Fig. 79), very badly battered, which had also been stacked up with many wall blocks, probably by McFadden workmen, just inside the north temenos wall. The capital type may be a simplification of Hellenistic Corinthian capitals of Alexandria, as transmitted through Petra to Cyprus.

In 1979 the author found an acorn decoration in the Archaic Precinct just west of the altar (Fig. 80). This apparently adorned a similar but larger capital. A second, smaller acorn was found in 1980 by John Rutherford west of the temple. The acorns were too large to fit the capitals of the Temple of Apollo, but they show that similar capitals were in use in other buildings around the site.

The original "Cypro-Corinthian" capital was tentatively dated by Scranton to the Augustan period, but this has not been confirmed; in fact, it was called into question by us in the 1979 campaign. The columns seen by Cesnola are all gone; their dimensions, as he gave them, do not seem appropriate for our capitals and we have, at Scranton's suggestion, posited a column of approximately nine diameters in height. Scranton did not discuss when or where the first capital was found, but we are now able to ascertain this from McFadden's diary. In an entry describing clearing operations east of the temple he notes:

> "East of Temple B delta-epsilon east 2-4, 4th stratum . . . Removed Cypriot capital lying on third stratum and dug epsilon to precinct wall south of it."[18]

Integrating this with the gridded plan for the Sanctuary by Joseph Last, one can see that this is almost exactly the location east of the temple that the capital was in when the preliminary site survey was conducted in 1977. The capital may have been among debris hurled down by the earthquake of July 21, 365 A.D. Supporting this idea is the fact that McFadden found rof tiles in the second stratum, along with the capital.

Scranton reported that another such capital was used in the gymnasium of Salamis in eastern Cyprus.[19] In the latter example, a sort of Doric *echinus*, or necking, was added beneath the capital. Another example much closer to home was cited from the acropolis at the Kourion City site, but Scranton was not able to recall the precise area. A detailed search of the extensive city site turned up five such capitals in a large colonnaded place north of the so-called gymnasium excavated by Demos Christou in an unpublished, fenced-in area excavated by M. Loulloupis. These capitals, larger than ours, lacked the echinus feature of those found at Salamis, but did contain column shafts (unfluted) and bases, perhaps like those now missing from our temple. Loulloupis most graciously allowed us to borrow these features from his unpublished site so that we could use them for our paper reconstruction of the Temple of Apollo Hylates; we felt the proximity of the two sites justified our borrowing. Another well-preserved capital (Fig. 81), from the House of the Achilles Mosaic on the acropolis of Kourion City, is on display in the Classical Gallery at the University of Pennsylvania Museum (No. 54-28-225). It is described as a simplified Corinthian capital.

Our capital also is of interest because its bearing surface projects out by a few millimeters and because the raised area has a circular form, which may reflect the diameter of the column shaft.

Figure 74. Finding of the Cypro-Corinthian capital by workmen of George McFadden in 1937 southeast of temple. Courtesy of Dr. Roger Edwards, University of Pennsylvania Museum (negative out of focus).

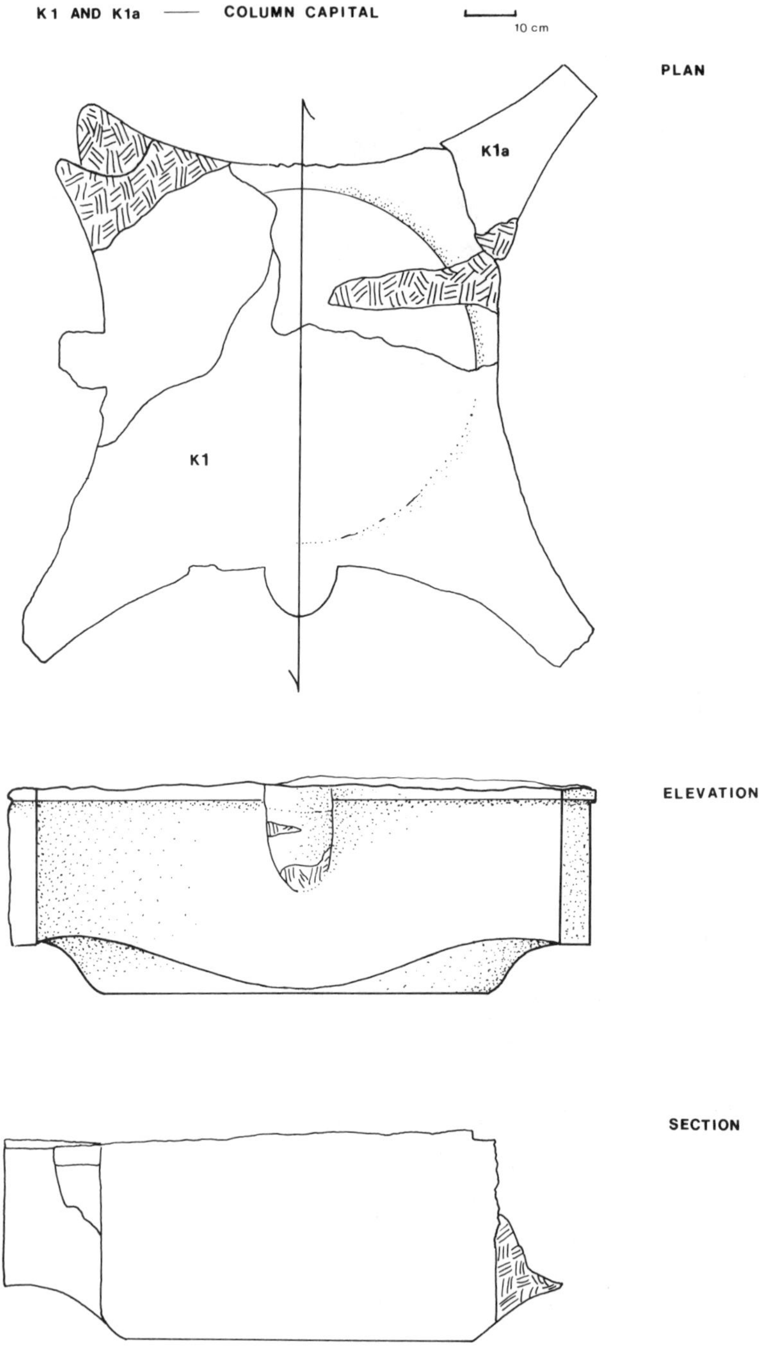

K 1 AND K1a —— COLUMN CAPITAL

10 cm

PLAN

K1a

K1

ELEVATION

SECTION

Figure 75. Drawing of Cypro-Corinthian capital 72 by Noelle Soren.

Figure 76. Cypro-Corinthian capital 72.

Figure 77. Cypro–Corinthian capital 72.

Figure 78. Cypro-Corinthian capital 72 with new "ear" 73 found in 1980 by John Rutherford.

Figure 79. Possible fragment of Cypro–Corinthian capital 126 found in 1980 by John Rutherford.

Figure 80. One of two acorn decorations from missing
Cypro-Corinthian capitals (89).

This observation, made by John Rutherford, not only gives us an
idea of the original column diameters for the second temple, but
also shows us that the builders wanted to keep the projecting
portion of the capitals from any load-bearing function.

Scranton also identified many architectural fragments which
appear to have come from the temple and which are at present
stacked just within the temenos wall north and west of the temple.
These fragments include a block, bearing part of the dedicatory
inscription, found in front of the temple; Scranton proposes that
this was the lintel, "the most probable place for the dedicatory
inscription to have appeared." The matter is, however, by no means
settled, and we have left it out of our facade reconstruction.

John Rutherford believes that the dedicatory inscription (Fig. 82) may have been part of a flat-arched lintel over the door of the pro-naos, owing to the slightly diagonal end of the block. Scranton has suggested a brief and convenient hypothetical completion of the inscription. Mitford noted that possible second and third lines of the inscription may have been erased, but he doubted the additional lines and ended up agreeing with Scranton. In 1980 Rutherford found a block roughly equal in height to the dedication block; it bears the letters *NIO* (Fig. 83). That the block is part of the temple dedication is suggested by the similarity in height and style of the letters on the two blocks and by the location of the lettering at the very top of each block.

The new block, like that found earlier, once bore a longer inscription, but parts of the three lines were either chiseled out or damaged. Was this the result of a *damnatio memoriae*? If so, for whom? Or was it simply the result of natural causes? Mitford is quite cautious about dating the inscription and can be of little

Figure 81. University of Pennsylvania capital from Kourion (No. 54-28-225).

Figure 82. Dedicatory inscription 78 from the temple found by George McFadden in 1947.

Figure 83. New fragment of inscription 113 found in 1980 by John Rutherford.

help. The inscribed blocks must have fallen from the second temple and should, when dated, show the time of dedication of the temple. Could it be Caligula, or even Nero, who suffered censure here, or some more local individual? Also, the new inscribed block has unusual cuttings on its back at an odd angle and these are not yet understood. Eugene Lane, who has studied the inscribed blocks, wrote in the Report of the Department of Antiquities of Cyprus for 1983 that the second temple may date to either 65 or 66 A.D., in the reign of Nero. The fascination of Nero for Apollo (and his music), of course, is well documented.

Among Scranton's other attributions are two "Cypro-Corinthian" anta capitals, along with a capital apparently from a corner pilaster (Fig. 84). He also believed he had found fragments of two other pilaster capitals. These discoveries, however, caused him a great deal of trouble, for he ended up having to fit his two anta capitals and three corner pilaster capitals onto the second temple, and this is one feature too many. He was then forced to suggest in his article that one of the pilaster capitals was left lying around from the first temple, which seems very unlikely.

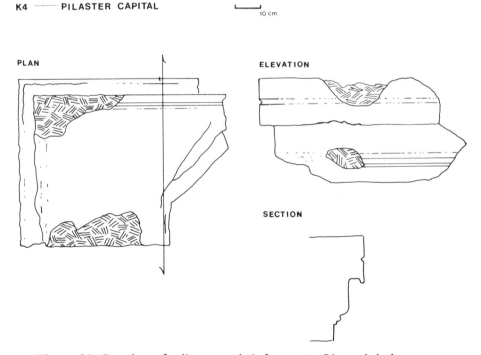

K4 ——— **PILASTER CAPITAL**

10 cm

PLAN

ELEVATION

SECTION

Figure 84. Drawing of pilaster capital fragments 74a and b by Noelle Soren.

There are, according to Rutherford, actually seven fragments of pilaster capitals, but they can, in fact, be fused to form two distinct capitals which fit the rear corners of the second temple and which measure seventy square centimeters. These capitals, combined with two anta capitals, fit nicely with the four corners of the temple (Fig. 85-88).

Also located were twelve fragments of what appear to be shafts of the corner pilasters (Fig. 89-91); these have greatly facilitated the reconstruction drawing of the flank of the temple by John Huffstot. The pilaster capitals originally were made in two pieces, and the anta capitals were joined from two pieces lengthwise just off the center cut line. This shows that the builders of the temple did, in fact, assemble these capitals in sections.

Scranton also found traces of thin slabs with double fasciae topped with a cyma reversa moulding, but he could not decide if this was an architrave for the temple or a wall crown only, running between the anta capitals at the side of the temple and the pilaster capitals at the rear (Fig. 92-95). This question was settled when the key corner architrave block was found. Scranton also had found an epistyle block, and he rightly suggested that there was a plain frieze course above the fasciated architrave (Fig. 96 and 97). The 1979 excavations confirmed Scranton's detective work by exposing much of the rear facade of the temple, which had been thrown down by the shear wave of the great earthquake of circa 365 A.D. that destroyed the sanctuary (Fig. 98-102).

This rear facade, originally found but not interpreted by McFadden in 1936, was still lying as it fell and represented much of the upper third of the cella wall of the temple, so that almost two-thirds of the lower part of the rear wall either remained upright or (less likely) toppled on top of this debris in an aftershock. The fallen blocks included the four rows immediately below the fallen architrave, as well as the epistyle course above it. The remaining parts of the temple, including the podium crown, column shafts, and capitals, were pillaged at a later date, while the six preserved rows of fallen stones went undisturbed and probably were covered with quake debris and forgotten.

When Scranton returned to Cyprus to study the quake stones in July of 1979, we decided to employ a three-fold approach: (1) attempt to reconstruct the facade and flank of the temple on paper, (2) raise funds to set up at least some of the temple again, and (3) accurately draw the temple in section and give an elevation so that it will be clear what we found *in situ* and what we have restored.

The paper reconstruction proceeded as follows. The actual remains *in situ* were considered first (Fig. 103-105). Most of the steps and podium of the second temple are well preserved and so formed the basis for all reconstruction work. By 1980 we had discovered some 150 blocks, which comprised circa twenty percent,

K2 AND K2a ——— ANTA CAPITAL   10 cm

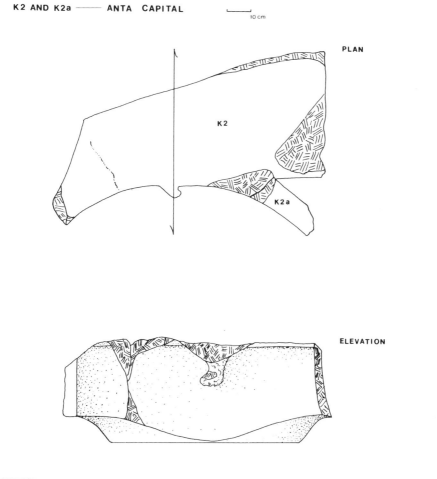

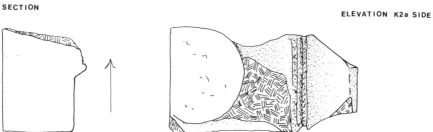

Figure 85. Drawing of anta capital 79 and joining fragment 80 by Noelle Soren.

Figure 86. Four joining pilaster capital fragments (74 a-c, 75) assembled in 1980 by John Rutherford.

Figure 87. Two joining fragments of anta capital (79, 80) assembled in 1980, shown upside down.

Figure 88. Two joining fragments of another anta capital (109, 110) found in 1980.

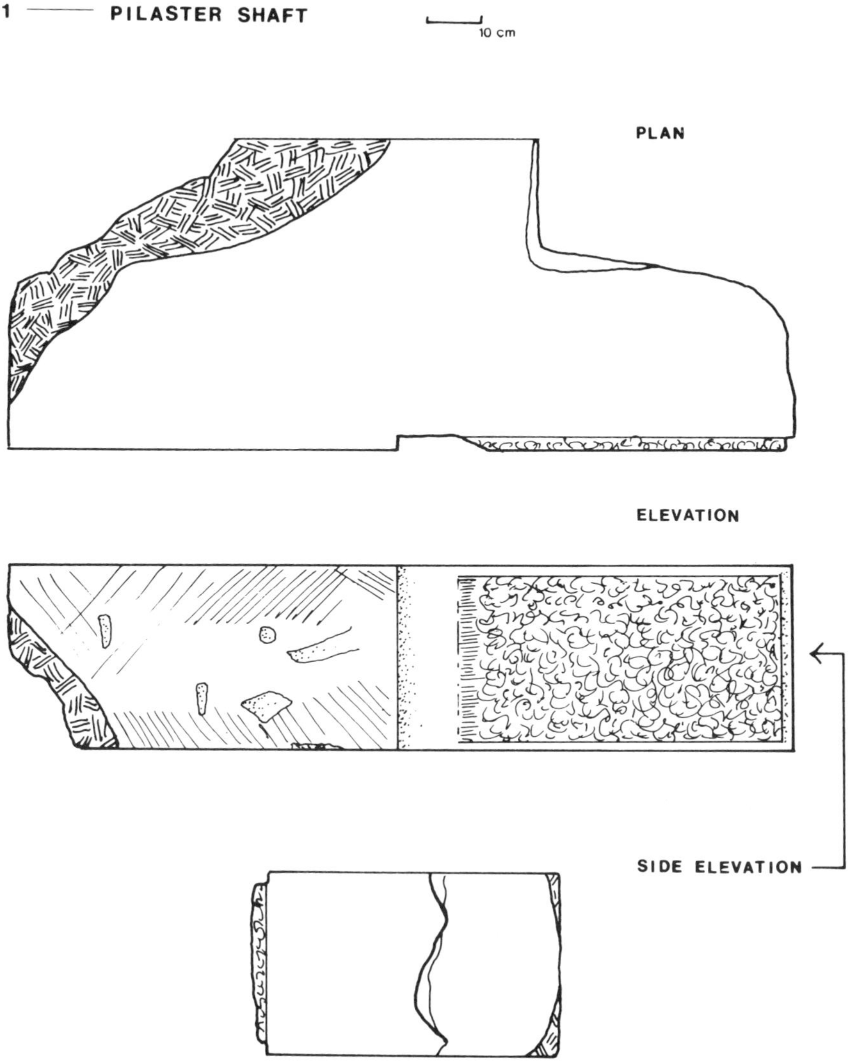

1 ——— **PILASTER SHAFT**

10 cm

Figure 89. Drawing of pilaster shaft block 77 from northeast corner of the temple.

Figure 90. Pilaster shaft block 77.

Figure 91. Pilaster shaft block 76.

Figure 92. Corner architrave block 61 found in 1980.

223 ——— **CORNER ARCHITRAVE**
10 cm

ELEVATION   **SIDE ELEVATION**

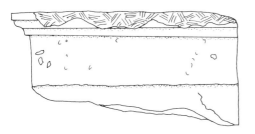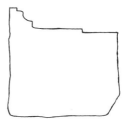

Figure 93. Drawing of corner architrave block S61.

or fifty square meters, of the original surface of the temple. The
column capitals were interpreted from the two now surviving, but,
as noted above, no trace of a necking moulding at the base of the
capitals was found, either here or on the similar capitals at
Kourion City (although the Kourion City examples have finished
volutes); therefore, none .has been added to the reconstruction
(Fig. 106 and 107). Because no columns or bases were found, despite
Cesnola's discoveries, the Kourion examples had to be borrowed.
The actual heights of the columns, temple entrance, and cella wall
are conjectural, but it is hoped that our approximations will not
seem unreasonable. The thickness of the column shafts that fitted
into the capitals was estimated at 80 cm by Scranton, but
Rutherford found such a thickness excessive; 68 to 74 cm seemed
more reasonable to him, based on the projecting area on top of the
capital described above.

Figure 94. Regular architrave block 67 from north wall fall.

35 ———— ARCHITRAVE

10 cm

SECTION   ELEVATION

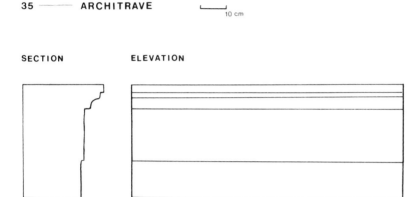

Figure 95. Drawing of arhcitrave block 67.

Rutherford also suggested that the floor of the second temple was higher than Scranton believed. If eighteen steps are allowed, the topmost would fall flush with the edge of the temple platform proper, some 2.2 m above the street. This would give the temple needed height and majesty, plus a commanding view over the Sanctuary to the Bay of Episkopi. And it would exhibit a comfortable relationship between the stairs of the temple and the podium. It would also give the podium needed height, especially if a podium crown moulding existed, as seems likely. The height of the cheek walls flanking the stairs was not known, but was set equal in height to the temple platform so as not to obscure the temple.

    The ashlar wall of the cella was drawn from the many fallen blocks in the area; the fasciated frieze and epistyle blocks are discussed above. We have assumed that these ran all the way around the temple. Cornice blocks with modillions were also cited by Scranton, but the treatment of the temple cornice (Fig. 108-114) proved more complicated than he was able to describe.[21] Rutherford located a corner cornice block of critical importance for understanding the treatment of the cornice, which was elaborated along the sides of the temple but lacked its uppermost cyma recta moulding when it continued horizontally around the front of the temple. This is evident when one compares the side profile illustrated in Figure 111 with the front horizontal cornice block seen in Figure 112.

The small upper moulding was instead carried diagonally above the tympanum and became part of the raking cornice. Rutherford has located nine cornice blocks besides the corner piece, and at least two of the cornice blocks are the simplified type from the front or rear of the temple. He also has found three fragments of raking cornice (Scranton had noted one). The pediment itself was represented by what appear to be tympanum blocks (Fig. 115). Scranton believed in 1962 he had found two such blocks with pitches varying from 1:3 1/6 to 1:4 3/4. Rutherford could find only two good fragments, which, although difficult to measure, had slope ratios of about 1:4. The battered corner cornice piece already cited seemed to measure between 1:4.5 and 1:5, but this is only approximate.[25]

Scranton's belief that the pediments of both the first and second temples were lying around need not be accepted. Only the remains of the second temple appear to be present. In 1980 Rutherford found the actual top block of the pedimental raking cornice (Fig. 116-118); it has a cutting in the rear to receive a beam of wood, possibly the ridgepole. Its slope was not measurable, but the ridgepole cutting was 20 cm wide by 22 to 28 cm high. Rear cuttings on other raking cornice blocks were 70 cm on center for beams 15 to 20 cm high placed at the lower part of the cornice. The horizontal cornice blocks from the long sides of the second temple have curious, slightly trapezoidal modillions separated by Y marks on the soffit, but this ornament is not found on the surviving pieces of raking cornice. The cornice blocks (Fig. 119-123) generally are large and have a long bearing surface to avoid tipping over when in place.

Figure 96. Epistyle block S68 from north wall fall.

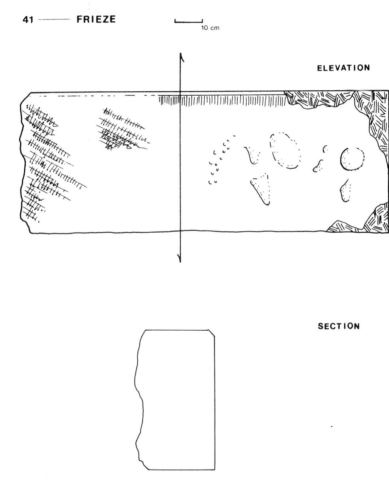

Figure 97. Drawing of epistyle block S68 by Noelle Soren.

Figure 98. Collapsed north wall of temple before final cleaning in 1979. Bipod photography by John Rutherford.

Figure 99. North wall fall after final cleaning.

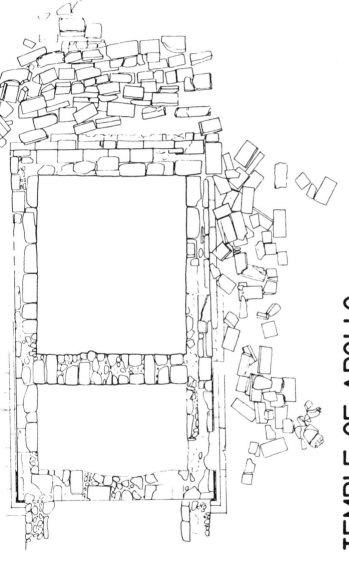

TEMPLE OF APOLLO
PLAN BY JOSEPH LAST
ca. 1935

Figure 100. Plan of temple with earthquake collapse, by Joseph Last during the McFadden excavations of 1935.

Figure 101. George McFadden (upper right) overlooks debris in view from temple steps in 1935.

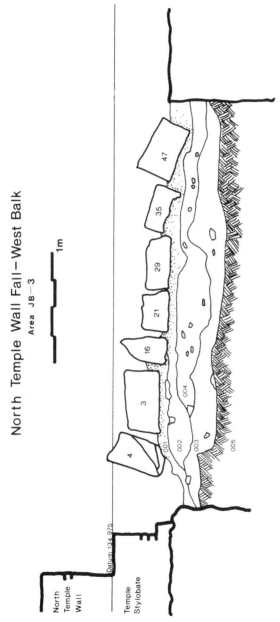

Figure 102. Section drawing of sounding in Jb 3 north of temple and under wall fall by Dana Karangelin.

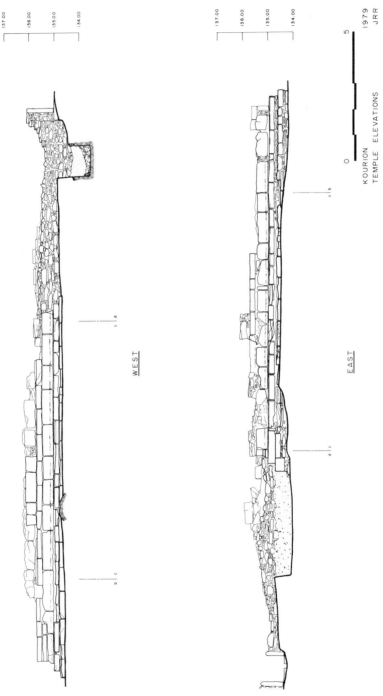

Figure 103. West and east side views of temple before restorations of 1980, by John Rutherford.

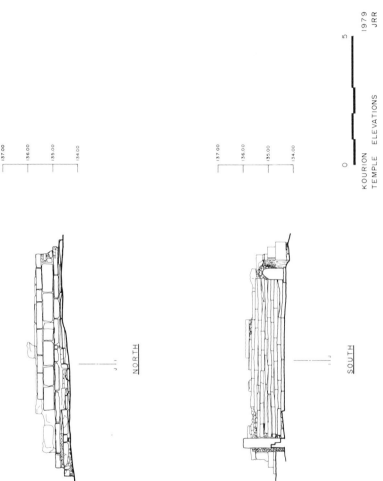

Figure 104. Elevations of north and south areas of temple before restorations in 1980, by John Rutherford.

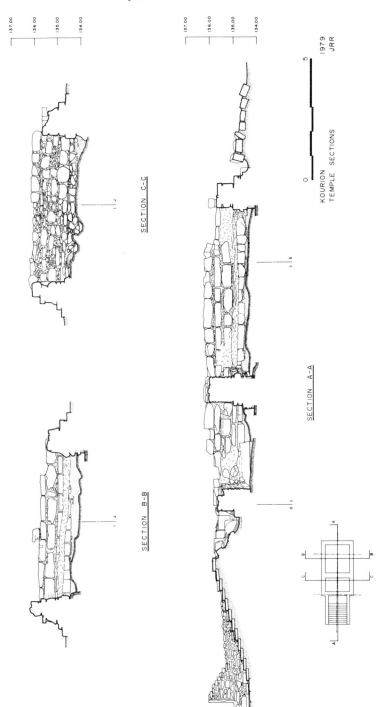

Figure 105. Elevation sections through temple by John Rutherford before restorations.

Figure 106. Proposed reconstruction of temple facade drawn by John Huffstot, supervised by John Rutherford with contributions by Alexandra Corn, Robert Scranton and Jan Sanders.

We have offered here a hypothetical reconstruction of the temple
facade in which there is the possibility of some error,
particularly in the podium crown, the columns and their spacing,
and the lack of bases owing to the absence of pilaster and anta
bases.[23] In preparing the reconstruction, we made some other
observations worth noting. Placing the floor level of the second
temple at a high level 2.2 m above street level would mean that the
height of the pithos found in the southeast corner of the cella in
1935 (discussed below) had to be studied to see whether it could
have functioned with the second temple, or whether it might have
been buried under it. According to Rutherford, if the pithos
functioned with the temple, it would have to have been set in the
floor where it was originally found and raised to a height of 1.4 m
to have reached the proposed level of the floor of the second
temple. The pithos is preserved to a height of 1.1 m, but it is
preserved only to the shoulder. Its neck would have to be only
27-30 cm high to reach the floor, and that does not seem
unreasonable. Also worth noting is that among the earthquake
stones, block number S114 (Fig. 124) proved to be a curious
right-angled piece probably reused here but originally a corner

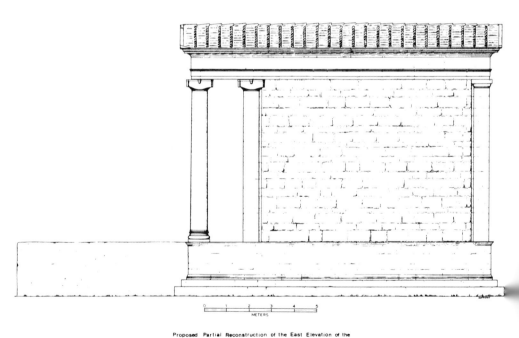

Proposed Partial Reconstruction of the East Elevation of the
Temple of Apollo Hylates at Kourion

Figure 107. Proposed reconstruction of temple flank.

block, perhaps for the first temple. From the quake fall it was also clear that the cella wall of the temple was laid in courses of varying height, rather than in courses of uniform height.

The attempt at a reconstruction was not the only work done on the temple. Trenches were dug inside the temple (1979) and outside against its northeast (1979) and southeast (1978) foundations (Fig. 125-130). The 1978 sounding was significant in providing information about the date of the second temple.

In this area McFadden had sunk his L-shaped Trench 4 in 1935, although he noted: "Only surface soil removed in this trench system."[24]

Our probe revealed that while McFadden did, in fact, reach bedrock in part of his Trench 4, he did not do so in the immediate vicinity of the Temple of Apollo. It was possible to define precisely where McFadden had made his trench (Fig. 131) because it corresponded to the area indicated on McFadden's original plan by Joseph Last. Most of the stratigraphy against the temple was undisturbed below the stylobate.

In the trench, located in grid area Jd1 and Jd2, the actual foundations of the first temple were found resting on bedrock. There were cuttings in the bedrock east of the foundation, presumably for use as planting pits. Layers of fill had been placed over the pits, putting them out of use, an action probably associated with rebuilding of the temple. Locus 006 was a fill for the second temple and was placed against the lower portion of the rubble foundation of the staircase wall. When originally found, Locus 006 had been mistaken for a foundation trench for the first temple.

The area immediately east of the east staircase of the temple was disturbed, as if there had been ancient trenching to adjust the staircase wall. The fills placed against the second temple and over the pits, which may have been associated with the first temple, held primarily material of the first century B.C. or the beginning of the first century A.D. The latest finds should give an idea of the date of the second temple, probably Julio-Claudian, and they agree with Eugene Lane's possibly Neronian date for the second temple, based on the dedicatory inscription. The Neronian date is particularly intriguing, since several areas of the site have finds of about that period. Lamps found beneath the street paving in front of the main stoa appear to belong to this date, and there are hundreds of surface finds of the time scattered throughout the West Enclosure. A large cistern (Cistern 3), located in the southeast area of the site but north of the street by the Palaestra, is full of finds suggesting that it was filled in at this time or just after. These areas are being written up for future publication, but catalogs of finds from the Temple of Apollo and an explanation of the *loci* are incorporated in this volume.

The east wall of the staircase of the second temple rested in part on bedrock; packed against it was a hard mortar shelf (Locus 002), which provided sturdiness and support. According to Sinos,

Figure 108. Corner cornice block S60 discovered in 1980.

Figure 109. Corner cornice block S60.

Figure 110. Front horizontal cornice S115 discovered in 1980.

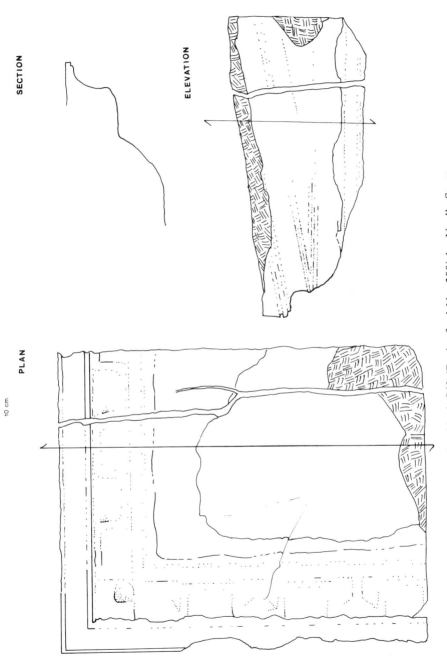

SECTION

ELEVATION

PLAN

10 cm

Figure 111. Drawing of corner cornice block S60 (Rutherford No. 200) by Noelle Soren.

this staircase wall may have been built or rebuilt to accommodate a final rebuilding of the temple staircase in the second century A.D. Among the fills over the rock-cut pits and probably contemporary with the second temple were Loci 003 (Baskets 3 and 5), 012, and 014, containing a preponderance of material generally datable to the first century A.D.; these dates correspond to the first century material found by us in the excavations of the rock-cut channels beneath the temple steps and in the rock-cut channels to the west of the temple. These channels were put out of use by the second temple.

Thus the second temple most likely dates to about the time of Nero and is, therefore, probably slightly earlier than the Trajanic date suggested by Scranton. The staircase cheek walls of the second temple were much less carefully built than were the walls of the first temple, and contain a reused, rusticated block. Sinos, who has taken over the reconstruction, believes the cheek walls and current staircase belong to yet a third period of the temple, a

221 ——— **FRONT HORIZONTAL CORNICE**   10 cm

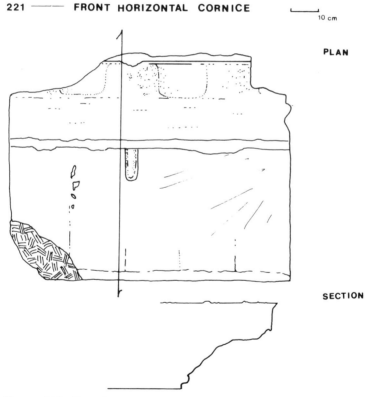

PLAN

SECTION

Figure 112. Drawing of front horizontal cornice S115 by Noelle Soren.

Figure 113. Fragment of raking cornice S69, discovered in 1980.

292 ——— **RAKING CORNICE**
10 cm

PLAN

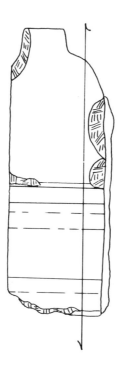

SECTION

Figure 114. Drawing of raking cornice S69 by Noelle Soren.

Figure 115. Possible tympanum blocks S204 and S205 discovered in 1980.

Figure 116. Top block of raking cornice S108 with cuttings for acroteria and beams, discovered in 1980 by John Rutherford.

Figure 117. Same as preceding.

304 ——— **PEDIMENT   PEAK**   [scale] 10 cm

ELEVATION

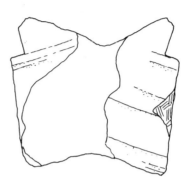

PLAN

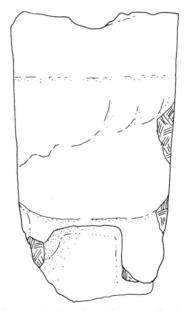

Figure 118. Drawing of top block of raking cornice/peak of pediment S108.

211 ——— CORNICE

PLAN

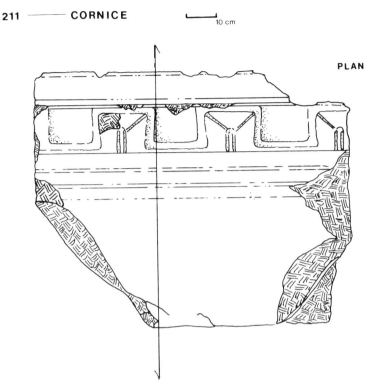

SECTION

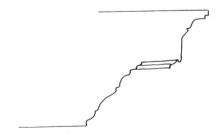

Figure 119. Drawing of side horizontal cornice S66 by Noelle Soren.

time of cosmetic change in the frontal area. Indeed, the walls seem hastily improvised when compared with the earlier finely prepared masonry and well bedded foundations of the pre-Roman temple. Scranton suggests that the temple was not completely rebuilt, but rather had its front remodelled, its interior divided, and its floor level raised in the Roman period to give it a more updated look than the simple, initial boxy structure.

Also, there is Cesnola's account of a broken pithos (Fig. 132 and 133) found along the eastern temple foundations beneath the now missing stone paving. This large jar fragment, which is discussed further below, is dated by Mitford to the Trajanic period (110 A.D.?), but the precise find spot of the pithos is still in doubt, as is its stratigraphic relation to the temple. If Cesnola found

299 ——— **RAKING CORNICE**

10 cm

PLAN

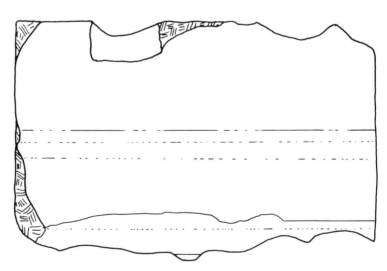

Figure 120. Drawing of badly weathered raking cornice S71 by Noelle Soren.

Figure 121. Side horizontal cornice S66.

Figure 122. Side horizontal cornice S66, additional fragments S66 a through f.

Figure 123. Raking cornice block S71 discovered in 1980.

Figure 124. Possible corner block S114 apparently reused in the second temple and found in north wall fall.

the pithos sealed under the second temple, it must date earlier than Mitford believed and could, in fact, be Neronian, unless the cella floor was redone under Trajan. If it is Neronian, this could mean that Nero was the first emperor to be called Apollo Caesar, and that Trajan simply followed this practice later on. The letter forms on the pot are more consistent with an *earlier* date.

Some further evidence for the post-Neronian altering of the staircase wall of the second temple comes from the glass dated by Andrew Oliver. One glass fragment (Gl 2), found sealed in the mortar of Locus 002 (the mortar shelf supporting the exterior of the southeast cheek wall), "could not pre-date 60 A.D. and should be later than the Hadrianic period," according to Oliver. He dates another fragment (Gl 47) from the same context to "probably the later second century."

In sum, the glass does not date the second temple, but only the cheek walls. The second temple of Apollo may, therefore, date to 50 to 75 A.D., and the first temple--the simple rectangular box with fine base mouldings--should be considerably earlier. In fact, a recently completed study of finds in the fill beneath its cella and

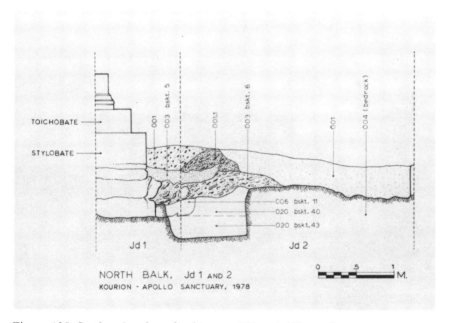

Figure 125. Section drawing of grid areas Jd1 and Jd2, southeast corner of the temple.

in the foundations for the walls suggest a *terminus post quem* around the mid to late sixth century B.C. for the initial structure.[24] Minor alterations to the front may have occurred in the second century. The reconstruction drawing we have done would thus represent the final version of the temple before its destruction in circa 365 A.D.

After unearthing the foundations of the first temple, our entire trench was cleaned, revealing several surprises. Under a fill (Locus 020, Basket 40), which now appears to have been placed with the construction of the second temple, and emerging from the north balk was a roughly oval pit, or cist, cut carefully into the bedrock and about three quarters visible (Fig. 128, 130). This pit would seem to have been installed, or at least to have functioned, with the first temple, since the filling over it is the same as the fill put in after the first temple and against the second. The pit began at bedrock level 133.73 to 133.95 (allowing for a slight slope) and continued to a depth of 133.46 above sea level. We initially speculated that the pit might be a tomb situated outside the Archaic Precinct, a plant or tree pit, or simply a storage pit for some foodstuff. A clue to its identity came from McFadden's Trench 4.

Figure 126. View of 1978 sounding southeast of temple with work in progress.

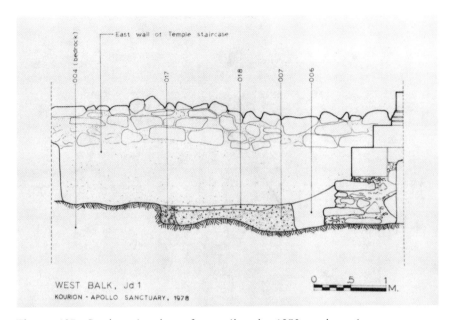

Figure 127. Section drawing of sounding in 1978 against the east staircase wall of the temple.

A cleaning in the southeast area of our probe revealed that within the old McFadden trench was another pit similar in width, in depth, and in the fact that it was cut down into bedrock. This second pit was, however, lined with a hard white mortar, which had been itself cut into on its eastern side at a later date, possibly when McFadden excavated in the area. The mortar curved up from the center and formed a circular depression 20 cm across and 40 cm below the surface of the pit.

The mortared outline may once have contained a large, wide jar, which could have held some offering of foodstuff, sunk into the pit with the upper part of the jar protruding above a floor level now gone, but possibly indicated by the cut-back ledge of bedrock at the top of the pit. An almost complete pithos found in 1935 in the southeast corner of the temple cella (discussed below) seems to have functioned in just this manner. The pit could just as well have contained a large flower or planting pot.

The date of this pit could not be determined, since McFadden had removed all the stratigraphy above it, but one wonders whether this area might not originally have housed plants, trees, or sacred stores for the cult of Apollo. A third pit was found just northeast of this sounding in a 1981 cleaning operation. It is well established from the inscriptions and finds of Cesnola and McFadden

Plan – Jd 1 and Jd 2

Kourion   1978

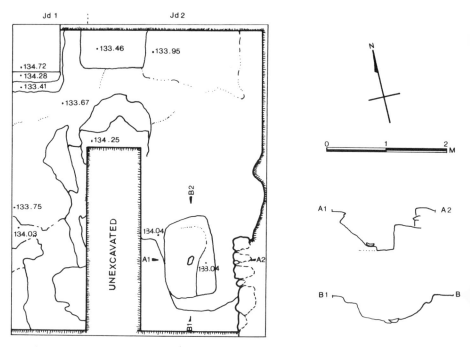

Figure 128. Drawing of pits discovered southeast of temple in 1978 in grid areas Jd1 and Jd2.

that the cult here frequently was associated with the dedication of jars and plants or trees. Evidence of pitting, apparently contemporary with the pits to the east, has been noted in the rock-cut channel west of the temple.

The question of two pithoi found in fragmentary form within the cella of the temple has long been a confusing one, but our work in 1979 went a long way toward untangling the problem.

Cesnola dug within the cella and found, as we saw above, "fragments of a very large earthenware jar inscribed in Greek letters with a dedication to Apollo Hylates . . . beneath the stone pavement of the temple."[25] This pithos still exists and, in addition to the two pieces found in 1875 and acquired by the Metropolitan Museum, four other fragments of it were found by McFadden in 1935.[26] The three pieces on the viewer's right in Fig. 132 were found on November 6 and marked McFadden's second find at the Sanctuary:

Inscribed fragment large terracotta water-jug found about twelve meters southwest of west end of Trench 1 . . . Now in New York, Metropolitan."[26]

McFadden described his discovery in more detail in 1938:

This was a sherd of a large water jar or storage vase of a coarse red Roman ware. It is inscribed by incision in two lines running around the neck of the jar . . . . This is significant as it establishes beyond doubt that this is the Sanctuary of Apollo Hylates of which mention is made by ancient authors, and to which there is reference in ancient inscriptions.[27]

The other fragment found by McFadden and cited by Mitford is a small triangular sherd that fitted onto the extreme left of the pithos. It was found just north of the Central Court in surface soil over the street.[28] All of the fragments of the vase were of local Kourion fabric. (The fragments formerly were housed in the University of Pennsylvania Museum, but the pithos has since been shipped back to Cyprus and the Episkopi Museum.) Mitford dated the jar to "ca. A.D. 110?"[29]

McFadden also found the base of yet another jar (Fig. 134) "bedded in the fill below the floor of the temple of a later period in the southeast corner of the cella."[30] The circular depression left by this jar, still visible at level 135.31, measured 24 cm across. It may have been sunk into the floor and provided, as Mitford suggested, a source for "oil or water or it may be corn."[31]

Was this jar, which Mitford said was "unfortunately not saved," the same jar Cesnola found along the east side of the temple? Mitford added: ". . . it's association with . . . [the other pithos] cannot now be demonstrated."[32]

Our 1979 excavations within the cella (Fig. 135 and 136) resulted in the reexcavation of McFadden's trench within the temple. Mixed with modern debris were some pithos fragments which, when mended, appeared to have come from the jar McFadden discovered in 1936 or one similar to it. The search for further traces of the lost pithos led to the questioning of citizens of Episkopi who were involved in the McFadden excavations. Socrates Savva, a store owner in the village and site guardian, distinctly recalled an attempt by a tourist (circa 1962) to steal the jar, which he says was definitely *in situ* up to that date (which preceded the writing of Mitford's book). He remembered putting the jar, now broken into fragments, in the site lavatory area behind and below the South Building for safekeeping, the room occasionally having been pressed into service for storage. Amazingly, some seventeen years later the fragments were still there, along with a few extraneous sherds. When mended, the fragments did indeed form a pithos, preserved up to its neck, just like the one illustrated in Mitford's book. Thus the mystery of the

Figure 129. View of 1978 sounding from the southeast just prior to discovery of the pits.

missing pithos was solved, but it was even more of a surprise when the sherds from the fill in McFadden's old trench actually joined the pithos.

All that remained to be done was to compare the pithos found by McFadden in 1935 with Cesnola's inscribed pithos, since both were of similar fabric. Drawings of both examples proved conclusively that they were two completely different jars.

Such jars, of course, have a long cult history on Cyprus. Sjöqvist described a pithos of apparently similar nature sunk in the ground in association with a *Kulstätt*, the major cult house of Aijia Irini during Late Cypriote III.[33] The location of the jar in the corner of a room in the heart of the most sacred building of a sanctuary parallels, to some extent, our jar placement. At Aijia Irini the pithos is associated with a hearth and offering table, and Sjöqvist believed that it was used as a "Sammelgefass für die Gussopfer."[34]

Since the cult at Aijia Irini has so many parallels to Kourion, it is instructive to note the sorts of offering materials recovered there, which could suggest the contents of the jar that stood in our Temple of Apollo. A large number of olive pits were found in the cult house, along with evidence of the use of oil for the pouring of libations on the sacred offering table. The aniconic

Figure 130. View of 1978 sounding from southwest showing the two pits in Jd at top center and right.

Figure 131. Overhead view of mortared pit found in cleaning of McFadden Trench 4.

image (baetyl) recovered from the archaic sanctuary at Aijia Irini also shows traces of periodic anointing with oil or something like it, according to Sjöqvist.[35] Such practices occurred widely in Greece and apparently were intended to raise the power of the fetish.

The temple on the acropolis of Amathus yielded another large jar, the colossal "vase d' Amathonte," in 1865. Now in the Louvre, it stands 1.85 m high and 3.2 m in diameter. A second vase remains *in situ* before the entry to the temple.[36]

Perhaps the Kourion jar should be considered a "Libationspithos," and as such deserve its place sunken into the floor in the heart of the temple, the sacred focus of the cult in Roman times. At any rate, McFadden's discovery of the jar within the temple suggests that Cesnola may have been right about finding his example in this area. This means that the alleged stone floor from the second temple, now missing, could be at least of Trajanic date, if Mitford is correct in his interpretation of the inscription on the Cesnola jar, or it could be earlier (i.e., Julio-Claudian), according to our own finds in the trench of 1978. Whether Cesnola's description of the findspot is entirely correct is still another variable to consider.

Figure 132. Pithos fragments discovered by Cesnola in 1875 with added pieces found by McFadden.

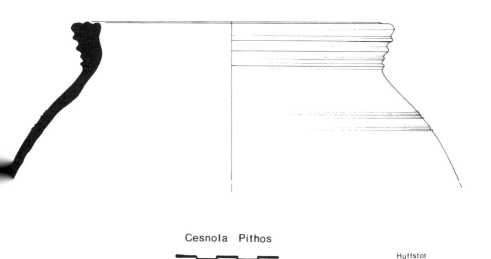

Cesnola Pithos

20 cm

Huffstot

Figure 133. Drawing of Cesnola pithos.

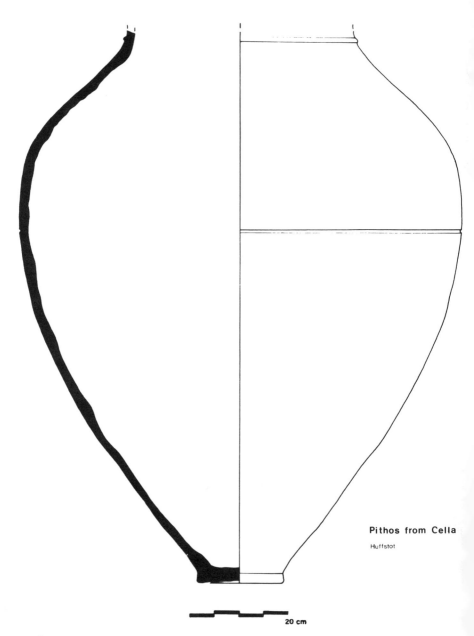

Pithos from Cella

Huffstot

20 cm

Figure 134. Drawing of McFadden pithos.

Figure 135. Overhead view of temple cella showing emplacement spot for pithos in southeast corner.

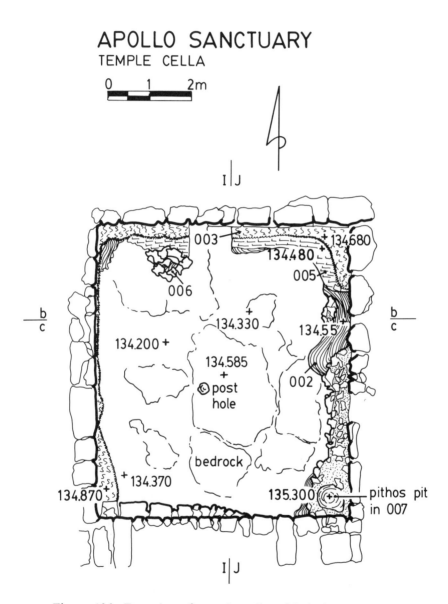

APOLLO SANCTUARY
TEMPLE CELLA

0   1   2m

Figure 136. Top plan of temple cella with loci.

In 1979 the entire cella was cleaned down to bedrock prior to reconstruction work by the Cypriote Department of Antiquities. The southern area of the cella had already been cleaned out by McFadden, who noted that the fill in that area was disturbed before he began digging.[37] The rest of the soil within the cella did not seem to have been disturbed below level 134.90, but neither did it contain the expected sherds of the Roman period. Instead, the stratified fill contained a large number of pottery fragments of the Archaic period (eighth through late sixth century B.C.), suggesting that the first temple was much earlier than had been thought. This material has recently been studied and the preliminary conclusions presented in this volume.

The soil layers and floor uncovered within the cella have shed some light on the history of the building and complemented the information recovered from our work against the southeast exterior corner of the temple. Starting at the bottom, one must cite first the irregular bedrock, undulating caliche, or, as Koucky prefers, kafkala (Locus 004), with its natural solution-sculptured surface showing the process of bedrock weathering and concentration. It disassociates readily, and chips of it, termed rock float by Reuben Bullard, are found in high concentration through the lowest soil levels above bedrock.

The soil layer just above bedrock is a natural deposit and was not given a separate locus number (Fig. 137 and 138). It is sterile terra rossa soil with angular rock float in a matrix of red-brown soil and soft friable decomposing caliche fragments. This product of the interaction of the atmosphere and the bedrock, the result of chemical leaching, yields the observed residual rock float and terra rossa.

Above the bedrock/terra rossa is Locus 002, an actual fill with crystals, selenite and cobble particles (Top Levels 134.895 in the east and 135.005 in the west, Bottom Level circa 134.895). Interspersed in this layer were limestone flagstone partings about 1 cm long. This locus, which had been disturbed in a number of places by McFadden or Cesnola trenches, animal burrowing, and/or rainwash, contained a volume of local Cypriote pottery and several imported pieces. This Locus 002 was a fill for the now missing floor of the cella of the first temple. It tapers slightly as it extends from the temple walls, perhaps as a result of sinking. Partially above 002 lay Locus 003, which represents the first documentation for the floor level of the cella of the first temple.

In the north and southeast areas of the cella the first temple floor foundation 003 was absent. Above 002 was Locus 001, a mix of 002 and rainwash. Some of 001 was stratified, but contamination from the surface could not be ruled out. In 001 was a coin of Ptolemy I Soter, datable between 312 and 305 B.C. In the southeast quarter of the cella a large pit (Locus 002, Baskets 9, 12 and 13) was cut into Locus 002. The soil in this pit was dug out by McFadden and was looser and often grayer than was the rest of 002 (10YR 5/4 yellow brown). It contained much chalk, as well as some

Temple Cella – East-West Section

View to North

1m

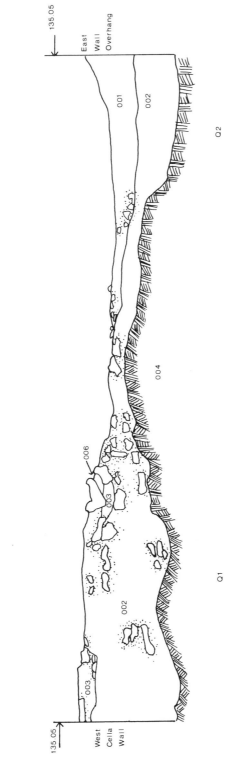

Figure 137. Section drawing of excavated cella east to west.

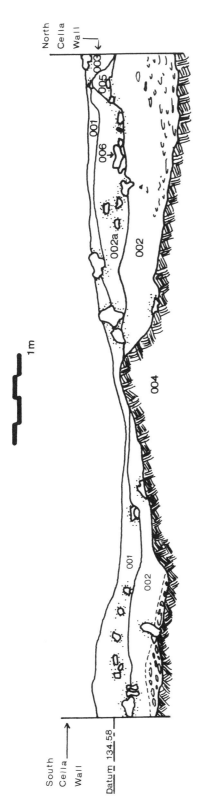

Figure 138. Section drawing of cella north to south.

modern material, including a bottle cap. But among the sherds were many pithos fragments, perhaps put in by McFadden's workmen after they were finished in the area in 1935. These fragments joined the rest of the pithos described earlier. The soil of the pit dug easily and ran under the narrow overhanging area in the southeast corner of the cella. The overhang, containing the depression from the emplacement of McFadden's pithos, was left undug by our team so as not to disturb this important area. The soil of the overhang was above Locus 003 and, therefore, was associated with the second temple. It consisted of medium to large cobbles set in mud, but appeared to lack any concentration of sherds.

Just over bedrock the foundations of the first temple walls were exposed. Because the bedrock undulated, levelling courses were placed in the depressions of bedrock and under the ashlars of the first temple. Locus 006 was a layer of cobbles and boulders and some brownish soil and sherds. Over this, particularly in the northeast corner of the temple, was Locus 005, which in this area lay immediately under the floor of the first temple (003) and helped shore up the corner.

Locus 005 was an ashy layer of dense bone, burned sherds similar in form to those of Loci 002 and 006, laminated pebbles, and cobbles. It was deliberately packed in between levels 134.755 and 134.535. Bedrock 004 in this northeast quadrant of the cella wavered between levels 134.680 and 134.120, a disparity of up to 56 cm.

In sum, the 1979 excavations within the cella determined the level of the cella floor at the time of the first temple and showed a fill and wall foundations containing material only from the Archaic period, giving an idea of a date for the first temple in the mid to late sixth century B.C. The lost pithos from 1935 was found again, mended, and compared to the Cesnola pithos of 1875, showing that they were two different jars.

Our work also provided the temples with approximate dates for construction, as well as the date for the destruction of the second temple by shear wave in circa 365 A.D. This quake appears to have hurled parts of the temple mainly north and east, suggesting an earthquake epicenter to the southwest. We have been able to combine the discoveries of Cesnola, McFadden, and Scranton with our own efforts to offer for the first time on Cyprus a reasonably accurate reconstruction of an entire Roman temple facade, flank, and rear, although modifications are to be expected. Curious pits located just east of the structure are contemporary with the first temple and may have been part of a sacred grove of trees and plants, or they may have served as sacred stores for the Sanctuary. The work of temple rebuilding (Fig. 139-141) is continuing in the hope of providing a worthwhile visual experience for tourist and scholar alike. By 1981 the northeast end of the temple had been built up to and included the pilaster capitals there. Stefanos Sinos, of the Athens Polytechnical Institute, has taken over the rebuilding project and will combine our data with his own studies.

Figure 139. Reconstruction of northeast corner of temple supervised by John Rutherford in 1980.

Figure 140. Blocks from the front pediment of the temple.

Figure 141

Figure 141. Blocks from the side entablature of the temple.

A few important loose ends remain to be discussed. The finds and dedicatory inscription suggest that the second temple could well have been built in 65 or 66 A.D., or at least erected between 50 and 75 A.D.

The Neronian period is a likely one for construction of the second temple. The period was one of reasonable prosperity for Cyprus, and sufficient resources were available to construct an aqueduct at Soloi. The theater at Kourion is known to have been rebuilt in 64 or 65 A.D., and a theater often is a useful measure of the urban well-being of an area.[39] According to Lane, a statue of Nero was dedicated in 65 or 66 A.D. by proconsul Lucius Annius Bassus, the very name that appears to be on our dedicatory inscription from the Temple of Apollo.[40]

The inscribed statue base could have been done to honor Nero for building the temple, and it is fascinating that Mitford is concerned that "it may well be that the city in A.D. 64/65 was overspending."[41]

The first phase of the structure may have looked like "a simple rectangular building with a cella and vestibule entered by a door--no columns, the entrance at ground level."[42] This early naos with its podium would have served cult requirements until the modernization of the northwest area of the site in the Roman period.

The remaining blocks and the capitals found near the temple apparently were used in the second temple. It also appears that the first temple was laid out in conjunction with many pits to its east, these possibly forming a grove. The rock-cut channel west of the structure appears to have been constructed to frame the first temple on its southwest side.[43]

It is hoped our analysis of the Temple of Apollo will shed new light on the Roman imperial building style on Cyprus, since this period had been so little studied there.

Since this article was originally written, Professor Sinos has been able to study our conclusions. He has made several important discoveries which will be presented by him in 1987. It is important here to note again that he has found that the current front staircase of the temple may not have been put in until the second century and that the "Neronian" second temple had its own staircase. A rough finished or rusticated ashlar block, common in the Claudian-Neronian period, has been reused in the making of the bordering wall of the east staircase. The staircase which we have drawn on our elevation may thus be later than the Neronian period (see Plate 106, left, on top of the staircase wall.) He also believes that there was a necking piece below the capital and that the central intercolumniation was wider and will offer evidence for it in his forthcoming article. Sinos thus will add to our rapidly growing knowledge of this important Cypriote temple, and we must await the justification for his new conclusions, which differ from ours.

CHAPTER 6, APPENDIX ONE:
SUMMARY OF THE TEMPLE BLOCKS

The scattered blocks and architectural fragments from the Temple of Apollo were studied preliminarily in 1979 by Robert Scranton, following up his original studies of 1962. The project was continued in 1980 in greater detail by John Rutherford, senior architect for the Kourion project. Every block in the vicinity of the temple was turned over and examined thoroughly.

About fifty square meters of wall surface, comprising some 150 blocks or fragments of blocks and architectural members, were tallied over a span of two months. Workmen for McFadden or for the Cypriote Antiquities Service had removed many fragments to the area of the temenos wall west and north of the temple, and many blocks scattered east of the temple were removed in 1978 prior to the backfilling of the cella by bulldozer in 1979. The following list includes the major architectural fragments recovered, primarily by Rutherford in 1980.

1. S55   Acorn fragment from missing capital found in the southwest area of the Archaic Precinct by David Soren during surface cleaning in 1979. It is similar to the well preserved acorn on the capital from the temple, but is smaller and probably not from the temple.

2. S60   Corner cornice block found just southwest of the temple in 1980 (see Fig. 108, 109, 111).

3. S61   Corner architrave block found north of the temple in 1980, in a stack of blocks by the temenos wall (see Fig. 92, 93).

4. S66   Seven cornice blocks from the sides of the temple and numerous small fragments found in block stacks (see Fig. 119, 121, 122).

5. S67   Twelve architrave blocks, six of which came from the north wall fall (see Fig. 94, 95).

6. S68   Six epistyle or frieze blocks from the north wall fall (see Fig. 96, 97).

7. S69   Three fragments of raking cornice found in 1980 in
   to   block stacks (see Fig. 113, 114, 120, 123).
   S71

8. S72   "Cypro-Corinthian" capital found by McFadden in 1935 southeast of the temple (see Fig. 74-78).

9. S73   "Ear" piece found in 1980 west of the temple; joins S72
            (see Fig. 78).

10. S74a   Four joining fragments of a pilaster capital from a
    and   rear corner of the temple, found in 1980 in block
    S75   stacks (see Fig. 84, 86).

11. S76   Two of twelve engaged pilaster shaft blocks from the
    and   rear corners of the temple, one from the southeast area
    S77   of the north wall fall (see Fig. 89-91).

12. S78   Block with dedicatory inscription found by McFadden by
            the steps southwest of the temple in 1949 (see Fig. 82).

13. S79   Anta capital and small joining fragment found stacked
    and   north of the temple (see Fig 85, 87).
    S80

14. S89   Acorn found in Archaic Precinct near S55 in 1980; this
            one is smaller and probably not from the temple (see Fig.
            80).

15. S108   Top block of raking cornice found southeast of temple
            near S72 in 1980 (see Fig. 116-118).

16. S109   Large and small fragments of a possible anta capital
    and   found stacked west of the temple in 1980 (see Fig. 88).
    S110

17. S113   Inscribed block related to S78 but found stacked west of
            the temple in 1980 (see Fig. 83).

18. S114   Reused right-angled block from north wall fall, found in
            1980 (see Fig. 124).

19. S115   Front horizontal cornice found in block stack west of
            temple in 1980 (see Fig. 110, 112).

20. S116a   Two joining fragments of a second corner cornice found
    and b   in block stacks in 1980.

21. S123   Three joining fragments of a second pilaster capital
            found in block stacks.

22. S126   Possible fragment of "Cypro-Corinthian" capital found ina
            stack west of the temple (see Fig. 79).

23. S201 Eight possible tympanum pieces found scattered about
    to   the temple area in 1980 (see Fig. 115).
    S208

Conjectural parts of the temple used in our reconstruction drawing include the following:

1. Column shafts and bases borrowed from the acropolis at Kourion City, where capitals very similar to ours have been found (see Fig. 106, 107).

2. Podium crown borrowed from the Temple of Nebi Safa, Syria, because the base moulding of the podium of the temple closely resembles that of the Temple of Apollo.

All other portions of the temple reconstruction are based on actual remains from the structure. The antae, cella wall, and pilasters probably had bases, but we did not feel that our reconstruction would allow us the freedom to include them without more evidence. Column and temple height are derived from the South Temple at Si in Syria, which closely resembles our temple and is close in date to it.

CHAPTER 6, APPENDIX TWO:
ARCHITECTURAL PARALLELS

The Temple of Apollo Hylates at Kourion has been restored on paper as a tetrastyle prostyle podium temple. Although Roman in its basic form, the architectural details of the temple show closer ties with the decorative scheme of monuments in the Roman east, particularly in the column and anta capitals. The latter are commonly found on the rock-cut monuments of the Nabataean cities of Petra[1] and Hegra, near Medain Saleh, in the first centuries B.C. and (especially) A.D.[2]

The Aramaic-speaking Nabataeans were among the latest of many nomadic Arab tribes to move in from the desert, settling in southern Jordan and Palestine. By the fourth century B.C. their capital city, Petra, was already an important trade center. Bitumen (necessary for the Egyptian embalming process),[3] frankincense and myrrh from southern Arabia, and spices from the orient traveled by caravan across the Arabian desert to Petra, the distribution center from which the goods went on to Syria, Palestine, Egypt, or Europe.[4] The Roman geographer Strabo, commenting on the Nabataeans in the first century A.D., mentioned that the route ran from "the Rock (Petra) of the Nabataean Arabians, as they are called, and to the Palestine country (probably Phinocolura) . . . whither all the neighboring peoples convey their load of aromatics."[5]

As merchants with access to both the Mediterranean and Red seas, the Nabataeans influenced and were influenced by currents from the east and west. This fact alone may well account for the presence of Nabataean capitals on Cyprus.

These simplified capitals, characterized by the horns or projecting ears that take the place of the volute of the Corinthian capital, and a boss in the center of the concave face of the abacus were recurring features in Nabataean architecture. The rock-cut monuments of Petra and Hegra fall into a well defined typological sequence.[6] The typologically earliest type, the Pylon type (Fig. 142), is a rock-cut tower, usually featuring a stepped crenellation resting on an Egyptian cavetto cornice. The door may be flanked by pilasters, occasionally capped with Nabataean capitals. The Hegra type (Fig. 143), so-called owing to its appearance at Medain Saleh, ancient Hegra, shows an increasing use of classical elements and features an unusual attic story. Pilasters with Nabataean capitals appear at the corners, as well as flanking the doorway, which receives a classical entablature.

Lastly, and most elaborate, are the temple tombs (Fig. 144). In this type, the gable that appeared above the doorway of the Hegra type becomes the crowning motif of the whole facade. Otherwise, the urn akroteria, Nabataean capitals, disc metopes, and columnar facade are motifs found on the typologically earlier tombs.

Figure 142. Petra rock-cut monument of pylon type (Brünnow and Domascewski, Plates 152-154).

Figure 143. Hegra: Rock-cut facade.

Although Petra was well established in the fourth century B.C., it was not until the first century B.C. that dressed masonry began to replace stone and mud architecture.[7] The earliest dated rock-cut monument, the Pylon type Tomb B6 at Hegra, first century B.C.,[8] coincides with this date. The area was annexed by Trajan in 106 A.D. as part of the Province of Arabia, but Nabataean monuments remained distinctive throughout the second century A.D. The typological sequence of the rock-cut tombs generally is considered to correspond to their chronological development, the Pylon type dating to the late first century B.C., the Hegra type dating to the first century A.D., and the Temple type, also called Roman Temple Tombs,[9] dating from the late first century A.D. into the second.[10]

Except for three variations,[11] the Nabataean capital appears on all types of rock-cut tombs; it is already fully developed on Tomb B6 at Hegra. Although there is little definitive material concerning its origin,[12] the derivation of the form is quite clear. The Nabataean capital is a simplified form of the late Hellenistic Corinthian capital, the proportions of which are squatter than those given by Vitruvius (IV.i.l).

> ". . . the height of the Ionic capital is only one third the thickness of the column, while that of the Corinthian is the entire thickness of the shaft."[13]

Figure 144. Petra: Temple tomb.

The late Hellenistic Corinthian capital appears in the Nabataea at Petra (Fig. 145),[14] at Soueida in the Hauran[15] and on the Temple of Dushara at Si in the Hauran.[16] The late Hellenistic Corinthian capitals are, however, most popular and achieve their fullest development in the area influenced by the art of Alexandria.[17] They were employed on the facade of the Temple of Augustus at Philae on the Nile.[18] Several examples are stored in the Greco-Roman Museum in Alexandria.[19]

The strikingly simple, "classic"[20] Nabataean capitals closely resemble the underlying structure, or blocked-out form, of the Alexandrian late Hellenistic Corinthian capitals. They would have, then, close affinities with the Alexandrian late Hellenistic Corinthian capital in its roughly quarried state.

The Nabataean type of capitals on the Temple of Apollo Hylates at Kourion are not unique to that site. A Nabataean capital was found associated with the Gymnasium at Salamis,[21] dated generally to the first or second century A.D. Three unfinished Nabataean capitals recently were uncovered in the quarries near Xylophagou, north of Larnaca. The capitals, along with five unfinished statues, apparently were intended for the same monument. A Trajanic date is suggested.[22]

In Egypt, on the islands of Philae near modern Aswan, are the remains of a Temple of Augustus, securely dated by inscriptional evidence to 13/12 B.C.[23] The restoration shows a tetrastyle prostyle podium temple approached from the northeast by a flight of stairs between cheek walls. The podium is restored without either base or crown mouldings. The columns, antae, and corner pilasters all share a similar base. The columns and antae carry Alexandrian late Hellenistic Corinthian capitals, while the two rear pilasters carry Nabataean capitals (thought by the excavator to be unfinished). The architrave has only two fasciae; the frieze is a Doric triglyph and metope.

In the Hauran, south Syria, in the mountains northeast of Bostra, was the sanctuary of Si, a Nabataean "high place." The sanctuary, including the Temples of Ba'al Shamin and of Dushara, is dated by incriptions to the end of the first century B.C.[24] In the late first century A.D.[25] the sanctuary was enlarged by addition of an outer courtyard to the east of the Nabataean gate. The courtyard, entered by a monumental arch, contained the South Temple, a tetrastyle prostyle podium temple similar in size to the Temple of Apollo Hylates. The South Temple is approached by a stairway between cheek walls (Fig. 146). There are remains of podium base and crown mouldings, as well as of column and pilaster bases. The column capitals are Nabataean, while the pilaster capitals are fine examples of the Alexandrian late Hellenistic Corinthian. The architrave and frieze have been restored. The two cornices, both with the same profile, appear somewhat less complicated than do those of the Temple of Apollo Hylates.

Close political, economic, and cultural ties existed between Greco-Roman Egypt, Cyprus, and the Nabataea. That these ties

Figure 145. Petra: Late Hellenistic Corinthian arched gate capital
(drawing by G.R.H. Wright).

touched the artistic world is evidenced by the derivation of the Nabataean capital and its occasional use outside the Province of Arabia, as well as by the widespread occurence of the Alexandrian late Hellenistic Corinthian capital in the eatern Mediterranean. These three geographically diverse Roman temples seem to share another Nabataean characteristic: quality work without a great deal of finely carved architectural decoration, as is common on contemporary Roman works.

Remains *in situ* of the Temple of Apollo Hylates show a general, but not exact, adherence to the basic principles of Vitruvius. The length is circa 3 m short of equalling twice the width, but the cella is in fact very close to the prescribed Vitruvian length, which must equal one plus one-quarter widths (IV.iv.l).

In discussing the podium (III.iv.5), Vitruvius maintains that "if the podium is to be built on three sides round the temple, it should be so constructed that its plinths, bases, dies, coronae, and cymatium[26] are appropriate to the actual stylobate which is to be under the base of the columns." Remains of the podium of the Temple of Apollo Hylates include the plinth, the base moulding, and the die, or vertical face. There is no evidence for the podium crown moulding or for the column, anta, and pilaster bases. Clearly, the temple was not highly decorated. Is simplification sufficient reason for this curious lack of crown moulding and bases, which otherwise are normal members of a Roman temple, or is the lack owing instead to the paucity of surviving remains?[27]

Several monuments in the Roman east have a podium base moulding similar to that on the Temple of Apollo Hylates. These include the Temple of Helios at Kasr Naus and Temple B at Hössn Sfiri (Fig. 147), both circa 10 km south and southeast, respectively, of Tripolis. An Ionic distyle in antis temple at Nebi Safa and the temple at Hibbariye, both situated between Tyre and Damascus, also have a similar podium base moulding.[28] Where remains are extant, the corresponding podium crown mouldings are all of a similar type, consisting of several rounded members with sharply articulated joins. The corona, the most laterally projecting member, has a strong vertical face.

A podium crown moulding appears as a most common feature on Roman structures. The simple form of the podium base moulding of the Temple of Apollo Hylates should suggest a correspondingly simple podium crown moulding, as on the temple at Mebi Safa.

That the Temple of Apollo Hylates should be restored with column, anta, and pilaster bases is strongly suggested by evidence from the Roman east, where even the simpler structures employ bases.[29] The most commonly used base is the Attic type of two roundels with an offset scotia between. Remains of Attic bases have been recovered from the Sanctuary of Apollo Hylates, but none fit the temple.[30] At Kourion City, Attic-type bases were used on columns with capitals similar to those of the Temple of Apollo Hylates.[31]

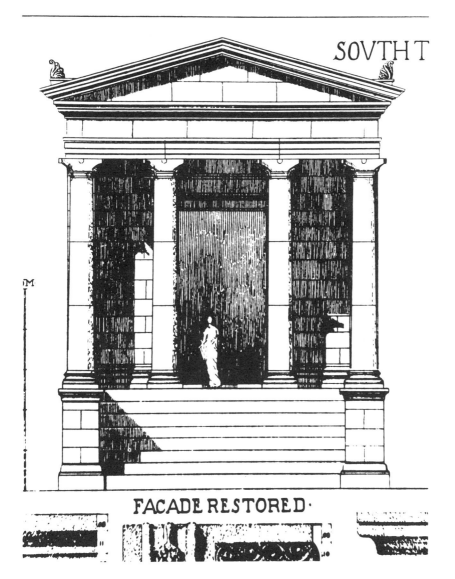

Figure 146. Si, South Temple. From Butler.

Mouldings of Near Eastern Temples
of
Roman Date

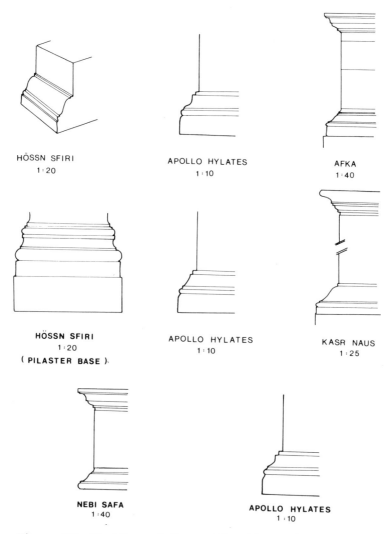

HÖSSN SFIRI
1:20

APOLLO HYLATES
1:10

AFKA
1:40

HÖSSN SFIRI
1:20
(PILASTER BASE)

APOLLO HYLATES
1:10

KASR NAUS
1:25

NEBI SAFA
1:40

APOLLO HYLATES
1:10

Figure 147. Mouldings of Roman Near Eastern Temples.

It would be unusual if such a conservative structure as this temple to a major divinity were to deviate from the conventional practice of bases. It is true that the Nabataean capital occurs on an engaged pilaster without a base on the facades of early rock-cut tombs, but this apparently is unique to those rock-cut monuments. In its first occurrence on a free-standing column on the South Temple at Si, the capital is balanced by an Attic base.[32]

The podium temple, prostyle or in antis, was a fairly common feature throughout the Roman world; along with the aqueduct and monumental arch, it was a symbol of *Romanitas*. On Cyprus, however, the type is unusual.

Sacred structures of the Hellenistic and Roman periods on Cyprus more often took the form of the court temple.[33] Initially an enclosed court with a cult room at one end, the court temple developed to include triple cellae with a forecourt, all enclosed within a temenos wall, forming a strongly symmetrical whole.[34] This type is without obvious connections to buildings that exhibit Greek or Roman influence, but owes its origins to both Cyprus and the Near East.[35]

The Temple of Apollo Hylates was one of several Cypriote temples[36] that varied from the court temple type. Fragmentary remains of the Temple of Zeus at Salamis[37] suggest a nearly square cella on a high podium approached by a flight of stairs from the north. It has been suggested that the structure had a peristyle[38] with a tetrastyle prostyle facade.[39] Only the foundation of the porch, however, gives evidence of supporting a colonnade. Several building phases were noted and an Augustan date was tentatively suggested for the original construction.[40] The excavators offer no restoration.

Although a podium temple is somewhat unusual on Cyprus, the position of the Temple of Apollo Hylates in relation to the entire Sanctuary is reminiscent of the position of the cult room in relation to the whole structure of the court temple. The Temple of Apollo Hylates was placed on an extension of the central court area specifically designed to receive it, at the end of the main axis, atop the highest point, and thus the focal point of the Sanctuary.[41] Such a position, as the focal point of an enclosed or at least delimited area, is a common feature of structures in sanctuaries throughout the Roman east. The South Temple at Si is placed within its own court, separated from the Temples of Ba'al Shamin and Dushara, each within their own courts.[42]

One aspect of the restoration remains questionable. The Temple of Apollo Hylates was reconstructed as a tetrastyle prostyle temple. This was not based on remains, but rather on architectural parallels, presumably with mainstream temple architecture of the first and second centuries A.D.[43] Although distyle in antis temples are not unknown in the Roman east, even well into the second century A.D.,[44] prostyle temples are more common. This is especially true when the temple is an isolated structure within an enclosure, or the focal point of an area with a controlled entrance or approach.[45]

The Temple of Apollo Hylates, as the focal point of the Sanctuary, was most likely tetrastyle prostyle. Since, by the time the Sanctuary received the Temple of Apollo Hylates it was a Roman center, it might be safe to assume that the podium base moulding should be complemented by a simple podium crown moulding and Attic type bases.

CHAPTER 6, APPENDIX THREE:
GEOLOGICAL REPORT

Archaeological geologist Frank Koucky, a member of the Apollo
Sanctuary team in the summer of 1980, studied the stones of the
temple in detail. Koucky pointed out that the different colored
stones employed in the podium of the temple probably were chosen
intentionally for contrast, a point also made by his predecessor at
Kourion, Reuben Bullard, in 1979.
   The lowest course of the podium may be termed the euthynteria,
consisting of small, long blocks. At the corners of the temple the
blocks are largely grey calcarinite. This is a shallow-bedded
(sometimes cross-bedded), shallow water-cemented limestone with
fine to medium sand-sized grains. It is rather coarse, easy to cut,
and hardens with exposure. Along the sides of the temple the grey
calcarinite yields to blocks of marly limestone. Both grey
calcarinite and marly limestone were quarried near the Kourion City
site.
   At that still visible quarry are found dense limestone, a
fine-grained precipitate rock interbedded in the cliff with grey
calcarinite, chalk, marly limestone, and coarse fossiliferous
limestone. On the temple above the lowest course is a course of
dark grey calcarinite mixed with occasional marly limestone and
occasional, probably reused, rusticated blocks.
   Above this appears the large base moulding of the temple in
yellow calcarinite. It has lost much of its definition to spalling,
a process which bears some explanation. Grey calcarinite has no
clay, while the yellow does. The clay absorbs and gives off
moisture, which is evaporated by the sun. The clay within the stone
expands and contracts, causing the surface to spall and flake away.
Stone like this, cut with a moulding, could keep its definition in
Cyprus for several years.
   The corner base moulding in the southeast area of the temple is
grey calcarinite, confirming a tendency to use the grey in
positions requiring strength and to avoid it in areas where color
coding or banding is desired. The brilliant yellow calcarinite is
found east and south of the Sanctuary, especially on Akrotiri
peninsula, and is more coarse-grained than the grey.
   The course above the yellow, so far as it is preserved, is
entirely grey calcarinite, although some restoration work in the
course includes other kinds of stones, even chalk. The stairs of
the temple also were the durable grey calcarinite of Kourion bluff,
with a few marly limestones and some fossiliferous limestone.
   The pilaster shafts are a mix of fossiliferous limestone
interbedded with marly limestone and grey calcarinite. This shows
that the stone suppliers for the temple were quarrying both from

217

the interbedding and from pure areas for wall areas of the temple, but *not* for mouldings, an example of economy of materials.

A few of the wall blocks are made of calcrete, unbedded or poorly bedded limestone. It can also be termed calicheated limestone, or even kafkala. The latter is the crust above limestone bedrock. This crust, on which the Temple of Apollo is placed, is hard and calicheated, as well as unbedded and often undulating. It results from carbonate leached from the rock below and is very hard to cut or quarry. The absence of bedding planes causes poor splitting. The calcrete is the area immediately below the kafkala. The term chavara can be used to describe soft material floating above the crust, a kind of "rock float" to the archaeologist, which flakes off easily.

The fill in the door of the first temple (presumably done during the construction of the second temple) contains some blocks of kafkala. The low foundations of the crosswall of the second temple are a mix of blocks of calcrete and grey calcarinite. Surprisingly the top block of the raking cornice is also calcrete.

Chapter 7
Pottery from the Cella
of the Temple
Luisa Ferrer Dias with Ines Vaz Pinto

The pottery from the Kourion excavations eventually will provide an opportunity to study a whole sequence in Cypriote pottery. As we have studied only chosen loci thus far, however, that is not yet possible.

The loci cited here are from the Temple of Apollo. The great bulk of pottery studied is of local manufacture. Most of it has parallels in Type IV of Gjerstad's typology (beginning of Cypro-Archaic I). After the studies of du Platt Taylor based on the Al-Mina (Syria) finds, and the revising of some Cypriote dates by Birmingham, the dates for this type of ware are agreed to be 800 to 700 B.C. In some loci Type V wares also occur, with dates ranging from 700 to 600 B.C. Some imports are present too: from Tyre (Phoenicia), one piece; from Greece come Attic Black Glazed and Black Figured wares (found in the Temple and Round Building) dated to the sixth century B.C., at least as late as 570 and possibly later.

In the catalog that follows we have identified the shape and briefly described the decoration of each fragment. Some coarse wares were cataloged along with the typical Cypriote wares. In the uncontaminated loci these wares are closely dated and will help other archaeologists dealing with Cypriote wares.

One important pattern in the pottery recovered from the foundation of both the Round Building and the Temple of Apollo is that the sixth century B.C. Attic pottery appears side by side with Cypriote wares presumed to be eighth to seventh century B.C. There may be several explanations for this recurring pattern: the dates for Cypro-Archaic pottery are less fixed than one thinks, these pottery types are longer lived than had been supposed, or (most simply) the Cypriote pottery is largely residual, resulting from a cleanup of the earlier Sanctuary in the sixth century B.C.

219

However, if the latter conclusion were true, one would expect to find imported Greek pottery of the seventh century B.C. mixed in, unless of course the seventh century B.C. Cypriotes were not importing such material in this area. It is necessary, then, to beg the question for the moment, and simply to urge other excavators not to feel too sure that all of the chronological problems of the Cypro-Archaic period have been solved. One must also remember that the sixth century is only a *terminus post quem* at this point.

The Pottery

Locus C 3, 002: fill within the cella (Locus 002) for the first Temple of Apollo. Occasional pitting by McFadden and Cesnola, together with animal burrowing and rainwash, left the layer circa 80 percent purely stratified. From this locus we studied only two fragments, although more than sixty fragments, primarily of Gjerstad Type IV, were noted for future publication. No. 1 (below) is from an Attic Black-figured type B panel amphora (Fig. 148). In the absence of an exact parallel for the siren, the closer examples, now in the Boston Museum, are dated between 580 and 550 B.C. No. 2 (below) is an Attic Black-glazed cup (Fig. 149) with a parallel in Cyprus published by Gjerstad. This type is usually dated toward the middle of the sixth century B.C. and just after.

Attic Black-figured, 1-(P 1785). Fragment of body and neck of a type B panel amphora (Fig. 148), black-glazed except for reserved panel with siren. Head turned right and part of both wings visible. Details incised but no incised outline. Traces of red paint on the wings. Very fine. Fabric close to 2.5YR 6/6 (light red); reserved panel 7.5YR 6/6 (reddish yellow); 7.5 R 2.5/0 (black) glaze; 2.5YR 4/8 (red) paint. No exact parallel with a siren was found in the available bibliography. Cf. With 2 horses in the reserved panel: *Corpus Vasorum* 19-fascicule 1 Plate 1.1,2 (dated 580 B.C.); with 1 horse: Id., ibid., Plate 1.3,4 (dated 560 B.C.); with a horseman: Gjerstad, 1977, Plate IV. 499, p.52 (found in Marion, *Necropolis* II, dated 550 B.C.). For the eye and wing treatment see also Boardman 1980, plate 56 by the Timiades Painter circa 565 -550 B.C. and plate 60 (Castellani Painter) of the same date.

Attic Black-glazed, 2-(P 1786 a). Rim of cup (Fig. 149). Very Fine. Between 5YR 5/6 (yellowish red) and 10YR 5/3 (brown); 10YR 2/1 shining (black) glaze. Diameter, 190 mm. Cf. Gjerstad, 1977, Plate XLVII.1, no. 470, p. 49; Sparker and Talcol 1970 XII, 1 no. 434, 435.

Locus C 1, 2, 3, 003: foundation locus bonded with the walls of the first Temple of Apollo. This locus had few of the typical Cypriote wares. Nos. 1 and 2 (below) are in red slip. Both are wheel burnished, a feature that comes to an end around 700 B.C., according to Birmingham. Nos. 7 and 8 (below) are base fragments in Attic Black-glazed. For no. 7 we found a possible parallel in Athens, with its probable *terminus ante quem* dated ca. 490 B.C. No exact parallel could be found for a coarse ware "fish-plate" with traces of slip (?) on the inside. The type is found in Al-Mina (Syria) in levels VIII through V.

Figure 148. Attic Black-Figured Panel Amphora. (P1785)

We believe this locus to be dated toward the end of the sixth century B.C.

Red Slip, 1-(P 77). Rim of bowl (Fig. 150), wheel-burnished. Medium fine with big white inclusions; 5YR 5/8 (yellowish red); 2.5YR 4/6 (red) Diameter, 130 mm. Cf. Gjerstad, 1948, Fig. XLII.12 (Red Slip II (IV) ware).

Black-on-red, 2-(P 76). Rim of bowl (Fig. 150), wheel-burnished. Medium fine with a few white inclusions; 7.5YR 6/4 (light brown); 10 R 4/8 (red). Diameter, 130 mm. Cf. Gjerstad, 1948, Fig XXXVII.1 (Black-on-Red II (IV) ware).

Plain White, 3-(P 78). Rim of bowl (Fig. 150). Medium fine with many white inclusions; 10YR 6/3 (pale brown); 10YR 7/2 (light gray) slip. Diameter, 110 mm.

Coarse ware, 4-(P 75). Rim of bowl (Fig. 150). Medium with white inclusions; 5YR 6/4 (light reddish brown) Diameter, 190 mm.

Idem, 5-(P 70). Rim of pot (Fig. 150). Medium with white and black inclusions; 5YR 4/6 (yellowish red). Rim blackened. Diameter, 252 mm.

Idem, 6-(P 71). Rim of pot (Fig. 150). Gritty with white and black inclusions; 2.5YR 4/6 (red). Rim fire-blackened. Diameter, 208 mm.

Attic Black-glazed, 7-(1796). Base fragment (Fig. 150), very fine. Color 5YR 5/8 (yellowish red); 10YR 2/1 (black). Diameter, 179 mm. Cf. Sparker and Talcott 1978, XII, Fig. 20. 574, p. 276 (dated before ca. 490 B.C.)

Idem, 8-(P 72). Base fragment (Fig. 150). Very fine with minute dark inclusions; 5YR 6/6 (reddish yellow); 2.5YR 2.5/0 (black) matte slip. Diameter, 50 mm.

Coarse ware "fish plate," 9-(1857). Base of "fish-plate" (Fig. 150). Fine. Color 5YR 5/8 (yellowish red), traces of slip on the inside (?). Diameter, 57 mm. Cf. No exact parallel. Some rims of "fish-plates" were found in Al-Mina. Taylor, 1959, Fig. 6.25 to 30, p. 82 (from Level VIII to V)

Locus C 1, 2, 3, 005: critically important Locus 005 was sealed completely in the foundations for the first temple. It is an ashy layer of dense bone, and some sherds were burned. It was packed *against* the cella wall beneath Locus 003, so that it clearly formed part of the foundations.

This locus had a great deal of Red Slip and Black-on-Red pottery. Some White Painted, Black Slip, and Plain White No. 1 in Red Slip have a parallel in Tyre (Phoenicia) in Strata II-III, with a date from 740 to 700 B.C.

Nos. 2 and 8 (below) are wheel-burnished, a rather rare feature among the Kourion finds. This feature comes to an end around 700 B.C., according to Birmingham. Nos. 3, 4 and 5 (below) have parallels in Al-Mina in levels VIII to VI. No. 11 is a problem piece; with a very fine paste, it is probably an import.

POTTERY — TEMPLE CELLA , KOURION

LOCUS 002

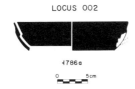

4786a

0   5cm

Figure 149. Attic Black-Glazed Cup. (P1786a)

POTTERY — TEMPLE CELLA , KOURION

0   5cm

LOCUS 003

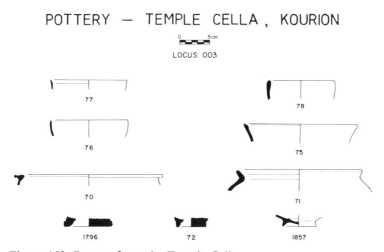

Figure 150. Pottery from the Temple Cella.

No parallel was found, except for the shape in Samaria-Sebaste in a deposit dated in the early seventh century B.C.

No. 12 (below) in Black-on-Red is a well known and well dated piece with parallels in Cyprus, namely in the cemeteries of Ayia Irini and Paleapaphos-Skales, as well as on the continent in Al-Mina and Tyre (Phoenicia) in Strata II-III. Nos. 13 and 14 (below) have parallels in type IV of Gjerstad's typology. No. 16 (below) has a parallel in Al-Mina in level VII-VI. No. 17 has been published here as possibly black-on-red ware, but Vassos Karageorghis believes it is an Ionian cup, although it lacks the fine pink fabric and shiny black glaze usually associated with Ionian cups. For No. 18 (below) in White Painted no close parallel could be found. A similar shape occurs in type II of Gjerstad's typology. For the rim of amphora No. 21 (below) the closer parallel is in type VI of Gjerstad's typology. Nos. 23 to 25 are in Black Slip with horizontal grooves, dated by Karageorghis as Cypro-Archaic I-II.

No. 26 is a fragment of the wall of inventory number 1785 in Cella 3, locus 002. This Attic Black-figured Type B panel amphora can be dated in the first half of the sixth century B.C., probably in the second quarter. Nos. 29 and 30 are terra cotta fragments. Both types are well known figurines with parallels in Kourion. No attempt has been made to date these common figurines of the Kourion Sanctuary.

We believe the date of the Attic Black-figured amphora to be the date of this locus.

Red Slip, 1-(P 94). Rim of bowl (Fig. 151). Fine with tiny white and orange inclusions; 5YR 5/8 (yellowish red); 10 R 4/6 (red) slip. Diameter, 140/150 mm. Cf. Bikai 1978, Plate IX. 9, 10 (Strata II/III).

Idem, 2-(P 82). Rim of bowl (Fig. 151), wheel-burnished. Medium fine with and black inclusions; 5YR 5/6 (yellowish red); 10 R 4/5 (red). Diameter, 207 mm. Cf. Karageorghis 1970, T. 41.5, p. 73 (Plain White V ware); Bikai 1978, Plate VIII A.5 to 19 and 23 to 27 (Stratum III) (Plate II, unslipped).

Idem, 3-(P 79). Rim of bowl (Fig. 151). Medium fine with black, white and orange inclusions; 7.5YR 6/4 (light brown); 10 R 4/8 (red) slip. Diameter, 158/172 mm. Cf. Taylor 1959, Fig. 6.13 (from level VIII).

Idem, 4-(P 93). Rim and wall of bowl (Fig. 151). Gritty with white and dark inclusions; 2.5YR 6/6 (light red); 10 R 4/6 (red) slip. Diameter, 158 mm. Cf. Taylor 1959, Fig. 6.37, p. 83 (unslipped, similar to others from Level VIII); Gjerstad 1948, Fig. XL.7 (Bichrome Red I (IV) ware).

Idem, 5-(P 90). Rim and wall of bowl (Fig. 151). Gritty with many white inclusions; 7.5YR 6/4 (light brown); 5YR 5/8 (yellowish red) worn slip. Diameter, 212 mm. Cf. Taylor 1959, Fig. 6.29 (from Level VII-VI).

Idem, 6-(P 86). Rim of bowl (Fig. 151). Gritty with white and dark inclusions; 7.5YR 5/4 (brown); 10 R 4/8 (red) slip. Diameter, 180 mm. Cf. Gjerstad 1948, Fig. XXXVII.14 (Black-on-Red II (IV) ware).

Idem, 7-(P 105). Rim of bowl (Fig. 151). Gritty with white inclusions; 5YR 4/6 (yellowish red); 2.5YR 4/8 (red) slip, with black spots inside. Diameter, 190 mm. Cf. Karageorghis 1983, T. 62.132, Fig. CXX, p. 145

Idem, 8-(P 83). Rim of bowl (Fig. 151), burnished. Medium fine with white inclusions; 7.5YR 4/6 (strong brown); 2.4YR 3/6 (dark red) slip. Diameter, 191 mm. Cf. Gjerstad 1948, Fig. XLII.11 (Red Slip II (IV) ware).

Idem, 9-(P 80). Small bowl (Fig. 151), lid(?). Gritty with many white inclusions; 2.5YR 5/6 (red); traces of 10 R 5/8 (red) slip. Diameter, 121 mm.

Idem, 10-(P 81). Pot(?) (Fig. 151). Medium fine with white and dark inclusions; 2.5YR 3/6 (dark red); 10 R 4/8 (red) slip. Diameter, 155 mm.

Red Slip(?), 11-(P 1852). Rim of bowl (Fig. 152). Very fine. Color 2.5 Y 7/2 (light grey); 2.5YR 4/8 (red) slip. Diameter, 180/193 mm. Cf. For the shape see Crowfoot and Kenyon 1957 p. 194.8, p.98 (from a deposit dated in the early seventh century B.C.).

Black-on-Red, 12-(P 1847). Rim of bowl (Fig. 152), set of concentric circles on rim; three horizontal bands and one large band on outside rim; black inside. Fine. Color 10YR 7/3 (very pale brown); 2.5YR 4/8 (red) slip; 2.5YR 2.5/0 (black) bands. Cf. Gjerstad 1948, Fig. XXXVII. 24 (Black-on-Red II (IV) ware); Taylor 1959, Fig. 5.12; Birmingham 1963, Ill. 1.22; Bikai 1978, Plate XI.21, p. 53, Strata II/III; Rocchetti 1978, 28.19, p. 56; Karageorghis 1983, Pl. LXXVII.60, p. 102.

Idem, 13-(P 103). Rim of bowl (Fig. 152), two horizontal bands between rim and body; black band on the inside. Medium fine, with dark inclusions; 10YR 7/4 (very pale brown); 2.5YR 4/6 (red) to 5YR 5/6 (yellowish red) slip; 2.5YR 2.5/0 (black) paint. Diameter, 188 mm. Cf. Gjerstad 1948, Fig. XXXVII.26 (Black-on-Red (II) IV ware).

Idem, 14-(P 95). Rim of bowl (Fig. 152), black bands on rim inside and outside. Gritty with black and white inclusions; 7.5YR 4/6 (strong brown); 10 R 5/8 (red) slip; 2.5YR 2.5/0 (black) paint. Diameter, 172 mm. Cf. Gjerstad 1948, Fig. XXXVII.14.

Idem, 15-(P 1849/85). Rim of bowl (Fig. 153), horizontal bands on outside wall; black band on inside rim. Color 7.5YR 5/4 (brown); 2.5YR 4/8 (red) slip; 2.5YR 2.5/0 (black) paint. Diameter 190 mm. Cf. Gjerstad 1948, Fig. XXXI.1 (Bichrome IV ware); Taylor 1959, Fig. 5.3 (Level VII-VI).

Idem, 16-(P 68). Rim of bowl (Fig. 153), horizontal bands on rim and inside. Gritty with white and dark inclusions; 7.5YR 5/6 (strong brown); 2.5YR 4/8 (red) slip; 2.5YR 2.5/0 (black) paint. Parallel in Al-Mina in level VII-VI. Diameter, 190 mm. Cf. for the shape, Taylor 1959, Fig. 6.33 (associated with Level VIII).

Idem, 17-(P 125). Base (Fig. 153), set of concentric circles on inner bottom. Fine. Color 10YR 7/3 (very pale brown); 2.5YR 6/6 (red), outside 7.5YR 5/0 (grey); 2.5 Y 2/0 (black) paint. Diameter, 28 mm. Cf. Gjerstad 1977, p. 17, Nos. 84-87 for similar feet, but of larger diameter; they are possibly Rhodian and date to circa 600 B.C. In the same volume (p. 33) Gjerstad comments on Ionian cups that may parallel this base: "There are Cypriote imitations of them in White Painted IV and Bichrome IV." The date again is circa 600 B.C.

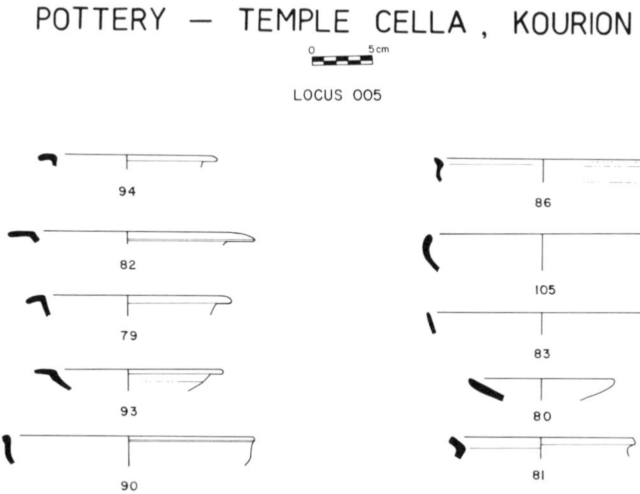

POTTERY — TEMPLE CELLA , KOURION

0 ____ 5cm

LOCUS 005

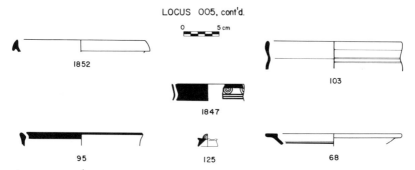

Figure 151. Pottery from the Temple Cella.

POTTERY — TEMPLE CELLA , KOURION

LOCUS 005, cont'd.

0 ____ 5 cm

Figure 152. Pottery from the Temple Cella.

POTTERY — TEMPLE CELLA , KOURION

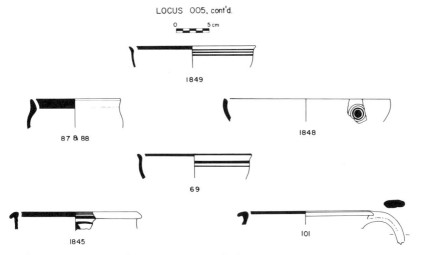

Figure 153. Pottery from the Temple Cella.

White Painted, 18-(P 87/P 88). Rim and wall of bowl (Fig. 153), black band on the inside rim. Gritty with dark inclusions; 10YR 7/2 (light grey); 7.5YR 2/0 (black) band. Diameter, 137 mm. Cf. Gjerstad 1948, Fig. XXIV.12 (Black-on-Red I (III) ware).

Idem, 19-(P 69). Rim and wall of bowl (Fig. 153), black rim inside and outside; two horizontal bands on the outside. Gritty with white and dark inclusions; 7.5YR 5/6 (strong brown); 7.5YR 7/6 (reddish yellow) slip; 7.5 Yr 2/0 (black) paint. Diameter, 172 mm. Cf. n.15 (1849/85) above.

Idem, 20-(P 1848). Rim of bowl (Fig. 153), six concentric circles. Fine with tiny white inclusions; 7.5YR 4/0 (dark grey). Outside possibly burnt. Diameter, 250 mm.

Idem, 21-(P 1845). Rim of amphora (Fig. 153), inside of rim black; horizontal bands on outside rim; wavy band on neck. Gritty with dark and white inclusions; 5YR 5/6 (brownish red); 10YR 8/3 (very pale brown) slip; 10YR 3/1 (very dark grey) paint. Diameter, 185/202 mm. Cf. Gjerstad 1948, Fig. LXX.2 (White Painted VI ware).

Idem, 22-(P 101). Rim and handle of amphora (Fig. 153), bands on

rim inside and outside. Medium fine with dark inclusions; 10YR 7/4
(very pale brown); 5 Y 7/3 (pale yellow) slip; 10YR 3/1 (very dark
grey) paint; Diameter, 184/206 mm. Cf. Gjerstad 1948, Fig. XL.3
(Black-on-Red II (IV) ware).

Black Slip, 23-(P 1846). Rim and neck of amphora (Fig. 154),
grooves on upper part of rim. Medium fine with big grey inclusions;
5YR 4/6 (yellowish red); 5YR 3/1 (very dark grey) slip. Diameter,
160/176 mm. Cf. for the kind of ware, Karageorghis 1983, Fig. I, p.
119 to 122, Plates XXI-XXII.

Idem, 24-(P 104). Rim of amphora (Fig. 154), grooves on upper
part of rim. Medium fine, with big white inclusions; 2.5YR 4/0
(dark grey); 2.5YR 2.5/0 (black) slip. Diameter, 164 mm. Cf. like
No. 23 (1846) above.

Idem, 25-(P 84). Rim and neck of amphora (Fig. 154). Medium
fine. Color 10YR 4/1 (dark grey); 10YR 3/1 (dark grey) slip.
Diameter, 226 mm.

Attic Black-figured, 26-(P 124). Wall fragment of 1785 (see Fig.
148); part of black stripe between reserved panels.

Coarse ware 27-(P 1851). Rim and neck of amphora (Fig. 154).
Gritty with white and dark inclusions; 7.5YR 5/4 (brown). Diameter,
214 mm.

Idem, 28-(P 102). Pot (Fig. 154). Gritty with many
white inclusions; 2.5YR 3/6 (dark red). Diameter, 112 mm.

Terra cotta, 29-(T 922). Head and part of body of figurine, low
pointed cap. Color 7.5YR 5/6 (strong brown). Traces of black paint.
Cf. Young and Young 1955, Plate 9.525, p.32. (from the Archaic
Precinct fill)

Idem, 30-(T 923 a). Head of an animal, probably a bull. Color
10YR 7/3 (very pale brown). Traces of black paint. Cf. Young and
Young 1955, Plate 12.855, p.42 (from West of Street 1).

Locus C 1, 2, 3, 006: similar to, but beneath, 005. In this
locus the bulk of the pottery again is in Red Slip and
Black-on-Red. Some White Painted, Bichrome and Black Slip with
horizontal grooves occur in smaller quanitities.

No. 1 (below) has a parallel in the Iron Age cemetery of
Palaepaphos-Skales in a piece dated by Karageorghis Cypro-Archaic
I. No. 2 (below) is a wheel-burnished rim of an amphora with no
close parallel in the same ware. The closest shape found is in
White Painted IV ware of Gjerstad's typology. Nevertheless, we
attribute more value to the wheel-burnishing, whose end has been
placed by Birmingham around 700 B.C. The Black-on-Red finds
cataloged have parallels in type IV of Gjerstad's typology. No. 10
(below) is the base of a "double-bowl." This is not a common find
in Kourion. The "double-bowls" found in Salamis have been dated by
Karageorghis to Cypro-Archaic I.

Although the pottery argues for a date of circa 700 B.C., a date
around the mid sixth century seems correct for this locus

POTTERY — TEMPLE CELLA , KOURION

LOCUS 005, cont'd.

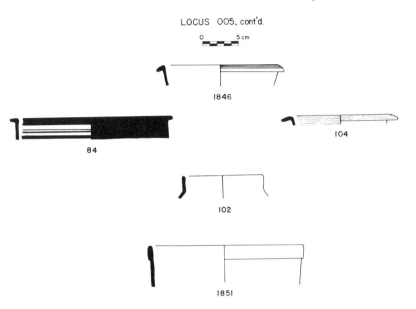

Figure 154. Pottery from the Temple Cella.

because a terra cotta horse head (TC 88 a and b) parallels closely
that reported in Young and Young 1955, p. 228.

Red Slip, 1-(P 110). Rim of bowl (Fig. 155). Medium
fine with white and dark inclusions; 7.5YR 5/4 (brown); 10 R 4.5/8
(red) slip. Diameter, 250 mm. Cf. Karageorghis 1983, T. 62.132,
Fig. CXX, p. 145 (dated beginning of CA I).

Idem, 2-(P 97/98). Rim of amphora (Fig. 155), wheel burnished.
Gritty with many white inclusions; 5YR 5/6 (yellowish red); 10 R
5/6 (red) slip. Diameter, 132/148 mm. Cf. Gjerstad 1948, Fig. LIX.
2 (White Painted VI ware).

Black-on-Red, 3-(P 1793). Rim of bowl (Fig. 155), black bands on
rim inside and outside. Color 7.5YR 6/6 (reddish yellow); 2.5YR 5/8
(red) slip; 2.5YR 2.5/1 (black) paint. Diameter, 231 mm. Cf.
Gjerstad 1948, Fig. XXXVII.16 (Black-on-Red II [IV] ware).

Idem, 4-(P 1794). Base of bowl (Fig. 155), set of concentric
circles. Fine. Color 10YR 7/4 (very pale brown); 2.5YR 2.5/0
(black) paint. Diameter, 30 mm.

Coarse ware, 5-(P 106/P 107). Rim of pot (Fig. 156). Gritty with white inclusions; 5YR 5/6 (yellowish red) surface smoothed; 5 Y 6/6 (reddish yellow). Diameter, 250 mm.

Idem, 6-(P 1795 a, b, c). Rim of pot (Fig. 156). ´Gritty with white and dark inclusions; 5YR 6/6 (reddish yellow). Diameter, 240/252 mm.

Idem, 7-(P 108/P 112). Rim of bowl (Fig. 156). Medium fine with a few white inclusions; 10YR 6/2 (light brownish grey); smoothed surface 10YR 7/2 (light grey). Diameter, 190 mm.

Idem, 8-(P 111/P 109). Rim of dish or shallow bowl (Fig. 156). Medium fine. Color 2.5 Y 2/0 (black). Diameter, 270 mm.

Idem, 9-(P 113 a, b). Small bowl (Fig. 156). Gritty with white inclusions; 10YR 6/6 (light yellowish brown). Diameter, 79 mm.

Idem, 10-(P 114). Base of "double-bowl." Medium fine clay with many white inclusions; 7.5YR 4/6 (strong brown). Diameter, 50 mm. Cf. Karageorghis 1973, T. 79.476, 477, Plate CCXXXII, p. 48, 49. (dated CA I).

Based on the pottery analyzed, the date of the original Temple of Apollo should fall within the sixth century B.C., at least as late as 570 B.C. Further evidence may well push the date a good deal later in the sixth century B.C.

POTTERY — TEMPLE CELLA , KOURION

LOCUS 006

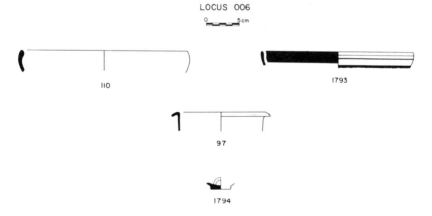

Figure 155. Pottery from the Temple Cella.

POTTERY — TEMPLE·CELLA , KOURION

LOCUS 006

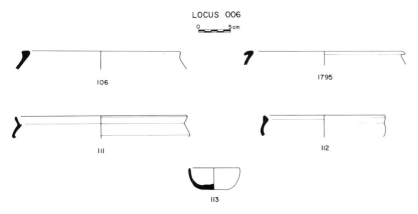

Figure 156. Pottery from the Temple Cella.

Chapter 8
Significant Pottery and Lamps from the Temple
Lucinda Neuru and David Soren

Materials recovered from the 1978 excavations immediately southeast of the Temple of Apollo and against its foundations are reported here. The significant finds discussed are, for the most part, fragments of ceramic vessels. The glass currently is under study by Andrew Oliver Jr., and will be published separately. Discussion of material recovered by George McFadden is appended to this chapter.

The ceramic evidence is listed first by major locus divisions, and then in order of fine, kitchen and common wares, lamps, and miscellaneous.

The fine wares fall into the standard categories of Arretine, Cypriote, Sigillata, and Eastern Sigillata A and B.[1] Arretine ware is well documented and needs no explanation here.[2]

The Cypriote fabric is generally smooth-textured, with lumps of lime both large and small occurring from time to time. The color range of the paste varies from red to a darkish maroon, very occasionally to dark brown or grey, and usually falls between Munsell 10 R 6/2 to 2.5YR 4/6. The thin slip is darker than the paste and regularly has a metallic lustre. Double-dipping streaks are frequent.

The fabric of Eastern Sigillata A ranges in color from yellow to a light orange (Munsell 10YR 8/4YR 7/6-8/6). The paste tends to be fine and powdery in the orange variant and is considerably coarser and more granular in the yellow. There are no obvious impurities.

The slip has a higher iron content than does the body clay, and so fires to a noticeably darker color, ranging from an orange-red to a maroon-red (2.5YR 4/6-4/8). The quality of the slip can approach that of Arretine Sigillata, particularly on the earlier examples with yellow body clay. A dull brownish red slip

(2.5YR 5/6) over a body clay of orangish buff (7.5YR 7/6) is sometimes found in the late Hellenistic period, while during the Roman period the slip tends toward a bright, glossy vermillion red over a powdery light orange clay. The slip on the interior surfaces frequently is smoothed with a small brush and tends to flake off in this small brush pattern, a phenomenon that can extend to the entire interior surface.

Some Hellenistic examples were deliberately fired black, and others exhibit a mottled red and black, a result of misfiring. A few examples from the Domitianic to Trajanic periods show a marbled or mottled surface, produced by sponging immediately after the application of the wet slip. This was perhaps intended to imitate bronze ware.

Eastern Sigillata B has two basic variants. B2 has a highly micaceous and very porous body clay, whereas B1 usually does not. The basic paste color is orange-red (10R 6/4), but a range between 2.5YR and 10 R 5/12 is possible.

The surface gloss is prepared from the same clay and is higher in iron content than are many other Asia Minor wares (except Candarli). This slip fires to a bright vermillion or orangish red (about 10 5/6). Many examples are deliberately fired black, and others are simply misfired, resulting in a surface color range from creamy white to dark chocolate brown (2.5YR 3/2-/4).

The mica, when it is visible, appears as fine, silvery flakes. There are no other visible impurities. The paste tends to be quite flaky, and obviously was easily broken and abraded, judging by many excavated examples.

The feel of the surface tends to be soapy or waxlike. It is considerably duller in appearance than is Arretine Sigillata. Double-dipping streaks appear on the B1 version; B2 usually is more thickly slipped and does not readily show the same streaking.

The fabric of the kitchen and common wares in the Temple of Apollo loci is somewhat different from the standard fabric found in the Cistern 3 deposit of late Flavian date.[3] Both are most certainly local, that is Cypriote, but there is always the possiblity that the wares came from two different production sites.

The color range of the kitchen and common wares in the Temple of Apollo deposits is red (Munsell 10R 3/6 to 4/6). The wares are fairly gritty with black and white inclusions, the latter being generally the larger.[4] The kitchen ware regularly is blackened. All examples may be assumed to be of this fabric unless otherwise indicated.

There are very few lamps in this deposit, and most are fragmentary. They are, for the most part, probably of local Cypriote production and can usually be dated to the first century A.D.

LOCUS 001

This locus consisted of a light yellow-brown surface soil (10YR 6/4) with little contamination; it appears to be fill put in for the second temple. It was much disturbed by the previous excavator. One glass fragment from this locus joins to another in locus 002.[5] Small quantities of terra cotta figurines of earlier date are intrusive in all loci. The locus was exposed by George McFadden in the 1930s, but only his trench in the south corner of the temple was excavated then.

Fine Ware

1. Rim/side, bowl (Fig. 157). Eastern Sigillata B, Hayes *EAA* early form 58. Date range: A.D. 50-75. See also: Robinson 1959, 24-5, pl. 61, No. G19; Knipowitsch 1929, 13-14, Typus 1a, Fig. 3.4, pl. 1, 1a, with a stamp KEP/△OS; Hellström 1965, 1, 67, No. 210, p. 35. (K78 Jd 1/2 001 67).

2. Three joining fragments of one bowl (Fig. 157), Eastern Sigillata B. Hayes *EAA* form 58 variant, slightly heavier profile. Flange and carination at turning point to base less delineated. Date range: presumably the same as no. 1. (K78 Jd 1/2 001 68-70)

3. Two fragments, rim/neck and shoulder of presumably the same jug (Fig. 157). Eastern Sigillata B. Rouletting on lip, interior and exterior surfaces, unusual. Three grooves around lower neck/shoulder, wide band of rouletting below. Date range: probably not inconsistent with above two examples. (K78 Jd 1/2 001 71-72).

Kitchen Ware

4. Rim collar, casserole (Fig. 157). Flared, overhanging lip. Interior ledge. Blackened exterior as indicated. (K78 Jd 1/2 001 74).

5. Rim, possible cooking pot (Fig. 157). Burnt. Tiny interior ledge, thick horizontal overhang. Pronounced horizontal ridging on exterior below rim. (K78 Jd 1/2 001 77).

6. Rim collar, casserole (Fig. 158). Thin, straight, flaring, with overhang. Small interior ledge. (K78 Jd 1/2 001 78).

7. Rim collar, flared with slight thickening at lip (Fig. 157). Small groove at turn to a probably bag-shaped body. (K78 Jd 1/2 001 79).

POTTERY — TEMPLE EXTERIOR, KOURION

JD I and 2, LOCUS OOI

Figure 157. Pottery from the Temple Exterior.

POTTERY — TEMPLE EXTERIOR, KOURION

JD I and 2, LOCUS OOI

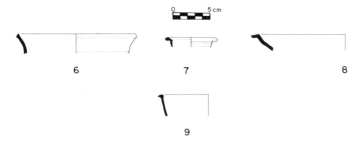

Figure 158. Pottery from the Temple Exterior.

Common Ware

8.   Rim/side of shallow flaring bowl or dish with broad flat rise
       (Fig. 158). Dusky red clay (2.5YR 3/2) fired to a paler shade
       on exterior surfaces. (K78 Jd 1/2 001 75).

9.   Rim, small cup (Fig. 158). Thin, slightly flaring walls, small hook at lip. (K7 Jd 1/2 001 76).

10.   Handle, jug; not illustrated. Hard, crisp, dark red fabric (2.5YR 3/6). (K78 Jd 1/2 001 73).

LOCUS 002.1-4

This level, consisting of a light grey soil (5YR 7/2) and containing randomly distributed chunks of mortar, lay against a shelf formed for the support of a retaining wall stair, or cheek wall, of the temple. This locus appears to have been slightly disturbed by installation of the cheek wall and thus should contain material associated with the second temple; if the cheek wall is a later addition, it is possible that even later material might be present. One glass fragment was actually sealed in the cheek wall and was dated "probably second century" by Andrew Oliver.

Fine Ware

11.   Base (Fig. 159), Cypriote Sigillata, forerunner of Hayes *EAA*, form 29. This form is common A.D. 100-150 at Paphos. Kourion example is shorter and squatter. Date range perhaps A.D. 50-100? (K78 Jd1 002.3, SDNR).

Kitchen Ware

12.   Rim, widely flaring, exterior "D" thickening under lip (Fig. 159). Slight groove just above beginning of thickening. (K78 Jd 1/2 002 199).

13.   Rim/handle of a presumably two-handled casserole (Fig. 159). Slightly thickened at lip. Plain, round handles. (K78 Jd 1/2 002 199).

14.   Rim, casserole (Fig. 159). Flat-topped lip, slightly wedge-shaped. (K78 Jd 1/2 002.1 611).

15.   Rim/handle, as above (No. 13), but flared rim with triangular overhang at lip (Fig. 159). (K78 Jd 1/2 002 200).

16.   Rim collar/side, similar to the bag-shaped "T" rim casserole with interior ledge (Fig. 159). Found also in Cistern 3, examples 4-8. This example has a higher collar. Date range: first century A.D. (K78 Jd 1/2 002.2 681 a and b). cf. article by A. Leonard in this volume (Fig. 54:i).

17. Rim/handle, casserole (Fig. 160). May be a variant of "T" rim collared type; cf. preceding example. (K78 Jd 1/2 002.2 682).

18. Rim, casserole (Fig. 160). Wedge-shaped and flared collar, with very prominent, sharply delineated interior ledge at end of slight concavity. (K78 Jd 1/2 002.2 683).

19. Rim, cookpot (Fig. 160). Straight, slightly flaring sides rising from carinated turn to base. Flat-topped horizontal rim. (K78 Jd 1/2 002.3 690).

20. Rim/side, bag-shaped casserole (Fig. 160). Slightly flared rim collar ending with outward nobbed lip. Very slight interior ledge. (K78 Jd 1/2 002.3 690).

21. Rim, cookpot (Fig. 161). Slightly flared, straight-sided vessel with slightly wedged, two-grooved interior edge. Severely blackened. (K78 Jd 1 ext. 002.4 1223).

Common Ware

22. Rim, basin (Fig. 161). Wedge-shaped lip, quite flared. Groove on interior just below lip. (K78 Jd 1/2 001 80).

23. Rim, simple thickened lip (Fig. 161). Amphora. (K78 Jd 1/2 001 81).

24. Rim/neck/handle stub (Fig. 161). Two identical rims of jar or amphora. Brown fabric (10YR 5/3). Square shape to lip exterior. (K78 Jd1 Ext 002.1 609).

Lamps of the First Century

25. Shoulder, Cypriote lamp with raised decoration; not illustrated. Cloverleaf? (K78 Jd 1/2 OO2 84).

26. Thin-walled lamp base/side; not illustrated. Reddish yellow buff clay with weak red surface gloss. (K78 Jd 1 002.2 684).

27. Base; not illustrated. Reddish yellow buff clay with red surface gloss. (K78 Jd 1/2 002.3 687).

Miscellaneous

28. Roof tile, fragment (Fig. 161). Standard local coarse ware fabric. (K78 Jd 1/2 002, 19).

POTTERY — TEMPLE EXTERIOR , KOURION

JD I and 2 , LOCI 002.1 to 002.4

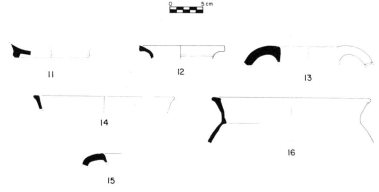

Figure 159. Pottery from the Temple Exterior.

POTTERY — TEMPLE EXTERIOR , KOURION

JD I and 2 , LOCI 002.1 to 002.4, cont'd.

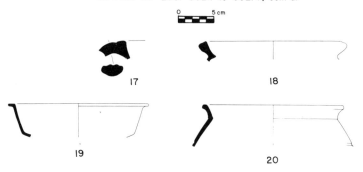

Figure 160. Pottery from the Temple Exterior.

29. Body fragment, probable lamp; not illustrated. Very pale brown
fabric (10YR 8/3), with a blotchy light brown surface (7.5YR 6/4).
Cypriote. (K78 Jd 1/2 002 SONR)

POTTERY — TEMPLE EXTERIOR, KOURION

JD I and 2, LOCI 002.I to 002.4, cont'd.

0   5 cm

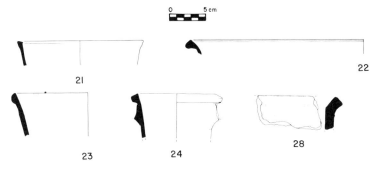

21

22

23   24

28

Figure 161. Pottery from the Temple Exterior.

LOCUS 002.5 (floor below cheek wall)

Under the light grey soil of the cheek wall is a layer of brownish soil with an admixture of mortar similar to that of the cheek wall. This brown soil level extended beyond the wall, covered most of the southern part of the trench, and probably was associated with the second temple. It may have been a temporary floor outside the temple and may never have been smoothed down before the cheek wall was installed. The disturbed area suggests the cheek wall may have been remodeled or intruded into the pre-existing fill, which would explain the earlier date of the fills in comparison with the glass in the cheek wall proper.

Fine Ware

30.   Base (Fig. 162), catillus(?). Arretine Sigillata. Central rectangular stamp within two circular grooves: L. Tettius Samia. See Oxè-Comfort, 1968, p. 456. This potter is documented at Arrezzo, 20-0 B.C. Residual in present deposit? (K78 Jd1 Ext. 002.5 1229).

31.   Rim (Fig. 163), Arretine Sigillata. Plate or cup, badly preserved. Residual? (K78 Jd1 Ext. 002.5 1230).

32.   Rim (Fig. 163), sigillata. Shallow dish or bow. Possibly Cypriote; light red fabric (2.5YR 4/6-6/6) with a red gloss. (K78 Jd 1 Ext. 002.5 1225).

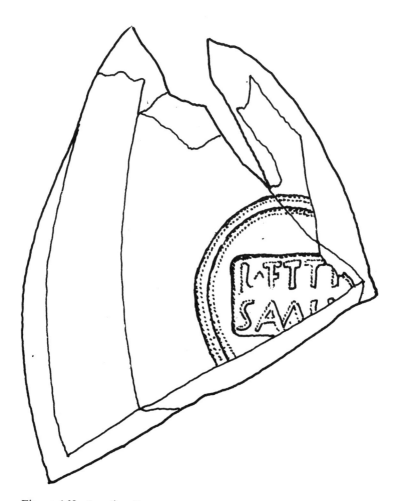

Figure 162. Arretine Base.

Kitchen Ware

33. Rim collar, bag-shaped casserole (Fig. 163). Local grey fabric. Slightly curved and outward-flaring walls. Lip turned back toward center. Series of small grooves immediately below. (K78 Jd 1 Ext 002.5 1226).

34. Rim collar, two-handled casserole (Fig. 163). Short, squat and wedge-shaped rim with small interior ledge. Parallels elsewhere on this site, e.g., Locus 003 and 013; both loci associated with second temple. (K78 Jd 1 Ext. 002.5 1217).

35. Rim, cookpot (Fig. 163). Straight sided, with flat horizontal rim. (K78 Jd 1 Ext 002.5 1218).

36. Rim, jar (Fig. 164). Simple, narrow rolled rim with horizontally mounted handle. Brown fabric (7.5YR 5/2). (K78 Jd 1 Ext. 002.5 1219).

37. Rim, small hemispherical bowl (Fig. 164). Very pale brown fabric (10YR 7/4). Rim curves inward at lip. This is one later example of a very long series of small, footed bowls. Proto-type is Hellenistic. (K78 Jd 1 Ext 002.5 1217).

Lamp

38. Shoulder fragment, lamp; not illustrated. Single groove around a rather deep discus. Reddish yellow buff (7.5YR 7/6) with a blotchy brown surface gloss (7.5YR 3/2). Likely Cypriote manufacture. Date range: roughly A.D. 50-100. (K78 Jd 1 Ext. 002.5 1224).

Miscellaneous

39. Rim collar, water pipe (Fig. 164). From the castellum line (?). Plain red fabric. (2.5YR 5/6). (K78 Jd 1 002.5 1220).

LOCUS 003 (fill for the second temple)

The fill consisted of yellowish-brown sandy soil containing chunks of mortar. In the southwest corner this level had been removed by the previous excavator's trenching; in the central area of the current trench the fill was quite apparent, but disappeared toward the north balk, where the light yellow-brown surface soil predominated. This fill was tightly packed with a slightly higher proportion of mortar chunks where it lay against the foundation of the first temple, and it was disturbed in the area of the cheek wall for the final staircase of the temple.

POTTERY — TEMPLE EXTERIOR, KOURION

JD I and 2, LOCUS 002.5

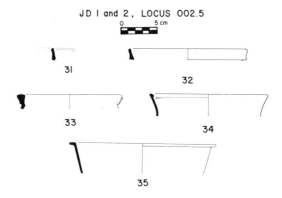

Figure 163. Pottery from the Temple Exterior.

POTTERY — TEMPLE EXTERIOR, KOURION

JD I and 2, LOCUS 002.5, cont'd.

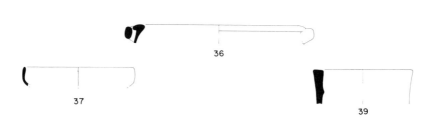

Figure 164. Pottery from the Temple Exterior.

Fine Ware

40.   Rim (Fig. 165), Cypriote Sigillata. Hayes *EAA* form 11 variant. Date range: very common A.D. 50-150. (K78 Jd 1/2 003 96).

POTTERY — TEMPLE EXTERIOR, KOURION

JD I and 2, LOCUS 003

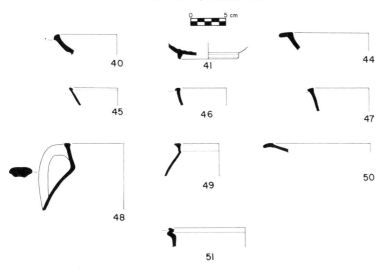

Figure 165. Pottery from the Temple Exterior.

41. Base, red gloss jug (Fig. 165). Fabric highly micaceous, Eastern Sigillata B? Interior not glossed. (K78 Jd 1/2 003 97) Possibly Hayes *EAA* form 106-8. Foot treatment suggests a date possibly similar to the preceding.

42. Base, badly preserved Eastern Sigillata A; not illustrated. (K78 Jd 1/2 003 95).

43. Handle, Eastern Sigillata A; not illustrated (K78 Jd 1/2 003 99).

44. Rim dish (Fig. 165). Red painted interior. Residual? Fabric color same as Cypriote Sigillata. (K78 Jd 1/2 003 95).

Kitchen Ware

45. Rim, thin-walled cookpot (Fig. 165). Nobbed toward interior, this side flattened. Rather sharp offset at base of interior nob. K78 Jd 1/2 003 102).

46.   Small rolled rim of cookpot (Fig. 165). Exterior grooved below lip. (K78 Jd 1/2 003 94).

47.   Rim collar, casserole (Fig. 165). Sharp triangle-shaped lip, small exterior groove below. (K78 Jd 1/2 003 94).

48.   Rim/side/handle, collared bag-shaped casserole (Fig 165). Rounded interior ledge. Lip as preceding example, but not so sharp. Ovoid handle, flattened top with finger pulls underneath. (K78 Jd 1/2 003 92).

49.   Rim/side, variant "T"-rim-collared, bag-shaped casserole (Fig. 165). Shorter collar with more of a wedge shape to the "T". (K78 Jd 1/2 003 93).

50.   Lid fragment (Fig. 165). Wide ovoid lip. Ridge on exterior at join to body. Sharp edge at interior junction between rim and body. (K78 Jd 1/2 003 201).

51.   Rim, S-shaped casserole (Fig. 165). Parallels for this type, presumably a one- or two-handled bag-shaped casserole, occur at Paphos in contexts of roughly the first half of the first century A.D. (K78 Jd 1/2 003 202).

Common Ware

52.   Simple rolled rim of amphora; not illustrated. 003 203).

LOCUS 006

A fill of dark brownish earth (10YR 4/6) was found packed against the second temple. The fill should date the second temple.

Fine Ware

53.   Base of bowl or dish (Fig. 166). Cypriote Sigillata? Possibly Hayes *EAA* form 28 or similar. Red gloss poorly adherent. Date range: first century A.D. (K78 Jd 1/2 006 292).

54.   Rim (Fig 166). Arretine, poorly preserved. Parallel: Goldman 1950 No. 577. Residual (K78 Jd 1/2 006 261).

55.   Rims of two cups (Fig. 166). Grooved lip, flared sides with rouletting on exterior. Eastern Sigillata A, Hayes *EAA* form 43, the Eastern version of Arretine Haltern 7 (Loeschke 1909). See also Vessberg and Westholm 1956 fig. 21, Nos. 6 and 13. Late Hellenistic 2, date range: late Augustan. (K78 Jd 1/2 006 300).

POTTERY — TEMPLE EXTERIOR, KOURION

JD I and 2, LOCUS 006

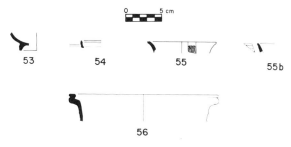

Figure 166. Pottery from the Temple Exterior.

POTTERY — TEMPLE EXTERIOR, KOURION

JD I and 2, LOCUS 006, cont'd.

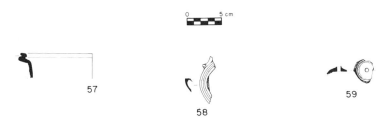

Figure 167. Pottery from the Temple Exterior.

Kitchen Ware

56. Rim, "S"-rim casserole (Fig. 166). See above, No. 48. (K78 Jd 1/2 006 291).

57. Rim (Fig. 167), as above. (K78 Jd 1/2 006 297).

Lamps

58.   Shoulder with three grooves and part of volute (Fig. 167).
       Beginning of deep discus. Light reddish brown fabric with
       blotchy brown gloss (5YR 6/4 to 5/4). Vessberg Type 10a. Date
       range: latter part of the first century A.D. Cypriote. (K78 Jd
       1/2 006 290).

59.   Discus undecorated (Fig. 167). Surrounded by two grooves and a
       row of multiply incised cross-hatching. Pink fabric, very
       blotchy surface gloss. Residual. (K78 Jd 1/2 006 296).

LOCI 001, 002 and 008
(extension of southeastern trench)

Locus 001 is a small rectangular extension of the original
trench Jd1 to the southwest along the exterior of the stair wall of
the temple. It contained surface soil, possibly a fill left undug
by the previous excavators. Locus 002 is similar; it probably is
slightly contaminated by previous excavations above and perhaps by
surface rainwash. Items 60-63 are from these two layers. Locus 008
is immediately below, but apparently is not contaminated. This
level contained only one thin-walled base, No. 64. All three loci
are associated with the second temple.

Kitchen Ware

60.   Rim collar/side, bag-shaped casserole (Fig. 168). See No. 6
       above. (K78 Jd 1 Ext 002 615).

61.   Rim/side/handle, basin (Fig. 168). Local fabric 1. Broad, flat
       rim, slanted downward toward center. Very wide horizontally
       mounted handles. (K78 Jd 1 Ext 002 612).

62.   Rim/handle, bag-shaped casserole (Fig. 168). Similar to No. 48
       above. (K78 Jd 1 Ext 002 614 a and b).

Lamp

63.   Thin, badly preserved fragment. Reddish yellow fabric, no
       gloss; not illustrated. Likely Cypriote. (K78 Jd 1 Ext 001
       613).

Thin-Walled Ware

64.   Base, thin wall vase (Fig. 168). Reddish yellow fabric (5YR
       7/6) with tiny black inclusions and some mica. (K78 Jd 1 Ext
       008 620).

POTTERY — TEMPLE EXTERIOR, KOURION

JD I EXTENSION, LOCI OOI, OO2 and OO8

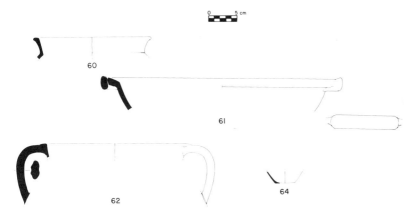

Figure 168. Pottery from the Temple Exterior.

LOCI 009-012

Each of these four loci is progressively deeper stratigraphically then 001, 002, and 008. All are composed of yellow-brown earth very similar to that in 008. They presumably are not contaminated and are fill associated with the second temple.

Fine Ware

65.   Base (Fig. 169), probably Arretine. Two concentric grooves on floor over foot. Similar to Goudineau p. 123, No. 12. Date range: early first century A.D. (K78 Jd 1 011 673).

66.   Rim, Arretine bowl (Fig. 168). Applied volute decoration. Haltern 8, Goudineau p. 207. Date range: ca A.D. 50. (K78 Jd 1 011 678).

67.   Rim, small rounded lip bowl (Fig. 169). Cypriote Sigillata, Hayes *EAA* form 11 early. Date range: A.D. 50-150. See also: Hayes 1967 form 10, p. 71-2; Robinson 1959, G 174, pl. 67; fig. 101. (K78 Jd 1 Ext. 012 1005).

Kitchen Ware

68.   Rim collar/side, bag-shaped casserole (Fig. 169). Variant "T"-rim casserole: Slight droop to outer half of flat lip. Sharp interior ledge, with additional offset. (K78 Jd 1 Ext. 010 605).

69.   Rim collar/side/handle stub, bag-shaped casserole (Fig. 169). Short, squat rim collar with plain flat lip, overhanging on exterior side. Remains of one handle; presumably two were present originally. (K78 Jd 1 011 677).

70.   Rim collar/side, bag-shaped casserole (Fig. 169). (K78 Jd 1 Ext. 013, 1002).

71.   Rim collar, with remains of interior ledge (Fig 169). Casserole, bag-shaped? Plain flared rim rising above interior ledge. Slight offset on lip. (K78 Jd 1 ext 012 1008 a, b, c).

72.   Rim collar (Fig. 169), as above. Interior ledge is sharper. (K78 Jd 1 Ext. 012 1006).

73.   Rim collar/handle, bag-shaped casserole (Fig. 169). Drooping wedge-shaped lip. (K78 Jd 1 Ext 012 1004).

74.   Rim, straight, slightly flaring side (Fig. 169). Oval nob at lip, slanting down toward center. (K78 Jd 1 Ext 012 1007).

75.   Rim, cookpot (Fig. 169). Broad, flattish lip, slanting downward toward center. Tiny upward hook at top exterior edge of a rounded lip. (K78 Jd 1 Ext. 012 1003).

Common Ware

76.   Rim, D-shaped, flared bowl or dish (Fig. 169). Diameter unknown. (K78 Jd 1 Ext 010 607).

77.   Lid, with sharply defined mid-way set oval lip (Fig. 170). Reddish yellow fabric (5YR 7/6). (K78 Jd 1/2 Ext. 009 618).

78.   Rim/side, small pot or jug (Fig. 170). L-shaped lip. Outward flaring straight sides. Kitchen ware fabric. (K78 Jd 1 Ext. 011 676).

79.   Rim, jug (Fig. 170). Simple rolled rim, light brown fabric (7.5YR 8/4). Local. (K78 Jd 1 Ext. 012 009).

POTTERY — TEMPLE EXTERIOR, KOURION

JD I and 2 EXTENSION, LOCI OO9 to OI2

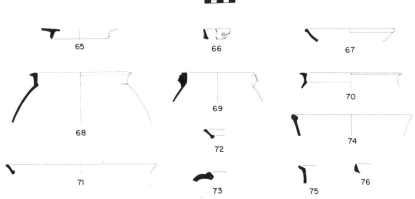

Figure 169. Pottery from the Temple Exterior.

POTTERY — TEMPLE EXTERIOR, KOURION

JD I and 2 EXTENSION, LOCI OO9 to OI2, cont'd.

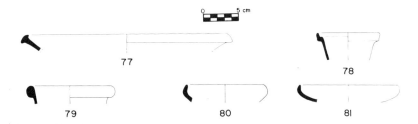

Figure 170. Pottery from the Temple Exterior.

Hellenistic Slipped

80. Rim, hooked toward center (Fig. 170). Small hemispherical bowl. Reddish yellow fabric with blotchy brown-black slipped surface. (K78 Jd 1 Ext 010 606).

81. Rim, small hemispherical bowl (Fig. 170). Less hooked rim profile. Interior surface is glossy dark red (7.5YR 3/6), exterior is blotchy red. Nos. 81 and 82 belong to a Hellenistic tradition that may have continued into the first century A.D. (K78 Jd 1 Ext. 009 616). They are particularly common from the French excavation at Amathus and at Salamis, where they are typically Hellenistic; thus they may be residual here.

Lamps of the First Century

82. Base/side of lamp; not illustrated. Pink fabric with blotchy brown surface (7.5YR 8/4 to 10R 4/4). (K78 Jd 1 Ext. 009 600).

83. Nozzle with bit of volute; not illustrated. Pinkish white fabric with a blotchy brown surface (7.5YR 8/2). (K78 Jd 1 Ext 009 601).

Tile

84. Rim, tile fragment; not illustrated. Gritty reddish yellow local fabric (5YR 7/6). (K78 Jd 1 Ext 009 619).

Locus 014

This locus contains earth mixed with chunks of mortar, but is similar to loci 002-002.4. Locus 014 pre-dates 013 stratigraphically. It is probably to be associated with the second temple.

Fine Ware

85. Rim, bowl (Fig. 171). Cypriote Sigillata, Hayes *EAA* form 11. Date range: A.D. 50-150. (K78 Jd 1 Ext. 014 997).

86. Rim, slightly hooked, flared sides (Fig. 171). Cypriote Sigillata, variant of preceding example? (K78 Jd 1 Ext. 014 995).

87. Rim, bowl or cup (Fig. 171). Cypriote Sigillata. (K78 Jd 1 Ext 014 1000).

POTTERY — TEMPLE EXTERIOR, KOURION
JD I and 2 EXTENSION, LOCUS 014

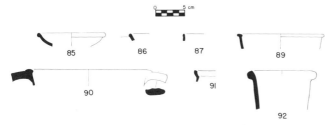

Figure 171. Pottery from the Temple Exterior.

POTTERY — TEMPLE EXTERIOR, KOURION
JD I EXTENSION, LOCI 015, 016 and 019

JC 3 and 4, LOCUS 001

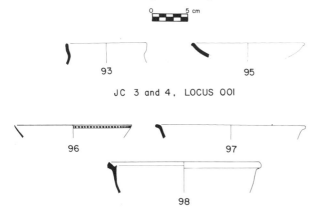

Figure 172. Pottery from the Temple Exterior.

88. Neck, jug; not illustrated. Cypriote Sigillata. (K78 Jd 1 Ext 014 1001).

Kitchen Ware

89. Rim, possible "T"-rim casserole (Fig. 171). Standard Temple fabric. (K78 Ext. 014 994).

90.   Rim collar/handle of "T"-rim (Fig. 171). Bag-shaped casserole. (K78 Jd 1 Ext 014 998).

91.   Rim, cookpot with interior ledge (Fig. 171). Diameter unknown. (K78 Jd 1 Ext 014 996).

Common Ware

92.   Rim, amphora (Fig. 171). Slightly flared sides with simple rolled rim. Probably not local: grey fabric (5YR 5/1). (K78 Jd 1 Ext 014 999).

LOCUS 015

This is a level of fill of similar earth below 014. It post-dates the first temple and appears to be associated with the second.

Kitchen Ware

93.   Rim collar, cookpot, bag-shaped casserole (Fig. 172). Very simple rounded rim. Collar not as sharply delineated as is usual in casseroles found on this site. (K78 Jd 1 Ext 015 1232).

LOCI 016 and 019

Loci 016 and 019 were fills excavated from below 002.5, which was similar in color. Only two fragments of ceramics were retrieved: one was a piece of badly preserved common ware of the fabric normal in the Cistern deposit, and the second was a piece of fine ware, described below. Probably associated with the second temple.

94.   Body fragment, common ware (K78 Jd 1 Ext 019 SDNR); not illustrated.

95.   Rim (Fig. 171), Cyrpiote Sigillata. Hayes *EAA* form 11. Date range: A.D. 50-150. (K78 Jd 1 Ext 019 1451).

NORTH EXTENSION (Jc 3/4).

A new sounding was begun north of Jd 1/2. Only surface soil was removed, and it was similar to Locus 001 of the first trench dug at the southeast corner of the temple.

96.   Rim, thin-walled vessel (Fig. 172). Straight, flared sides. Reddish yellow fabric (5YR 7/6). Interior is slipped a dark red (10R 3/5). Exterior is white-slipped with horizontal lines and dots of dark red (10R 3/4). Reminiscent of third and

second century B.C. Hellenistic series of bowls. Residual. (K78 Jc 1 Ext 001 206).

97.   Rim, cookpot (Fig. 172). Broad, flat rim slanting toward center. Bag-shaped casserole? (K78 Jc 3/4 001 209).

98.   Rim, bowl (Fig. 173). Broad rim with exterior offset and grooved at almost the lowest point of rim concavity. Answering groove on underside of rim. Very slight carination at turn toward base. (K78 Jc 3/4 001 208).

REMARKS AND CONCLUSION

There is little fine ware that provides a really precise date for any of the above deposits. Of the twenty pieces of fine ware illustrated and discussed, nine may be dated to A.D. 50 and later (Nos. 1, 2, 11, 40, 66, 67, 86, 87), while one example is found throughout the first century A.D. (No. 53). The remainder are probably residual.

Table 2, summary in chart form, shows date range, based on the fine ware, for the loci from the main trench, dug at the southeastern corner of the temple, and for the loci of the southwestern extension. The material retrieved from the northeastern extension from a surface sounding is not included; the artifacts would neither refute nor support any conclusions drawn.

Of the ten loci examined, one, a group composed of 001, 002, and 008 from the extension, shall be ignored: this is surface material, and quite possibly contaminated.

Four loci, 001, 003, and 006 of the main trench and the group composed of 009-012 from the extension, were obviously fill for the second temple. Three are datable to post-A.D. 50, and one to the first century, generally speaking.

The fill flanking the cheek wall of the temple, 002.1-4 of the main trench and 014 of the extension, dates to post-A.D. 50, and, in any case, is probably associated with the second temple. The final form of the cheek wall is of possible second century date, as Sinos has recently suggested.

The floor levels below the cheek wall date to the first century A.D. generally, both in the main trench and its extension. In the southwest extension, two levels excavated from below this floor also are associated with the second temple. These two levels, 016 and 019 from the extension, yielded only two ceramic artifacts. One was a piece of badly preserved cooking pot. The second, from 019, the lowest level, was a fragment of Cypriote Sigillata, Hayes *EAA* form 11, datable from A.D. 50 to 150.

The forms of the kitchen wares in these loci are solidly within a Hellenistic tradition that continued throughout the first century A.D. There are two qualities about the fragments

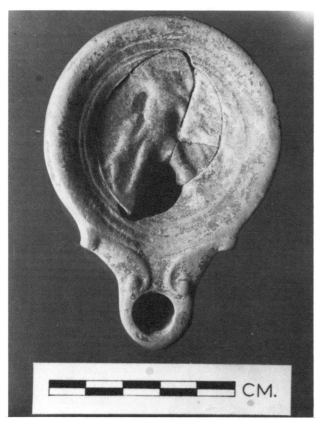

Figure 173. Lamp from McFadden Excavations. (L283)

Table 2: *Dating Summary*

Locus Identification		Fine Ware Type	Date Range
Main Trench:			
001	Fill, Second Temple	ESB 58 early	A.D. 50-75
002.1-4	Cheek Wall, Second Temple or later addition	CS 29 Variant	A.D. 50-100
002.5	Floor below Cheek Wall	Arretine residual	1st century A.D.
003	Fill, Second Temple	CS 11: ESB 106-8 variant	A.D. 50-100
006	Fill, Second Temple	CS 28	1st century A.D.
Extension:			
001, 002, 008	Surface, contaminated (?)		1st century A.D.
009-012	Fill, Second Temple	CS 11	A.D. 50-150
014	Disturbed Cheek Wall	CS 11	A.D. 100-150
015	Floor below Cheek Wall	residual	1st century A.D.
016, 019	Levels below Floor	CS 11	A.D. 50-150

that distinguish this group from the Flavian group of Cistern 3. First, the fragments from the Temple of Apollo exhibit a different fabric color, on the whole, than do the fragments of the Flavian group found in Cistern 3.

Second, as a group, the forms found in the Temple of Apollo loci are similar to, but not the same as, the forms found in the Flavian group that do not occur in the cistern. The bag-shaped "T"-rim casserole, found in the cistern, does not occur in the Temple loci, except for examples that are possible variants. The kitchen ware sherds from the Temple of Apollo loci tend to resemble each other more closely than they resemble those from the cistern.

This difference allows for the possibility of a difference in date: on this site at Kourion there may well have been a change in source of supply; that is, at the date of the temple deposits the residents received their supply of kitchen wares from one production center, and during the late Flavian period, the date of the

Cistern 3 deposits, they purchased from another source. As stated above, the forms from the Temple of Apollo loci belong to a general and long-lived Hellenistic tradition; this is also true for the forms found in the cistern. But this in no way negates the very real possibiltiy that some forms were made only in some places and not in others. Even if these forms overlap in date, it is quite possible that a temporal difference on one site may be detected by observation of the differences in these kitchen ware groups from one deposit to another. With this possiblity in mind, it appears that there is a temporal difference, perhaps not much, between the deposits of the cistern and the Temple of Apollo.

The common ware sherds are of no real use, except insofar as they fail to refute a general date in the first century A.D. The lamp fragments tend to be Vessberg Type 10/11 or related, and are only roughly datable to the latter half of the first century A.D.

Considering all information furnished by the stratigraphy and ceramic artifacts, it appears unlikely that the Temple of Apollo loci are contemporary with the cistern of late Flavian date. This leaves only the possiblities of a date in the third quarter of the first century or of a post-Flavian date. A date in the second century is unlikely for the second temple fill: the common Cypriote Sigillata 11, the most commonly found piece of fine ware in these loci, is probably representative of the earlier years of the series rather than the end, that is, A.D. 50-100 rather than A.D. 100-150. The kitchen wares do not appear to differ very much in date.

Most loci were associated with the construction of the second Temple of Apollo. The ceramic evidence from all contexts tends to suggest much activity here in roughly the third quarter of the first century A.D. Happily, this appears to be supported by the inscription that may date the dedication of the Temple to approximately A.D. 65.[6] It certainly appears, in any case, that the actual construction of the second Temple of Apollo is not too distant in time from that suggested date of A.D. 65.

SUMMARY

The majority of the finds from the soundings made against the southeast area of the Temple cannot be dated precisely, but they still are of interest in that a large number of them associated with the second temple can be dated to the first century A.D. Objects generally date in the first half of the century. There was, however, a decided lack of material from this area to date the first temple.

Several conclusions may be drawn from all this. Most of the fills would seem to have been put in for the second (possibly Neronian) temple. The fills would have replaced fills for the first temple, which must have been removed in this area to put in the stairs of the second temple. The latest finds that can be directly associated with the second temple are not earlier than circa A.D. 50.

The pottery connoisseur will be frustrated by the possibility of contamination and by the absence of solid floors, but the overwhelming presence of first-century material does allow one to hypothesize that some of the undated pot forms must date to that period. Future work can put this to the test.

ADDENDUM: MCFADDEN'S FINDS

The following is a list of additional finds from the temple area recorded by McFadden:

1. L283   Roman lamp (Fig. 173 and 174) of fabric 7/6 5YR reddish yellow and very poorly adherent red gloss. Discovered and noted by McFadden in his unpublished diary, p. 290. Decoration on molded bowl features figure with club driving off attacking dog. Perhaps Heracles and Cerberus. Voluted nozzle similar to Deneauve Italian type VA, early to middle first century A.D. Deneauve 1969 no. 411 has a similar Heracles but different subject. Found "east of Temple B A-b 2-4" on April 12, 1936. This is about 2 to 4 m east of the southeast corner of the temple, very near Jd 1 and 2. The object and its date fit well with material we recovered here, though no depth of find spot is given.

2. T1789   Small model (Fig. 175) of an offering table(?) in clay of uncertain fabric with red (stippled on drawing) and black painted decoration on the buff surface. Found by McFadden December 3, 1935, and noted in his diary, p. 61. It was found in loose soil over the temple steps. Perhaps part of a votive group.

3. ST444   Marble fragment of nose from statue (Fig. 176), found November 21, 1935, by McFadden just east of the mound of earth that would later yield the temple. The marble is not Cypriote and may be Cycladic. Diary, p. 19.

4. ST445   Marble fragment of right eye and forebrow (Fig. 177) of exceptional quality found by McFadden on November 25, 1935, just east of the temple in loose surface soil. Diary, p. 19.

5. I76   Marble inscription found in surface soil west of temple on April 20, 1936. Diary, p. 333. Published by Mitford 1971 (p. 328) and dated late first or early second century. Four other fragments were found scattered around the central court area of the site. Find spot H2-Ib ab-d10.

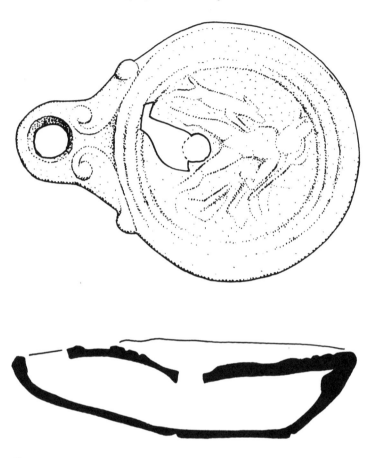

Figure 174. Lamp from McFadden Excavations. (L283)

6. 185   Fragment of inscribed marble plaque found on November 14, 1935, just west of the bottom of the steps of the temple. Diary, p. 19; Mitford 1971 (p. 345). Second century.

7. M138 Small bronze animal (Fig. 178; deer, bull, dog?) found in April of 1937 west of the temple at H-70-0, west 3.70. This is 3.70 m west of the rear northern corner of the temple. Found 30 cm below grass level.

Figure 175. Offering Table. (T1789)

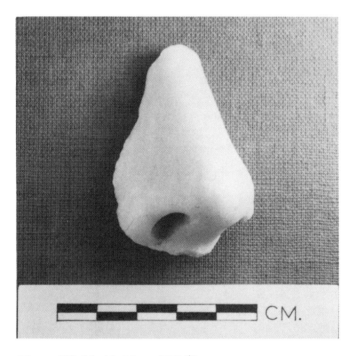

Figure 176. Marble Nose. (ST444)

Figure 177. Marble Eye and Brow. (ST445)

Figure 178. Small Bronze Animal. (M138)

Chapter 9
Roof Tiles
John Huffstot

When George McFadden focused his efforts on exposing the
architecture of the Sanctuary of Apollo, he published no studies of
the many roof tile fragments found. Some of the more complete ones
were cataloged, as were the few upon which he noticed inscriptions,
but most of the tile fragments were stacked neatly in the West
Enclosure. Two large stacks of tile fragments remain to this day
within this area, and additional heaps are scattered elsewhere
about the site. The modern surface is littered with fragments, too,
and it is impossible to say with certainty how much subsequent
removal or repositioning has occurred over the years. Lacking a
precise context, it nevertheless seems safe to assume that all of
the fragments recovered by the author from the various sources on
the site were, in fact, in use at the Apollo Sanctuary. This
surface material, taken together with the stratified tiles
recovered by the current excavations, now provides a clearer
picture of the types of roof tiles in use at the Apollo Sanctuary
from perhaps as early as the Archaic Period to the Sanctuary's
destruction in circa 365 A.D.

Briefly stated, the tiled roof elements at the Sanctuary, all of
fired clay, are most closely paralleled by the flat Corinthian
"pan" type. However, they are not as simple, and occur in at least
three styles. No curvilinear Laconian-type pan tiles have been
identified.[1] Extensive water conduit systems were installed during
the Roman period, incorporating tubular segments of terra cotta.
Small fragments of these water pipes sometimes resemble roof tiles,
but there is little chance of confusion because the water pipes
have been encountered almost exclusively *in situ*. The covering
tiles that protected the side edges between the pans are varied; no
fewer than twenty-six types have been identified, most of them
pentagonal (an angular peak supported by vertical or nearly
vertical walls).[2]

263

Fragments of some rather large cover tiles, perhaps intended for installation above the ridge pole, have been found, but other tiles with specialized purposes, such as eaves tiles, antefixes, simas, and proper two-way peak tiles, have not been identified at the Sanctuary. One might expect that attractive elements such as antefixes and simas might have been removed over the years by souvenir hunters, but their absence more probably indicates that the provincial architecture at the Sanctuary lacked such features altogether. Projections on one corner cornice block from the Temple of Apollo and a flattened platform at the peak of the pedimental block suggest that acroteria once decorated the building.

The principles of tiled roof construction at the Apollo Sanctuary were the same as those found elsewhere in the ancient Greek and Roman world, and are still widely practiced to this day. A course of flat (pan) tiles, each with up-turned side edges, is placed side by side along the bottom edge (eave) of the roof. At the eave itself, the tiles presumably are laid directly onto the cornice stones. Proceeding up the roof, the tiles are set either directly onto the timber elements of the roof structure or upon a setting bed, which may include clay, rushes, and one or more layers of light sheathing boards.[3] Another course is then laid, and another, and so on up to the peak, each course overlapping the top edges of the tiles in the course below. The seam between the up-turned side edges is then protected by narrow cover tiles mortared into place, once again beginning at the eaves and proceeding up to the peak, each tile overlapping the upper end of the tile immediately below. The peak of the roof must be covered with specialized two-way tiles, which constitute the uppermost course on each side of the roof and which must conform as well as possible to the pitch of the roof, that is, to the angle formed at the top of the pediment. One could also use a number of the cover tiles to protect the sides of the pan tiles, if the peak tiles were not available. The larger these tiles, or the wider their "splay," the easier this task would be. The fragments numbered 35, 45, 46, 47, and 48 in the catalog that concludes this chapter may have served in this capacity. If the architects at the Sanctuary cared little enough to provide such visible embellishments as antefixes and simas, they may have cared equally as little about a perfect roof peak; if so, they were probably content with a functional (if not beautiful) peak, finished off with regular or oversized "common" cover tiles.

The architects at the Sanctuary adopted a design for the pan tile--types X and Y in particular (Fig. 179 and 180)--that was actually somewhat more complicated than necessary. The pan tiles were provided with a lip on the underside at the bottom edge which was meant to hook over a ridge on the upper side at the top of the pan tile immediately below. This feature must have been perceived as providing a more weather-proof seal than simpler pan tiles, and perhaps it did, although a bit of mortar in the same position would probably have achieved the same result. Considering the extra work

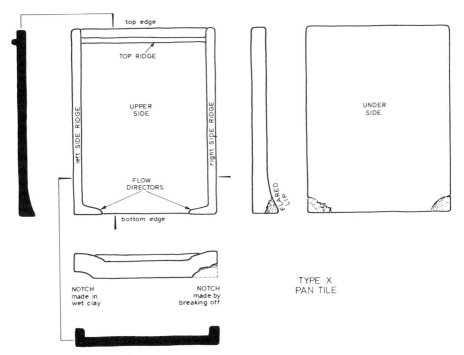

Figure 179. Type X Pan Tyle.

called for by the tile mason in trimming the lip at the sides of
the tile in order to fit it between the side ridges of the tile
beneath, the whole scheme could hardly have been worth the effort.
The superiority of a simpler design seems to have finally become
apparent by the first century A.D., when a flat-bottomed pan tile
comes into use.

On the basis of stratigraphic evidence, two similar pan tile
designs may have been in use at least as early as the first century
A.D. and may have continued in use until the final earthquake in
365 A.D. These are types "X" and "Y" in the catalog. The few tiles
preserving their original dimensions show that the type X pans
ranged from 51 by 61 cm to 54 by 59 cm, and were approximately 2 cm
thick. No complete type Y tiles have survived. In both types the
lateral edges on the upperside of the pan are built up to form
thick ridges approximately 2 to 2.5 cm high and 3 cm wide. These
side ridges run the full length of the tile from the top (up-slope)
edge to the bottom (down-slope) edge. On the upperside of the pan,
at 2 to 2.5 cm from the top edge, is an additional ridge, 1.5 to 2
cm high and 2 cm wide, running parallel to the top edge of the tile
and abutting the taller and thicker side ridges. Still on the upper

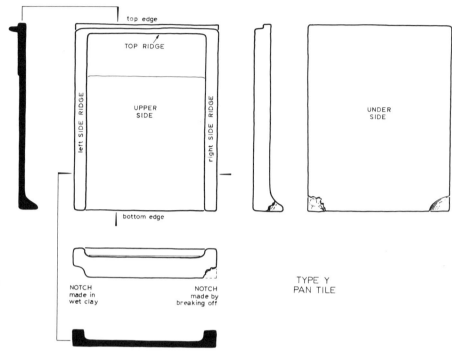

Figure 180. Type Y Pan Tile.

side of the tile, but at the bottom (down-slope) end, the side ridges turn the 90-degree corner and run an additional 4 to 10 cm until they taper off into the upper pan surface, sometimes in triangular wedges and sometimes abruptly. These short elements would direct the rain run-off generally toward the centerline of the tile and are henceforth referred to as "flow directors." On the underside of the tile, at the bottom end, is a tapering flared lip, 3 to 4 cm in the vertical dimension at the extreme bottom edge. As evidenced by traces of mortar preserved on many of the fragments, this flared lip was hooked over (positioned just down-slope of) the top ridge on the tile in the course immediately below.

In order to hook the flared lip of the upper tile down over the ridge on the surface of the lower tile, the flared lip of the upper tile had to be removed at each lateral end so as not to rest upon the raised side ridges of the tile in the course below. There are tile fragments that do not have the sockets necessary for this, and it may be surmised that these particular tiles were installed at the eave or in some other special configuration. Most of the tiles had some type of "cut-away" corner at the lateral ends of the flared lip, which was executed while the clay was still wet. However, it appears that these sockets were seldom large enough to

actually function properly, and it is very common to find tile
fragments which have both pre-formed sockets and additional
knocking and trimming performed during installation. This trimming
was achieved with one or two sharp blows from a striking
instrument. One tile fragment, No. X61 (Fig. 181), exhibits
parallel grooving along what would otherwise be the broken edge of
the tile. These are possibly the marks left behind by a trimming
device as the tile was shaped crudely to fit into a peculiar
position after it was fired.

Type X pan tiles occasionally are inscribed on the upper surface
with groups of Greek letters or are otherwise marked with what
should be interpreted as decoration or code indicating the
workshop, or perhaps a particular destination of use. The tiles
were inscribed by drawing a fingernail or similar instrument
through the clay. Two fragments, numbers X64 (Fig. 182) and X67
(Fig. 183), are inscribed with an upper case Δ (upside down if
viewed in the position as installed), followed by a short vertical
stroke which may represent another letter, but which is not in
keeping with the character of the Δ. Another fragment, number X66
(Fig. 184), is inscribed with an upper case Δ (rightside up),
followed by a vertical stroke which may or may not be an incomplete
letter, the tile being broken away at this point. X65 is inscribed
with what appears to be an upper case Φ (perhaps followed by a
dot); the letter unfortunately is incomplete as a result of
breakage of the tile. Fragment X62 has a row of thirteen
(preserved) nicks, each about 3 cm long, aligned in parallel 5 cm
from the bottom edge. Fragment X63 has a wavy line drawn with two
fingertips running down the centerline of the tile. Judging from
the casual application of mortar to the *exterior* of the cover tiles
(see below), the builders demonstrate a pronounced lack of
aesthetic regard for a tidy appearance to the final roof, and a
surprisingly unpolished quality must have prevailed.

The type Y pan tile is far less frequent than the type X, even
though the stratigraphic evidence suggests that similar types
existed as early as the first century A.D. and were certainly in
use as late as 365 A.D. Type Y is fundamentally the same as type X,
but with several differences that may reflect the efforts of a
different workshop. No complete examples of type Y tile have
survived, but it is possible to reconstruct its form from
fragments.

Type Y tile has no flow directors. The juncture of the side
ridge and the flat pan surface is rounded on type Y, whereas that
on type X is roughly right-angled. The flared lip on the underside
of type Y is steeper and slightly larger than that on type X. The
top ridge of type Y is the same height as the side ridges, unlike
that of type X, which is lower. On type Y the side ridges do not
extend all the way to the top edge, but turn to become the top
ridge. An unusual feature of type Y tile (demonstrated in only one
fragment) is a shallow (2-3 mm) step that appears to run from side
to side on the upper surface, 15 cm from the extreme top edge.

Perhaps this feature is an indexing mark to guide the tile mason in the placement of cover tiles during installation. No type Y tiles have been found bearing the fingered decoration or inscriptions found on type X tiles.

By circa 65 A.D. another type of pan tile appears at the sanctuary. The type Z tile (Fig. 185) represents a marked departure from the established forms in use. The one complete type Z tile that survives (No. Z95; Fig. 186 and 187) is 47 by 57 cm, smaller than the preceding X and Y types. The underside is flat, lacking the flared lip characteristic of the X and Y types. As a result type Z tile could probably be installed considerably faster, since the bottom edge of one tile would simply overlap a bit and rest on the top ridge of the tile below, with no need for trimming or fitting. The upper side is simplified as well. The flow directors, side ridges, and top ridge are all formed by a single, continuous ridge, lying flush with the edge of the tile and of uniform height (2-3 cm) and width (2-3 cm). The flow directors usually terminate more abruptly than on type X tile.

Aside from the different design, the type Z pan tile is further differentiated from the X and Y tiles by the more profuse embellishment of features drawn by the manufacturer into the wet clay using fingertips and pointed instruments. The underside of the type Z tile usually has a large "X" that connects the opposing corners; these "X"s may be stroked with one, two, three, or four fingertips. This feature might be interpreted as a notation of the "batch" of manufacture or use. One group of type Z tiles distinguished by a number of common characteristics (catalog 295-97) also has the word OΔONTY inscribed on the underside at the bottom edge. Probably Οδοντῦ is a late genitive treatment of a proper name, perhaps Οδοντῦσ,a hypocoristic name, typically ending in ῦσ derived from Οδοῦσ, "tooth." No such name is attested in Bechtel,[4] but G. Neumann discusses the occurrence of such hypocoristic names on Cyprus in pre-Roman times and even has an example from Kourion.[5] If we can compare the fingered letter forms on our tiles to papyrus writing in Egypt (manners of writing characterized by similar flexibility and spontaneity and which could be expected to produce similar letter forms), the closest parallels for our Delta, the two-stroke Upsilon, and perhaps the Pi (on the upper side), suggest a third-century date.[6] The presence at Kourion of a tilemaker called "Toothy" (whose name probably was derived from an obvious physical feature) sometime during imperial times, therefore, seems quite likely. If these tiles are "from the workshop of Toothy," it would be the first atelier identified in this area during this period.

On the upper side of the type Z tile, arcs (as in the case of 295) are stroked into wet clay to enclose the flow directors in the bottom corners; again, arcs may be drawn by one, two, three, or four fingertips. As these marks are on the upper (visible) side (see Fig. 186), it is tempting to interpret them as decoration, but the question is just how visible they would have been. They

Figure 181. Tile Fragment. (X61)

Figure 182. Tile Fragment. (X62)

Figure 183. Tile Fragment. (X67)

Figure 184. Tile Fragment. (X66)

probably should be viewed as having a utilitarian, coding purpose.
In addition, letter groups are often incised on the upper side
(Fig. 188,189). One group is inscribed φι within the arc in
the lower left corner (2102, 2103). The group with the ΟΔΟΝΤΥ
inscription on the underside also carries the inscription θπ in
upper case Greek letters arranged vertically in a column between
the arcs; another group is more difficult to interpret, but appears
to be ου in lower case Greek letters arranged in column (Fig. 190,
and 191; note cover tile number 35 for a similar inscription). The
"Omicron Upsilon" interpretation of this inscription is suggested
by the fact that all other inscriptions on tiles at the Sanctuary
are Greek. However, the possibility that the inscription could be
"CO" in Latin should not be excluded. The interpretation of this
inscription is addressed in greater depth in the catalog that
concludes this chapter.

The type Z tile fragments (numbers Z102, Z105 and Z106) are
decorated (?) with a wavy line drawn down the center of the tile
with two fingertips in the same fashion as on type X tile number
X63. Fragments of type Z tiles are common throughout the site, but
not so common as type X.

The cover tiles from the sanctuary present a multitude of styles
(Fig. 192 and 193). All appear to be manufactured upside-down in a
trough. Depending upon how much clay was molded into the trough and
how uniformly it was spread out by the tilemaker, a great deal of
variation in the thickness and internal shape can result.
Consequently, these characteristics are not taken as distinguishing
different types of cover tiles. The shape of the trough--that is,
the dimensions of the elements constituting the trough and the
angles formed by their arrangement--are the factors that determined
the exterior dimensions and configuration of the finished tile, and
these are the criteria used to identify the different types.

The twenty-six types of cover tile identified fall into four
general categories, each with variation of its own:

1. Pentagonal tiles with sloping surfaces meeting in an angular
   peak, supported by straight, vertical or nearly vertical walls.
   Included in this category are types C-1, C-2, C-3, C-4, C-5,
   C-6, C-7, C-8, C-9, C-10, C-11, C-15, C-17, C-22, C-23, and
   C-24.

2. Triangular tiles with sloping surfaces meeting in an angular
   peak, but without supporting walls. Included in this category
   are types C-12, C-13, C-21, and C-26.

3. A round "vault" or curvilinear design. Included in this category
   are types C-14, C-16, and C-25.

4. Oversized tiles similar to category 1. Included in this category
   are types C-18, C-19, and C-20.

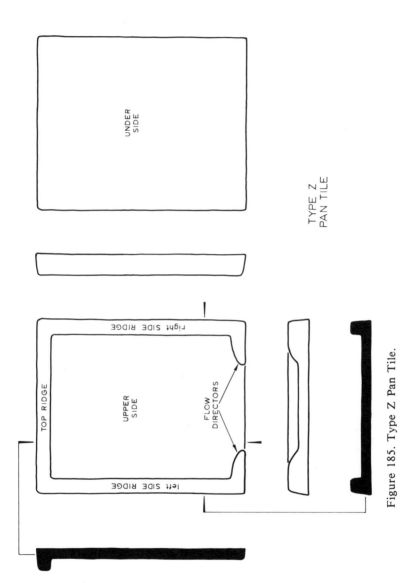

Figure 185. Type Z Pan Tile.

Figure 186. Type Z Pan Tile. (Z95)

Figure 187. Type Z Pan Tile. (Z95)

Figure 188. Type Z Pan Tile. (Z102)

Figure 189. Type Z Pan Tile. (Z103)

Figure 190. Cover Tile. (35)

Most of the types at the Sanctuary are of the first category, and
the type C-1 fragment is the most abundant cover tile at the site.
The only complete cover tile, number 20 (see Fig. 193), displays
the general design features of a typical cover tile. It is 58.6 cm
long, roughly the same length as the type X pan tile with which it
presumably functioned. Between 6.2 and 10 cm (depending upon the
individual type) from one end is an abrupt ridge or step on the
exterior surface, where the tile grows in height and width anywhere
from 1 to 6 mm. Though often negligible in size, this ridge is
always easy to see. This end, henceforth referred to as the
"designated end," is consequently slightly smaller in overall
height and width than either the other (non-designated) end or any
other point along the tile where a section is measured side to
side. The immediate conjecture is that this smaller designated end
was meant to nestle within and under the interior of the cover tile
immediately above, but in practice this simply did not work.
Because the interior is narrower and shaped differently, a tight
fit was never possible. At best, the upper cover tile rested upon
the top surfaces of the lower tile (if it touched at all). The
cover tiles probably were positioned on the roof with the
designated end at the top, the designating ridge serving only as a
rough guide mark for indexing the next cover tile into place, a
task which could probably be accomplished just as easily without
any such guiding marks at all. The length of the designated end

Figure 191. Type Z Pan Tile. (Z99)

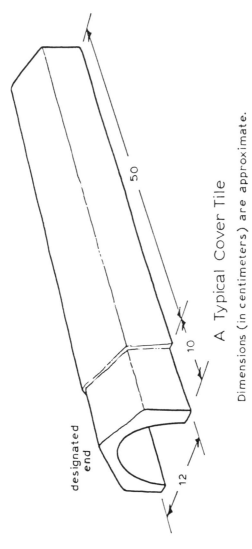

designated
end

50

10

12

A Typical Cover Tile

Dimensions (in centimeters) are approximate.

Figure 192. Cover Tile.

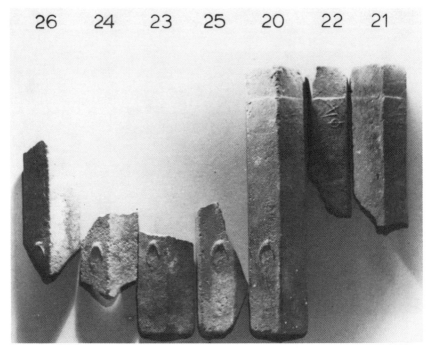

Figure 193. C-4 Type Cover Tiles.

corresponds roughly to the amount of overlap in the pan tiles, so
that perhaps this was the reason it was done in this way.

The cover tiles were secured in place with lime mortar in a
matrix of tiny blue pebbles. Some fragments of cover tiles have
preserved mortar on the inside (underside) of the tile, but
tell-tale traces on the exteriors of cover tiles, combined with the
position of mortar preserved on many pan tiles, testifies to the
fact that the cover tiles were often, if not usually, mortared
along the exterior of the cover tile; the morter then would have
been exposed to the elements and perfectly visible. This would seem
to be both impractical and an aesthetic nuisance, yet the evidence
is clear and implies either poor joining work and planning, or
repair. In some instances traces of mortar survive on the surfaces
of pan tiles in a line just below the top ridge, at the joint
between the pan and the bottom edge of the tile above. Considering
the frequency of earthquakes on Cyprus in antiquity, as well as
today, large scale consolidation of partially damaged structures
may have been undertaken, perhaps more than once. Cypriote Roman
architecture also is noted for reusing and recycling materials.

Of the twenty-six types of cover tiles identified at the site, nineteen are represented by only a single specimen, which might suggest additions on a rather small scale to existing structures or isolated repairs to damaged roofs.

The three examples in the fourth category (types C-18, C-19 and C-20), though incomplete in section, are all from tiles that clearly were considerably larger than the other typical tiles. As suggested earlier, these tiles could have been used to bridge the peak of a roof. Numbers 35 and 48 are splayed widely enough that they also could have served this function without difficulty.

Graffiti appears on cover tiles of two types. Tile number 35 (see Fig. 190), the only example of type C-10, is incised within the designated end with letters that may be interpreted as "CO" (may be incomplete) in Latin or ου in lower case Greek. The same inscription occurs on pan tiles number Z98 and Z99. Three examples of type C-4, numbers 20, 21, and 22, bear the inscription ΦΔ close to the designated end and in identical relief letters (see detail of number 22, Fig. 194). All seven of the type C-4 examples seem to be the product of one workshop and a single mold. In addition to the ΦΔ inscription on tile number 20 (the complete tile), there is a large crescent or oval shaped flaw (?) 18 cm from the non-designated end. The remaining four fragmentary type C-4 (numbers 23, 24, 25, and 26) exhibit the identical flaw. All of the inscribed cover tiles are surface finds, and so are not datable.

Type C-1 cover tiles have been recovered from strata of early dates and from debris of the earthquake of ca. 365 A.D., indicating a long-lived tradition. Of the other types, almost all examples were recovered on the surface or within contexts that are not securely datable. The only exception is tile number 47 (type C-20-one of the oversized fragments), which comes from a locus perhaps deposited in the sixth century B.C.

Included at the end of the following catalog are three fragments of what appear to be tiles of aberrant design. We should not exclude the possibility that they could belong, instead, to some of the votive terra cotta groups that are so plentiful at the Sanctuary. If they are in fact from such figures, the scale would surely be larger than most, but still well within the range of those excavated.

Cover Tiles

In the catalog of cover tiles, the first dimension is the preserved length of the fragment, the dimension in parentheses is the length of the designated end, when preserved, and the fabric is a local reddish gritty mix known as 1A, unless otherwise described.

Throughout the catalog, tile fragments that contain "west enclosure surf" in the registration number are from McFadden's stacks of fragments in the west enclosure area.

Figure 194. Cover Tile (22)

TYPE C-1

1.   K80-0m4-007-2262 (Fig. 195a). Preserved length 47 cm, designated end (10 cm). This locus is datable to ca. 365 A.D. or earlier.

2.   K78-Km2-013-1495. P.L. 20 cm.

3.   K80-Hg3-007-1926a. Basket #46. P.L. 17 cm, neither end is preserved.

4.   K80-Hg3-017-1943b. P.L. 14 cm, neither end is preserved. This locus is datable to the early first century A.D. or earlier.

5.   K80-Hg3-020-1932. P.L. 11 cm, neither end is preserved. This locus is datable to the early first century A.D. or earlier.

6.   K78-Hh4-005-1180. P.L. 13.5 cm, neither end is preserved.

7.   K80-Hh3-003-2345. P.L. 8 cm, neither end is preserved. This locus indicates a date of ca. sixth century B.C., with some possibly later.

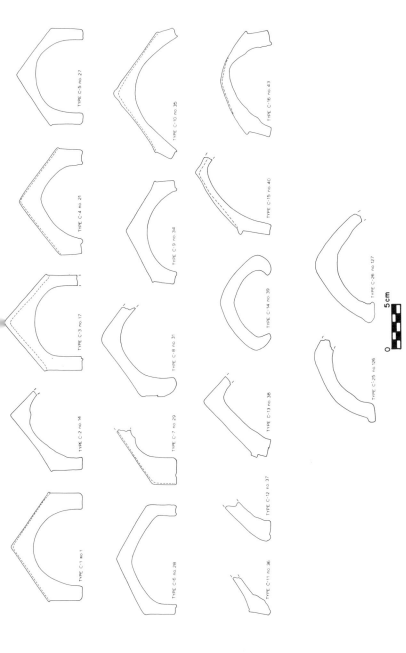

Figure 195. Cover Tiles C-1 to C-16, C-25, C-26.

8.   K80-Gh2/Gg4-046-2335. P.L. 13.5 cm, neither end is preserved. This locus is first century A.D. with earlier material.

9.   K80-Gh2/Gg4-034-2333. P.L. 9 cm, neither end is preserved. This locus is first century A.D. with earlier material.

10.   K80-Gh3-008-1084. P.L. 9 cm, neither end is preserved.

TYPE C-2

11.   K80-Ic-surf-2311. Thirteen joining fragments comprise 50 cm of the tile, providing a complete section. Neither end is preserved. Found in surface cleaning 2.5 m west of the Temple of Apollo.

12.   K80-Om4-007-2307. P.L. 31.5 cm, includes the designated end (10 cm). Locus datable to ca. 365 A.D.

13.   K80-Om4-005-2265. P.L. 16.5 cm, includes the designated end (10 cm). Locus datable to ca. 365 A.D.

14.   K80-Om4-007-2264 (Fig. 195b). P.L. 13.5 cm, neither end is preserved. This locus is datable to ca. 365 A.D. Section is illustrated.

15.   K80-McF. 1509-2376. P.L. 19.5 cm, included the nondesignated end.

TYPE C-3

16.   K80-Ib-surf north of Temple-2288. P.L. 12 cm, includes 1.5 cm of the designated end, but not the very end.

17.   K80-surf, Peribolos wall-2231 a & b (Fig. 195c). Two joining fragments comprise 14.6 cm of the tile, including the designated end (8.5 cm).

18.   K80-Gh2/Gg4-034-2334. P.L. 11.1 cm, neither end is preserved. Locus is first century A.D. with earlier material.

19.   K81-Fg-007-2533. 8.5 cm, neither end is preserved. This locus is datable to not later than the later first century A.D.

TYPE C-4

All of the type C-4 tiles in the catalogue were manufactured in the same mold.

20.   K80-surf-2228. This is the only intact cover tile and the only complete cover tile from the site; found in 1980 in the

storeroom built into the southeast corner of the South Building. The original find spot is not known. P.L. 56.8 cm, designated end (7 cm). On the right sloping surface, just beyond the designated end, is an inscription ΦΔ in relief. On the left sloping surface, 18 cm from the non-designated end, is a large crescent or oval-shaped mark, also in relief.

21. K80-surf-2273 (Fig. 195d). P.L. 35 cm, includes the designated end (7 cm) and the inscription. This, and all of the remaining Type C-4 tile were located by the author in a stack of tiles at the southeast corner of the Palaestra.

22. K80-surf-2272 (see Fig. 194). P.L. 32.5 cm, includes the designated end (7 cm) and the inscription.

23. K80-surf-2269. P.L. 22 cm, includes the non-designated end and the flaw.

24. K80-surf-2263. P.L. 19 cm, includes the flaw, but neither end is preserved.

25. K80-surf-2270. P.L. 28.7 cm, includes the non-designated end and the flaw.

26. K80-surf-2268. P.L. 29.5 cm, includes the flaw, but neither end is preserved.

TYPE C-5

27. K80-McF. tray #1645-3 -2258 (Fig. 195e). P.L. 28.5 cm, includes the non-designated end. Located in the eastern storeroom behind the Museum/dig house in Episkopi in a tray marked "1645 (3)," and assigned our number 2258 in the register.

TYPE C-6

28. K78-Km2-001/002-1425 (Fig. 195f). P.L. 30.3 cm, includes the non-designated end.

TYPE C-7

29. K80-Gj/Fj-surf-2018 (Fig. 195g). P.L. 18.3 cm, includes the designated end.

TYPE C-8

30. K80-Hg3 ext.-017-1943a. P.L. 13.2 cm, neither end is preserved.

31. K80-Ib-surf north of Temple-2233 (Fig. 195h). P.L. 24 cm, neither end is preserved.

TYPE C-9

32. K80-McF. tray #1267-2260. P.L. 30 cm, neither end is preserved. Located in the eastern storeroom behind the Museum/dig house in Episkopi in a tray marked "1267," and assigned number 2260 in the register.

33. K80-west enclosure surf-2237. P.L. 21 cm, neither end is preserved.

34. K80-surf-2275 (Fig. 195i). P.L. 31.4 cm, neither end is preserved, fabric 40.

TYPE C-10

35. K80-surf-2271 (Fig. 195j). P.L. 26 cm, includes the designated end (6.7 cm). Tile is inscribed within the designated end, either "CO" in line or "OU" in column. The characters were inscribed into the wet clay with an instrument. The inscription may be incomplete, as the tile is broken away at the inscription (note pan tile fragments nos. Z98 and Z99 for a similar inscription).

TYPE C-11

36. K78-Jd 1 ext-009-619 (Fig. 195k). P.L. 8.4 cm, neither end is preserved; context is first century or earlier. Section is illustrated.

TYPE C-12

37. K80-west enclosure surf-2236 (Fig. 195l). P.L. 8.2 cm, neither end is preserved.

TYPE C-13

38. K80-surf-2274 (Fig. 195m). P.L. 28.8 cm, neither end is preserved, fabric 1 A but with larger than usual inclusions.

TYPE C-14

39. K80-Hg3 ext-surf-2230 (Fig. 195n). P.L. 13.8 cm, includes the non-designated end. The trench Hg3 extension was excavated during the 1978 season. The author picked this tile fragment up from the "surface" of the bottom of the trench in 1980 after the winter rains.

TYPE C-15

40.   K78-Km2-001/002-1424 (Fig. 195o). P.L. 18.7 cm, includes the designated end (7 cm). From cistern.

TYPE C-16

41.   K80-Ii-005-2235. P.L. 13.3 cm, includes the designated end (8 cm). This locus is datable to the first century A.D. with some earlier intrusion.

42.   K80-Ii-005-2287. P.L. 10.5 cm, includes 3 cm of the designated end, but not the very end. This locus is datable to the first century A.D. as above.

43.   K80-Ii-005-2234 (Fig. 195p). P.L. 18.8 cm, includes 5 cm of the designated end, but not the very end. This locus is datable to the first century A.D. as above.

TYPE C-17

44.   K80-Ic-surf-2312 a & b (Fig. 196a). Two joining fragments comprise 28.5 cm, including the designated end (8.3 cm). From beneath a tumbled cornice block, Temple quake fall, west of the Temple of Apollo.

TYPE C-18

45.   K80-Hh3-003-2343 (Fig. 196b). P.L. 16.5 cm, neither end is preserved. The section is incomplete, but it is evident that this was an unusually large tile. Context is sixth century B.C. with possible later material.

TYPE C-19

46.   K80-Gh2/Gg4-034-2322 (Fig. 196c). P.L. 9 cm, neither end is preserved. The section is incomplete, but this, too, was a large tile. First century A.D. and earlier.

TYPE C-20

47.   K80-Gh3-012-2373 (Fig. 196d). P.L. 11 cm, neither end is preserved. This fragment is very poorly preserved, but would seem to be from the thickest, most massive, and possibly the largest cover tile yet found at the Sanctuary. This locus indicates a date of the sixth century B.C.

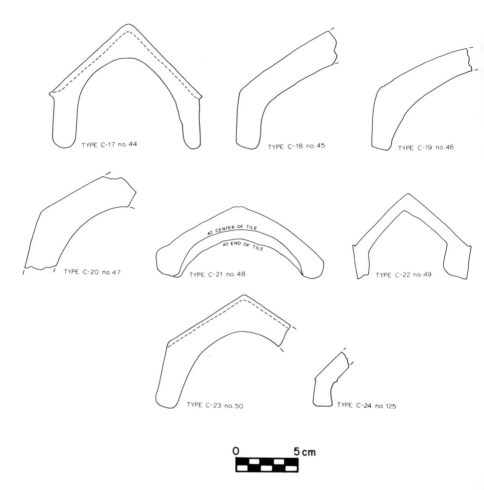

Figure 196. Cover Tiles C-17 to C-24.

TYPE C-21

48.   K81-Jc-surf-2645 (Fig. 196e). P.L. 19.5 cm, includes the non-designated end, fabric 42. Surface cleaned by the author, 3 m east of the Temple of Apollo.

TYPE C-22

49.   K81-Fg-007-2504 a through d (Fig. 196f). Four joining
        fragments comprise 14 cm, neither end is preserved, but the
        section is complete, fabric 7 B. The tile has a curious
        in-turned shape. This locus indicates a date of ca. 65 A.D. or
        earlier.

TYPE C-23

50.   K81-Nr-surf-2721 (Fig. 196g). P.L. 22 cm, includes the
        designated end (6.2 cm).

TYPE C-24

125.   K78-Jd1 & 2 -002-198 (Fig. 196h). P.L. 9 cm, neither end is
        preserved. This locus has material of the second century A.D.
        and earlier.

TYPE C-25

126.   UAK84-Apollo-surf-268 (Fig. 196q). P.L. 17 cm, includes the
        non-designated end.

TYPE C-26

127.   UAK84-Apollo-surf-269 (Fig. 195r). P.L. 31 cm, neither end is
        preserved.

PAN TILES

In the catalog of pan tiles the following conventions are
followed:

Terms such as "lower right, upper left," etc. are determined by
orienting the flat pan tile as it would have been installed on the
roof, with the upper side up, and the bottom edge (the edge with
the flared lip and flow directors) down.

"Corners notched" means that the lateral ends of the flared lip
may have been removed during manufacture (while the clay was wet),
in order to facilitate installing the tile over the tile coursed
below. "Corners knocked" means that the tile was made without this
provision, and that the corner was removed by striking it after the
tile was fired, presumably during installation.

Fabric is 1 A unless otherwise described.

For ease of recognition, an "X" precedes the catalog number of type X pan tiles, a "Y" precedes the catalog number of type Y pan tiles, and a "Z" precedes the catalog number of type Z pan tiles.

TYPE X

General Characteristics: The top ridge is lower than the side ridges; the tiles have flow directors at the bottom corners; the angle formed at the juncture of the side ridges and the flat pan surface is generally squared off; the flared lip (on the underside, bottom edge) is more gradual than the flared lip on the type Y tile; the side ridges extend all the way to the top edge.

X 51.   K79-D1-004-basket 7-1919. Fifteen joining fragments comprise most of the tile. Both finished dimensions are preserved, 54 x 59 cm. The lower right corner is notched *and* knocked. This is an unusual variety of type X pan tile with a very small (almost nonexistant) flow director. The lower left corner is not preserved. This locus is datable to ca. 365 A.D.

X 52.   K80-Om4-007-2306 a through i. Nine joining fragments comprise most of the tile. Both finished dimensions are preserved, 51.4 x 62 cm. The lower right corner is knocked. The lower left corner is not preserved. Flow director as tile no. X 51. There is much mortar preserved along the interior of the left side ridge. This locus is datable to ca. 365 A.D.

X 53.   K78-Hh4-019-796. Lower right corner and 13.2 cm of the bottom edge. This tile has a variation of the notched corner, which is smaller than usual. The flow director also is small, extending only ca. 3 cm toward the center of the tile.

X 54.   K80-west enclosure surf-2245. Lower right corner and 14 cm of the side ridge. This tile has a small flow director similar to tile no. X 53. The corner notching on this tile is unusual also. The notch is small, decidedly squarish, and very carefully made.

X 55.   K80-west enclosure surf-2246. Lower left corner and 21.5 cm of the side ridge. This tile is identical to tile no. X 54, except that the corner has also been knocked off a bit.

X 56.   K80-Gj/Fj-surf-2020. Lower left corner and 17.5 cm of the side ridge. Similar to tile no. X 55, corner notched *and* knocked. The fabric is 1 A, but with larger than usual inclusions.

X 57.   K80-west enclosure surf-2253. Top corner and 11.5 cm of the top edge. Same fabric as tile no. X 56.

X 58.   K80-west enclosure surf-2248. P.L. 29 cm of a side ridge.

X 59.   K80-Hg3-017-basket 58-1943. P.L. 13.2 cm of the top edge and ridge. This locus is datable to the later first century A.D. or earlier.

X 60.   K80-Hg3-007-basket 46-1926. P.L. 11 cm of bottom edge (flared lip).

X 61.   K80-west enclosure surf-2250. P.L. 4 cm of a side ridge. This fragment is notable for traces of tool marks(?), perhaps made while trimming the tile during installation(?). This is one of only three tile fragments discovered by the author to exhibit this feature.

X 62.   K80-Om4-007-2267. P.L. 26 cm of bottom edge (flared lip). The fragment has row of nicks (decoration?) running parallel to the bottom edge on the upper surface. This locus is datable to ca. 365 A.D.

X 63.   K80-west enclosure surf-2238. Bottom right corner and 37.5 cm of the bottom edge. Wavy line drawn with two fingertips down the centerline of the tile on the upper side (note tile fragments Z102, Z105, and Z106 for similar line).

X 64.   K80-McF. St. 9 -2308 a through l. Twelve joining fragments comprise most of the lower portion of the tile; the maximum preserved width (incomplete) is 49.5 cm. The corners are notched and knocked. The tile is inscribed on the upper side, ∇ or ∇I . This tile was registered by McFadden as "St. 9," and according to his notes was from " . . . room NE of altar 2".

X 65.   K80-west enclosure surf-2240. P.L. 11 cm of bottom edge (flared lip). The fragment is inscribed on the upper side with a partial Φ(?), followed by a dot(?). The tile is broken away through the inscription.

X 66.   K80-Om4-003-2257. Lower left corner and 25.5 cm of the bottom edge. The fragment is inscribed on the upper side Δ or ΔI . This locus is datable to ca. 365 A.D.

X 67.   K80-Om4-003-2261. P.L. 23.5 cm of the bottom edge (flared lip). The fragment is inscribed on the upper side VI . This locus is datable to ca. 365 A.D.

X 68.   K80-McF. St. 14 -2309 a through i. Nine joining fragments comprise most of the tile, including both finished dimensions, 51 x 61 cm. The corners are notched and knocked. This tile was registered by McFadden as "St. 14".

X 69.   K80-Om4-003-2305 a & b. Two joining fragments comprise the lower portion of the tile. The entire bottom edge is preserved, with a finished dimension (width) of 51 cm. The side edges are preserved for 25 cm. This locus is datable to ca. 365 A.D.

X 70.   K78-Hh4-005-1181. P.L. 7 cm of the bottom edge (flared lip). This locus is datable to not later than the early first century A.D.

X 71.   K78-Hh4-019-795. Top left corner and 8.5 cm of the left side. This tile exhibits a variation in the tip ridge, which slopes down to meet the flat pan surface ca. 5 cm from the side ridge. It is finished this way, not broken off.

X 72.   K78-Km2-001/002-1416. Top left corner and 22 cm of the left side.

X 73.   K78-Hh4-005-1179. P.L. 8 cm of the top edge and ridge.

X 74.   K78-Hh4-005-1178. P.L. 11 cm of the top edge and ridge.

X 75.   K78-Hh4-005-1181. P.L. 6.5 cm of the bottom edge (flared lip).

X 76.   K78-Hh4-005-1182. P.L. 7.8 cm of the side ridge.

X 77.   K80-Hh3-003-2344. P.L. 8.5 cm of the bottom edge (flared lip). Dark red 1 A fabric. This locus is datable to the sixth century B.C. with some possibly later material.

X 78.   K80-Gh2/Gg4-034/2 -2336. P.L. 17 cm of the side ridge. This locus datable to first century A.D. with earlier material.

X 79.   K80-Gh2/Gg4-034-2320. Top left corner and 18.5 cm of the left side. This locus is datable to first century A.D. with earlier material.

X 80.   K81-Fg-08-2651. Lower left corner and 11 cm of the left side. This tile is similar to X 53, with the same type of corner notching and small flow director. This locus is

datable to not later than ca. 100 A.D. (and probably not
later than ca. 65 A.D.) with some earlier material.

X 81. K80-Id-008-1987. P.L. 6.5 cm maximum preserved dimensions
(mpd). It is difficult to say with certainty what this poorly
preserved fragment is, but it is probably a bottom right
corner. It is included in the catalog because of its unusual
fabric, 7 B. This locus is datable to ca. 65 A.D. with some
earlier material.

X 82. K81-Hc ext-003-2556. P.L. 8 cm of the bottom edge (flared
lip). The fabric is orange 1 A. Locus datable as the previous
entry.

X 83. K81-Hc ext-002-2555. Top right corner and 10 cm of the
right side. The fabric is orange 1 A. Locus datable as the
previous entry.

X 84. K81-Gg4-107-2552. P.L. 8 cm of the side ridge. This locus is
datable to the sixth century B.C. with some possibly later
material.

TYPE Y

General characteristics: the top ridge is the same height as the
side ridges; the tiles do not have flow directors; the angle formed
at the juncture of the side ridges and the flat pan surface is
rounded; the flared lip (on the underside, bottom edge) is steeper
and more pronounced than the flared lip on the type X tile; the
side ridges do not extend all the way to the top edge; the flat pan
surface has a shallow "step" running from side to side on the upper
surface, 15 cm from the extreme top edge. (This feature is
observed on only one fragment).

Y 85. K80-west enclosure surf-2255. Lower right corner and 28 cm
of the right side. The corner is knocked.

Y 86. K80-west enclosure surf-2244. Lower left corner and 17.6 cm
of the bottom edge. The end of the flared lip has no notch
at all.

Y 87. K80-Ii-002-2232. Upper left corner and 13.5 cm of the top
edge and ridge. This locus contains first century A.D. and
earlier material.

Y 88. K80-west enclosure surf-2252. Upper right corner and top
edge, the flat pan surface preserves 24.5 cm of width (mpd).
This fragment exhibits a step (2-3 mm high) running from
side to side, 15 cm from the top edge.

Y 89.   K80-west enclosure surf-2350. Lower left corner and 11 cm of the bottom edge, corner notched.

Y 90.   K80-Gh2/Gg4-034-2321. P.L. 7 cm of the top edge and ridge. First century A.D. and earlier.

Y 91.   K80-Hh3-003-2346. Upper right corner and 10 cm of the top ridge. This tile is a variant of the normal type Y tile. The side ridge continues all the way to the top edge of the tile, but because the top ridge is the same height as the side ridge, it is classified as a type Y tile. The fabric is dark red 1 A. This locus is datable to the sixth century B.C. with some possibly later material.

Y 92.   K80-Hh3-003-2347. P.L. 11.5 cm of the side ridge. The side ridge is 3.4 cm wide, which is wider than usual. The fabric is dark red 1 A.

Y 93.   K80-McF. 1509-2377. P.L. 13.5 cm of the top ridge.

Y 94.   K80-McF. 1509-2378. Upper right corner and 9.5 cm of the top ridge.

TYPE Z

General characteristics: type Z pan tiles consist of the flat pan surface, and one un-interrupted ridge, flush on the edges, which forms the flow directors, the side ridges, and top ridge, all of uniform height (ca. 2 cm) and width (ca. 2 cm); there are no flared lips on type Z tiles, just a flat bottom; there is much embellishment upon the tiles in the form of lines and arcs drawn into the wet clay with the fingertips. This decoration/notation occurs on the upper surface and the underside. On the upper surface the marks are generally arcs in each of the bottom corners (the center of these arcs would be the corners themselves). Examples exist of arcs drawn with one, two, three, or four fingers. On the underside there is usually a large "X" drawn, connecting the opposing corners of the tile, and again with one, two, three, or four fingertips. Some small fragments have been observed with finger-drawn lines on the underside which do not seem to be heading toward the opposing corner, but instead to a point roughly in the middle of the opposite side.

The THETA PI Group

The following three tiles share these features: the upper side is decorated with arcs drawn with one fingertip; situated between the arcs and a few centimeters from the bottom edge is a two-letter inscription in the upper case Greek characters Theta Pi, arranged in column. The letters are inscribed into the wet clay with a fingernail or an instrument, with the bottom of the inscription toward the bottom edge of the tile; on the underside, a few centimeters from the bottom edge, is the word OΔONTY, incised with a fingernail or instrument, oriented with the top of the inscription toward the bottom edge of the tile; the "X" on the underside is drawn with two fingertips.

Z 95. K80-2310 a & b. This unlabeled tile was found with the McFadden material in the apotheke at the Museum/dig house in Episkopi. It is the only complete pan tile that survives. It is broken into two joining fragments that comprise the whole tile; finished dimensions 47 x 57 cm. This tile is illustrated by Scranton 1967 p. 5, fig. 1, b.

Z 96. K80-McF. St.6 6-2227. P.L. 26 cm of the bottom edge. The OΔONTY inscription is incomplete.

Z 97. K80-surf-2229. Lower left corner and 21.5 cm of the side edge. The "Theta Pi" inscription is not preserved on this fragment. The OΔONTY inscription is incomplete. This fragment was located by the author in a stack of tile fragments at the southeast corner of the Palaestra.

The OMICRON UPSILON/"CO"(?) Group

The following two tiles share these features: the upper side is decorated with arcs drawn with two fingertips; the "X" on the underside is drawn with four fingertips; the two tile fragments perhaps share the same inscription. Tile no. Z99 clearly preserves either "OU" (if Greek) arranged in column, or "CO" (if Latin) arranged in line (and written sideways up the tile). All other type Z tiles are inscribed with Greek letters in this position, which would support the Greek interpretation. However, in all other cases, these two-letter Greek inscriptions are in upper case characters, and the upsilon on tile Z99 would be in lower case. The inscription on tile Z98 is incomplete, but consists of an "O" preceded by another character which is only partially preserved. The preceding character seems to be a "C", but this time the inscription is written in line, from left to right, sideways across the tile. Perhaps these two tile fragments do not share a common inscription, since they are not arranged on the tile in the same fashion. If the inscription is Greek and arranged in column (as are all other inscriptions in this position on other tile fragments), then this is the only observed instance of a lower case letter in this position. If the inscription is Latin, "CO" is the only Latin inscription found on any of the tile fragments from the Apollo Sanctuary. (Note cover tile fragment no. 35 for a similar inscription.)

Z 98.   K80-McF. tray 1267 -2259 a & b. Lower right corner and 26.5 cm of the right side. Two joining fragments, inscribed on the upper side with an "O", and with traces of another letter ("C"?) visible at the broken edge, where it would precede the "O" in a linear arrangement.

Z 99.   K78-Om4-007-TC 223. Lower left corner, 40 cm (mpd). The fragment is inscribed on the upper side with "CO" or "OU." This locus is datable to ca. 365 A.D.

The PHI IOTA Group

The following five tiles share these features: the upperside is decorated with arcs drawn with two fingertips; the two-letter inscription on the upper side is positioned within the arc surrounding the lower left corner; the two-letter inscription ΦΙ is arranged in line; the "X" on the underside is drawn with four fingertips; all five of these fragments were found by the author in a stack of tile fragments at the southeast corner of the Palaestra.

Z 100.   K80-surf-2280. 25 cm of the left side, close to the lower left corner. The Φ and Ι are partially preserved in the upper side inscription.

Z 101.   K80-surf-2279. Lower left corner and 13.5 cm of the left side. Only part of the Φ is preserved in the upper side inscription.

Z 102.   K80-surf-2278. Lower left corner and 26 cm of the left side. The ΦΙ inscription on the upper side is complete. This tile also has a wavy line drawn (with at least two fingertips) down the center of the tile, similar to X 63, Z 105 and Z 106.

Z 103.   K80-surf-2277. Lower left corner and 22 cm of the left side. The ΦΙ inscription on the upper side is complete.

Z 104.   K80-surf-2276. P.L. 15 cm of the bottom edge. Because this fragment comes from the center area of the bottom edge, no "X" strokes are found on the underside. On the upper side, the ΦΙ inscription is incomplete, and only the bottoms of the vertical strokes are preserved. In fact, the inscription might be "ΙΙ" or something else all together.

The remaining Type Z tile fragments are not inscribed.

Z 105. K80-surf-2284. Lower left corner, 30 cm (mpd). The "X" on the underside is stroked with three fingertips. The upper side is decorated with arcs in the lower corners, drawn with three fingertips, and a wavy line, drawn with two fingertips down the centerline of the tile parallel to the sides. (Note tile fragments X 63, Z 102, and Z 106 for similar decoration.)

Z 106. K80-surf-2282 a & b. Top left corner and 34 cm of the left side. Two joining fragments. The "X" on the underside is stroked with four fingertips. The upper side is decorated with a wavy line drawn with two fingertips down the centerline of the tile, parallel to the sides. (Note tile fragments X 63, Z 102, and Z 105 for similar decoration.)

Z 107. K80-Id-004-2285. A top corner fragment, 23.5 cm (mpd). The "X" on the underside is stroked with two fingertips. This is a typical type Z fragment. This locus is datable to ca. 65 A.D. with some earlier material.

Edges of Pan Tile
(without corners preserved)

These fragments are included in the catalog because they demonstrate variety in design (or perhaps just casualness in manufacture), or variety in fabric, or because they come from stratified contexts that are datable. None have finger strokes on the underside.

111. K80-west enclosure surf-2249 (Fig. 197a). 20.5 cm of side ridge.

112. K80-Om4-005-2266 (Fig. 197b). P.L. 14.5 cm of side ridge. This locus is datable to ca. 365 A.D.

113. K80-west enclosure surf-2241 (Fig. 197c). P.L. 14.3 cm of side ridge.

114. K80-Ii-005-2235 b (Fig. 197d). P.L. 7 cm of side ridge. This locus is datable to ca. 65 A.D. or earlier.

115. K80-west enclosure surf-2242 (Fig. 197f). P.L. 21 cm of top ridge.

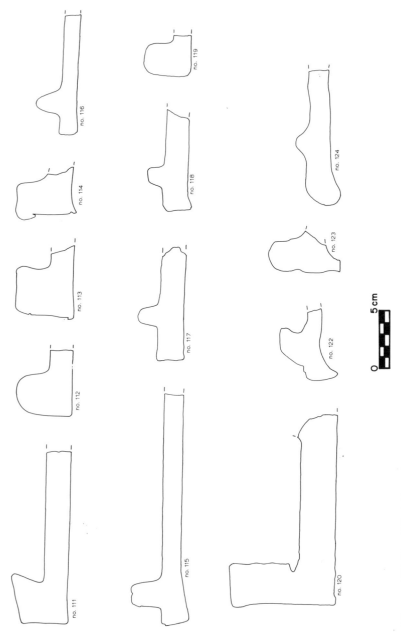

Figure 197. Pan Tile Edges (111 to 120, 122-124).

116. K78-Om3 ext.-012-1130 (Fig. 197e). P.L. 7.5 cm of top ridge; fabric 38.

117. K78-Km2-001/002-1419 (Fig. 197g). P.L. 16.3 cm of top ridge; fabric is coarse and soft 38.

118. K78-Km2-001/002-1420 (Fig. 197h). P.L. 9 cm of top ridge; fabric is coarse and soft 38.

119. K81-Fg-008-2513 (Fig. 197i). P.L. cm of side ridge. This locus is datable to ca. 65 A.D. or later, but not later than then first century A.D.

120. K80-west enclosure surf-2293 (Fig. 197j). P.L. 33 cm-long fragment of a large artifact of fired terra cotta. This may not be a roof tile at all. Possibly part of a water system. There is mortar preserved along the inside edge of the vertical ridge. There is evidence of up-turning along the broken edge opposite the ridge.

121. K80-Gh2/Gg4-033-2319. This is a fragment from the flat pan surface. There are no edges preserved. It is 2.2 cm thick and 9.5 cm (mpd). The fabric is similar to 7 b. First century A.D. and earlier material.

Aberrant Edges (of pan tiles?)

122. K80-west enclosure surf-2254 (Fig. 197k). P.L. 19 cm of an edge with a ridge. Section is illustrated.

123. K80-west enclosure surf-2251 (Fig. 197l). P.L. 15.4 cm of an edge with a ridge. Section is illustrated.

124. K80-Om4-003-2256 (Fig. 197m). P.L. 20.5 cm of an edge with a ridge. This locus is datable to ca. 365 A.D. Section is illustrated.

125 to 127: See the entry following no. 50.

Notes

NOTES: Chapter 1

1. The classic statement on stratigraphic excavation and three-dimensional recording is Mortimer Wheeler's *Archaeology from the Earth* (1954), based on his pre-World War II work in India and Great Britain. Kathleen Kenyon applied the same method in the Near East at Samaria (1930s) and Jericho (1950s) and summarized her experiences in *Beginning in Archaeology* (1961). American excavators in the Near East adopted what by then had become known as the Wheeler-Kenyon method for work at Samaria (West Bank, Palestine), Pella (Jordan), Khirbet Shema (Upper Galilee) and Gezer (Israel) in the 1960s, and at Tell el-Hesi (Israel) and Idalion (Cyprus) in the 1970s. All of these American excavations produced their own field manuals (some published, others privately circulated) describing excavation and recording techniques based ultimately on Wheeler's initial formulations. These include: Toombs in Wright 1965, Toombs n.d., Lance 1967, Walker 1971, Strange 1972, Seger 1972, Dever and Lance 1978, and Blakeley and Toombs 1980.

2. Dever 1973.

3. Only for Idalion is there a published and/or privately circulated excavation handbook: Walker 1971; see also the general comments in the first Idalion preliminary report: Stager, Walker and Wright 1974:6-8.

4. Wentworth 1922.

5. See Harris 1975 for an initial exposition of the idea of sequence diagram (which he terms a "matrix"). See also the comments on Harris' article in Barker 1977:196-199.

6. Blakely and Toombs 1980 p. 114.

NOTES: Chapter 2

1. The text of Cesnola's letter follows; Cesnola 1877 p. 343. For the reference to the letters I thank Mr. Brian McConnell and Nancy Mueller. They are from the Baker Library collection, reprinted by permission of the library and the Dartmouth Classics Department. For a general discussion of Cesnola including the Hitchcock letters, see Elizabeth McFadden 1971. For the Cesnola discoveries, see John L. Myres 1914.

Island of Cyprus
Curium October 7, 1875

My Dear Friend--

Your letter with the photograph coming from Denver, the former dated Aug. 16 has just reached me in these mountains, far away from all civilization, more or less, like the spot, I suppose, from which you have written to me--I am *very very* happy to hear, that your mining is going well, and I hope that you will be able to make up for your former losses. See what it is to have a *good heart*? But never mind; it is better to be victim of our good heart, than to see around us victims, made from our want of heart--towards them.

I believe, my dear friend, that we resemble to each other in this respect, and I am glad of it--I showed to my Chief Digger the photograph you enclosed, and told him you were the "*American Consul*" digging for *antiquities* in a *far away country*! He looked at the faces of the "gang" and then seriously said "I don't like their faces; they look, as if they would put into *their pocket any gold things* found *in the tombs*!!--The reference to *gold things* is due to the fact, that your friend Cesnola has just made the Discovery of *many gold* things, beneath a Temple here; the quantity and quality of which throws into shade Schliemann's so called "Treasure of Priam." There are among other things two massive gold armlets weighing nearly 3 pounds--They have engraved upon both a *Cypriote* inscription which I read thus/votive offering/"of Eterandes King of Paphos."

I have received the enclosed letter from Mrs. Chew, and another from Mr. Baracri (formerly Secretary of our Legation at Constantinople, and now employed at the "Centennial Exhibition.") Read them both attentively, and about that of Baraer's give me your opinion. If I should exhibit my "gold, silver, and precious stones Collection" which I possess, and 19/20 of which have been found now under a Temple here, [it] would create a great interest, and attract the *lady* visitors at the Exhibition more than anything else, and perhaps decide the Philadelphia people (*males,*) to buy my entire Collection, which I now have here for their new Art Museum. At any rate, I am not in a hurry; and I am going to see what offer the British Museum is going to make me--Mr. Gladstone wrote to me a long letter and sent all the pamphlets on Vaticanism, his own and those of Manning Dr. Newman and other of his adversaries--From the New York Museum no letters no money, nothing about my new Collection sent to them in last February! It becomes too long this affair! Yet I understand quite well that during the summer months Johnston Prime Blodgett How etc. are all out of town--I have written to Johnston to Blodgett and to Prime a few weeks ago. What *donkeys* they are if they let the 2 sarcophagi and the last splendid findings be purchased by another Museum! I am afraid however that it will be so. There is no *real* interest in them.

  . Give my best respects to your good lady and believe me ever

Affly your friend

L. B. Cesnola

2. For the accuracy of Cesnola's claims, see Terence Mitford 1971 pp. 2-3. See also Myres 1914, footnote 1.

3. See McFadden 1938, pp. 10-17; 1940 pp. 22-8; 1950, pp. 14-26. Additional articles appear in McFadden 1951, pp. 167-168; 1952, pp. 128-129, as well as *ILN* 1952, pp. 588-590.

4. Scranton 1967.

5. Joseph Last (and Roger Edwards) 1975.

6. John and Suzanne Young 1955.

7. See note 2. New inscriptions are being studied by Dr. Ino Nicolaou of the Cyprus Museum.

8. Dorothy H. Cox 1959 notes in her introduction: "Although occupied from the eighth century B.C. to about the end of the fourth A.D. there was little stratification of use in dating the coins. In fact, nowhere at Curium was there important stratification, nothing to show the growth or decline of the city."

9. Strabo 14.6.3 According to Dr. Giraud Foster, the altar area was rich in sheep or goat bones, some cut for eating. For goat sacrifices at the Apollo Sanctuary at Ayia Irini, Cyprus, see E. Sjoqvist, 1933, p. 314. W. F. Albright, 1957, p. 244 discusses goats pushed over cliffs in the *Mishnah*. If an altar existed in the center of the Round Building, it might be the one meant by Strabo and it would have been better protected from violators. An inscription (Mitford No. 104) refers to dancing around the sacred altar in Roman times but this would be hard to do with the altar of the Archaic Precinct.

10. Dr. Reuben Bullard, project geologist in 1979, believes the site of the Sanctuary was selected because it was "above the area of maximum vertical bluffs of this region of Cyprus." He has also traced metalling (man-made abrasion) on the caliche bedrock between the Sanctuary and the cliffs approximately one mile away: "Traffic could have caused the abrasion which lines up with the cliff, and there is a local tradition as well as traces of ancient construction on the edge of the cliff itself." The altar stones were of caliche, but slightly different from all other stone in the Archaic Precinct. The single curb of stones has been added by Dr. Buitron.

11. See D. Buitron and D. Soren, 1979, p. 29 for a discussion of perforated stones on Cyprus. See also S. Swiny in Helena Swiny 1982, pp. 151-152.

12. Rutherford connects the base of this curved monument which is *in situ* with five curved inscribed blocks from a dedicatory monument found in the Central Court just east of it. Mitford 1971 pp. 91-94 describes the blocks as composed of mottled, reddish marble, but his drawing on page 92 is inaccurate. The description itself belongs to a base for statues of Demetrios of Thessaly, Commandant of Kourion, his wife and their children, dating between 200 and 193 B.C., and found on June 6, 1939 by McFadden.

13. Diana Buitron 1982 has reported "a long narrow building was erected in the Archaic Period (7th-6th century B.C.) to serve as a sacred storeroom for the Sanctuary, while cult activity took place to the south, in the Archaic Precinct. Details are not available at this time. For the dating of the altar itself see the Buitron reports in *RDAC* 1979 pp. 316-320, 1982 pp. 144-147 and 1983 pp. 228-231 and the *Walters Art Gallery Bulletin* Vol. 34 No. 3 1981 p. 3. The pots she cites are Gjerstad Type IV, the dating of which is still difficult to establish precisely (see the article on the pottery in this volume). It is still not certain that altars, first

temple and first Round Building are not contemporary and only the future publication of the Buitron pottery will throw light on this. Other articles about the altar area by Dr. Buitron include the *Walters Bulletin* Vol. 33, No. 3 1980 and the ASOR Newsletter Vol. 35 No. 4 1984.

14. Scranton 1967, pp. 73-74 believed that the Augustan period saw major rearrangements and a new axis of focus which we actually may now show is hundreds of years earlier.

15. Professor Sinos of the Athens Polytechnical Institute has revised and updated our studies of the Temple of Apollo and will be publishing his own reconstruction shortly.

16. See the article by the author in the 1984 *RDAC*. On the possibility that the quake levelling Kourion was the Ammianus quake see also N. N. Ambraseys, 1965 p. 6, D. Soren and Eugene Lane, 1981 pp. 178-182 and Eric Pace, 1984 p. 20E.

17. These channels were illustrated but not discussed in George McFadden, 1950 p. 15 where a site plan by Joseph Last is published.

18. Buitron and Soren, 1978 p. 41.

19. There are six fragments of Attic black-glazed pottery recognizable so far from among 230 pottery pieces from the foundations of the temple. A Corinthian oinochoe was found in the area of the Semicircular Altar in the Archaic Precinct and was dated to the later sixth century B.C., see Terence Mitford, *Inscriptions of Kourion*, pp. 38-39.

20. For the tholos at Delphi (dated ca. 580 B.C.?) see D. S. Robertson, 1969 p. 85, and bibliography p. 363. For Euelthon and his dedication in the Corinthian treasury at Delphi see Sir George Hill, 1949 pp. 115-116 and Herodotos iv, 162.

21. Bernard Dietrich 1978 pp. 1-18, has argued that the roots of Greek religion went deep into the Bronze Age so that the hybrid quality of the sixth century site should not be completely surprising. Whether or not the chief god was a syncretized Apollo at this early date is difficult to establish. References to Apollo Hylates are not found until well into the Classical period on Cyprus (Kourion, Drymou, Chytroi) and the well-known Paphian sanctuary has been assigned to the later fourth century B.C. by Tolanta Melynarczyk, 1980 p. 243. Evagoras I (435-374) is usually seen as the "disseminator of Greek refinement in the Eastern Mediterranean" (see Constantinos Spyridakis 1974 p. 28). But the current evidence of the architecture and pottery suggests that Dietrich is right in pointing out the continuity of a Greek awareness mixed with Near Eastern influences even in pre-Classical

times but one cannot yet say that the presence of a tholos at an early date at Kourion is significant evidence for the Apollo cult at Kourion before the Classical period.

22. For a discussion of Julio-Claudian water systems at Keryneia (Claudius) and Soloi (Nero), see Terence Mitford, 1971 pp. 203-204.

23. Mitford 1971 (p. 204) cites the bilingual inscription of proconsul Q. Julius Cordus. On possible Neronian overspending see Mitford p. 156.

24. Scranton p. 62, cistern 2. The term Cistern 3 instead of 2 is used throughout McFadden's field diary and in the Kourion Museum finds registry.

25. For this see Diana Buitron, 1980 p. 320.

NOTES: Chapter 4

1. Shackleton 1969, p. 379.

2. Benson 1972, p. 133, plate 35 no. 5, B1323, B1351.

3. McFadden 1946, pp. 488-489, plate XLVIII, no. 140.

4. Reese, David S., *Excavations at Kition*, forthcoming.

5. Demetropoulos 1977, plate XXVIII.

6. Westholm, 1935, p. 17, fig. 6, no. 2.

7. Christodolou 1967, p. 63 note 4, plate XV, no. 15.

8. Demetropoulos, A. 1970, fig. 2.

9. Demetropoulos, A. 1973, pp. 270-272, plate LIII.

10. Nobis, G. 1977, p. 296.

11. Shaw 1980, p. 223, plate 160 c and d.

12. Reese, David S, Corinth Sanctuary, forthcoming.

13. N.J. Shackleton, personal communication, 1980.

14. Bate 1918, p. 221.

15. Brown 1926, p. 535.

16. Brown 1926, p. 535.

NOTES: Chapter 5

1. The author would like to express his appreciation to V. Karageorghis, Director of the Department of Antiquities of Cyprus, for his many kindnesses and logistical support during our work at Kourion. Thanks are also due to David Soren and Diana Buitron, co-directors of the University of Missouri--Walters Art Gallery excavations at the Apollo Sanctuary, for their help and encouragement.

2. Our team consisted of eight members, all of whom worked long hours in a variety of roles: Michael Arwe, Hillary Browne, Joseph Greene, Cynthia Johnson, Annie Lee Jones, James Rehard, Jan Sanders and Anne Seaver. Without their hard work and dedication the survey would have been impossible.

3. Cesnola 1877, pp. 296-298; Walters 1900: pp. 57-86; and McFadden 1946: pp. 449-489.

4. McFadden 1951, p. 167.

5. Walters 1900, pp. 56 and 60.

6. This feature, as well as many of the ancient tombs of the akrotiri, was shown to the author by H. C. Heywood. See now, Heywood 1982, especially p. 169 and fig. 126 where the Akrotiri piece is identified as a millstone.

7. McFadden 1946, pp. 449-489. Although this feature appears to be in the area of Walters' Tomb 14 (Walters 1900, p. 60, Map of Site B) it should not be confused with it, for Walters elsewhere describes this tomb as a "surface grave" (p. 82).

8. For a discussion of the chapel and its patron saint, see Swiny, H. W. 1982, pp. 148-150 (Information supplied by M. Proussis). The cemetery is discussed in the same work by A. Oliver, Jr. (Oliver 1982).

9. Last 1975, pp. 58-59.

10. It is probable that these are the inscriptions noted by Nicolaou (1982, p. 94 and note 8) which she dates to the 6th century B.C.

11. Gjerstad 1948, p. 48.

12. Gjerstad 1948, p. 52. Notice the shift toward greyish-black paint in White Painted II Ware.

13. Christou 1978, p. 145 and Pl. XII: 3. The wavy line on rim with more complicated neck decortion can be seen on Pl. IV: 52 (WP IV, p. 145) at the site and on a WPV amphora from Politiko, (Hadjisavvas 1978, P. XI: 3).

14. Gjerstad 1948, p. 60. On the relationship between Bichrome and White Painted Wares, cf. Benson 1973, p. 94.

15. Tomb G. 314. Deshayes 1963, pp. 158, 167, 219-220 and Pl. XXXIX: 2 and frontispiece (color).
For an imitation Cypriote amphora with triangular rim similar to Pl. 10 traded to the Greek mainland cf. Williams 1969, p. 57. For a similar occurence in Athens, cf. Sparkes and Talcott 1970, pp. 191-192.

16. Gjerstad 1948, p. 68.

17. These fabric groups are intended to provide general working descriptions of the pottery for the sake of convenient discussion in this report. They should not be construed as an attempt to arrange the material into a universal system of classification.

18. The noticeable absence of third to fourth century A.D. material at Ayios Philon prompted du Plat Taylor and Megaw (1981) to suggest a possible abendonment of the site before the Early Christian complex was built (p. 216).
For the severity of the disruption caused by the earthquakes of the fourth century A.D. cf., *inter alia*, Adovasio et al. 1975, pp. 251-286. A succinct survey of the history of the island can be found in Purcell 1969, (especially pp. 74-118).

19. Catling 1972, p. 24, Pl. 23: P465, etc.

20. cf. *inter alia*, Robinson 1959, p. 19, F84, 85 and Lapp 1961, *passim*. The narrower-necked variant (such as Pl. 13:l) is said to be the more popular in the Herodian (Roman I) deposits at Samaria, cf. Kenyon 1957, p. 294 and fig. 67.4.

21. Catling 1972, p. 61, fig. 34: P445, etc.

22. Catling 1972, p. 62, fig. 32: P130. The form of rim 13:a is not, however, restricted to cooking pots as can be seen by its appearance on earlier amphorae (in a pinkish-buff fabric) in Tombs 16 and 20 at Tsambres, Dray et al. 1949, pp. 45-48 and fig. 52:3.

23. Catling 1972, p. 33, fig. 20: P375.

24. Catling 1972, p. 61, figs. 23: P125, 24: P416, etc.

25. du Plat Taylor and Megaw 1981, p. 221 and fig. 45: 381 and 383. Cf, also Diederichs 1980, p. 28 and Pl. 7:75.

26. Robinson 1959, p. 100, Pls. 25: M171, 27: M222, etc. Similar in both rim profile and grooved neck are the smaller diameter variants of the Types 3 and 5 jugs from the Roman tombs at Vasa, du Plat Taylor 1958, pp. 32-35, and Pl. 15 and 17.

27. Pl. 54:n could be related to some of the examples of Vasa jug Type 2, du Plat Taylor 1958, p. 29 and Pl. 14.

28. The 'groove' on the top of the lips of Pl. 55:e and f seems to be more common in Palestine. Cf., at Samaria, Kenyon 1957, p. 302 and fig. 71:6 (Roman 3a) and p. 304 and fig. 72: 10 (Roman 4); and possibly on vessels of small aperture, Zayadin 1966, Pl. XXX: 84 (Early Hellenistic); and on larger vessels dated to the Byzantine Period (5th-7th century A.D.) from the Amman theater, Hadidi 1970, p. 15 and Pl. V: 26.

29. For first century B.C. examples, cf. Group F from the Athenian Agora, Robinson 1959, p. 18, Pl. 72: F77; for the persistence of the type into Catling's Period III, see fig. 27: P192, 28: P137, etc.

30. Catling 1972, p. 64, fig. 23: P470.

31. Catling 1972, figs. 7: P42 and 36: P177.

32. Catling 1972, p. 60, fig. 35: P202.

33. Catling 1972, figs. 5: P35; 6: P114, and possibly 6: P217. It is not impossible that fig. 57:n may be related to large bowls in a finer fabric from 1st-2nd century A.D. contexts in the Athenian Agora, Robinson: 1959, p. 29 (G77) and Pls. 4, 67.

34. Catling 1972, p. 73, fig. 33: P213. Cf., how-ever, a 1st-2nd century A.D. piece from the Athenian Agora, Robinson 1959, Pl. 67 (G77).

35. Catling 1972, fig. 37: P447. A rounder and less complicated rim appears on a large diameter vessel from Hellenistic Hama, Christensen and Johansen 1971, p. 45 (No. 192) and figs. 21 and 22.

36. Catling 1972, p. 69, fig. 40: P578 and P579.

37. Catling 1972, p. 64, figs. 28: P137; 32: P128, P129, etc.

38. Pl. 57:e--cf. Ayios Philon Period VII du Plat Taylor and Megaw 1981, p. 221 and fig. 42: 365; and Ktima, Deshayes 1963, p. 261 and Pl. XX.8 (P337). Pl. 16:f-For the general shape, cf. below

Pl. 22:j and references. Similar forms have also been identified as knobbed lids, cf. Ayios Philon, du Plat Taylor 1980, p. 118 and fig. 13:118 (Period II). Pl. 16:g-Ayios Philon Period II, du Plat Taylor 1980, p. 176 and fig. 12: 100; and Period VII, p. 221 and fig. 42: 366. Ktima, Deshayes 1963, p. 260 and Pl. XX:4 (P305); Aghia Irini, Quilichi 1971, p. 131 and fig. 83: 96. Beyond Cyprus compare Chios (Kofina Ridge) Anderson 1954, p. 170 and fig. 10:m; and Samos (Kastro Tigani), Tolle-Kastebein 1974, p. 118 and fig. 120: d. It is not impossible, however, that we are dealing with a shape more similar to the Plain White Ware vessels from Philamoudhi Vounari, Al-Radi 1983, Pl. XLV: 6. Pl. 16:h and/or i, cf. below Pl. 22:h and references and Ayios Philon, du Plat Taylor and Megaw 1981, p. 247 and fig. 61: 438; Aghia Irini, Quilichi 1971, pp. 131, 144 and figs. 83:85, 95:198; and possibly Chois, Anderson 1954, p. 170 and fig. 10:f.

39. Catling 1972, p. 73, fig. 5:P88. Note also similar forms in a "pinkish-buff ware" in an Early Christian (Period VI) deposit at Ayios Philon, du Plat Taylor and Megaw 1981, p. 219 and fig. 40:333 and 334.

40. Catling 1972, fig. 34:P203. Note also a similar rim on a painted vessel from a Period IV (second century B.C.-early first century A.D.) context at Ayios Philon, du Plat Taylor 1980, p. 205 and fig. 31:270.

41. Catling 1972, p. 64, fig. 32:P128 and P129. A similar rim may appear on a smaller necked vessel (amphora) from Tsambres Tomb 15, group V and VI (third century B.C.), Dray et al. 1949, p. 102 and fig. 52:7.

42. Catling, 1972, p. 70, fig. 33:P244, etc.

43. du Plat Taylor and Megaw 1981, p. 240 and fig. 56:423 (Period VIII).

44. Catling and Dikigoropoulos 1970, pp. 48, 57 and fig. 3:9.

45. Catling 1972, figs. 32:P243, P257; and 38:P270. Cf. also Robinson 1959, Pl. 21: M 77; and possible Pl. 68:P11259. Similar rims appear frequently on Hellenistic vases from the Agora. Thompson 1934, *passim*, but not--evidently--on vessels related in shape to fig. 10:p.

46. Catling 1972, fig. 21:P555. For Athens, cf. Robinson 1959, pp. 10, 18, 19 and Pls. 3 and 72. For Khirbet Qumran, cf. de Vaux 1954, fig. 5:5.

47. Catling 1972, pp. 25, 72, fig. 17:P514.

48. Catling 1972, fig. 22:P503.

49. Catling 1972, p. 61, fig. 34:P491. Not dissimilar in the stance of the lip and the presence of grooving is a vessel from the Athenian Agora dated to the late 3rd century A.D., Robinson 1959, p. 105 and Pl. 27.

50. Both the hollow-and solid-stem variants of this ubiquitous vessel-type appear in Period IV (second century B.C. and early first century A.D.) deposits at Ayios Philon, du Plat Taylor 1980, p. 206 and fig. 32:283-285 where Augustan parallels at Tarsus and Athens are cited (p. 206).

51. Hayes 1976, p. 35, nos. 166 and 167.

52. Jugs and juglets with rims similar to fig. 12:a can be seen in the Roman tombs at Vasa, du Plat Taylor 1958, figs 7:e, 8:d and 10:d.

53. Catling, 1972, fig. 17.

54. Catling and Dikigoropoulos 1970, p. 48, fig. 3:9. Note the similarity to the "Palestinian transport and storage amphora" imported to Corinth, Williams and Zervos 1983, p. 29 and Pl. 11:77, 78 in a similar fabric. Other possible parallels from the Athenian Agora include: Thompson 1934, pl. 18:M12, in a gritty grey-buff clay with a buff slip dated to the 1st half of the 1st century A.D., and Robinson 1959, p. 120(M391) and Pls. 34, 58 in a pale buff micaceous clay and slip thought to be of the late third to early fourth century A.D.

55. Perhaps from Kos as at Ayios Philon, du Plat Taylor 1980, p. 210 and fig. 35:305; or at Kambi, du Plat Taylor 1958, p. 38 and fig. 15:D.
    On the other hand, double handles do occur on local Cypriote vessels, cf., *inter alia* Karageorghis 1972, p. 167 and fig. 11:11 a White Painted V Pitcher from Tomb 1 at Patraki.

56. Early Chian amphorae are said to be characterized by such a bulge. Anderson 1954, p. 168-169 and fig. 8:51, etc. On Cyprus compare Ayios Philon, du Plat Taylor and Megaw 1981, p. 221 and fig. 42:362 (higher handle angle) and Tsambres, Dray et al. 1949, p. 107 and fig. 106.1, but see also fig. 57:2 from Rhodes.

57. Ayios Philon Period II, du Plat Taylor 1980, p. 177 and fig. 12:99 a "knob base" with references to Salamis. For general profile and "hollow" stem, cf. Deshayes 1963:Pl. XX:4 and 5.

58. A "pie-crust" rim of some sort appears on sherds from the Aphrodite Sanctuary at Morphou (Nikolao 1963, Pl. IV upper right and fig. 2) possibly in context with Syrian *mortaria* (op. cit. p. 28, fig. 8). For the latter, cf. now Hayes 1967.

59. du Plat Taylor 1980, p. 193 and fig. 22:214 in a "pinkish-buff clay with white surface," not dissimilar to the general appearance of the present fabric IV.

60. In order to facilitate future comparisons, the surface colors of these pieces are as follows: fig. 63:a, slipped: 7.5YR 8/2 (Pinkish White) to 5YR 8/3-8/4 (Pink); fig. 63:b, plain: 10R 6/6-6/8 (Light Red); fig. 63:c, plain: 2.5YR 5/8 (Red); fig. 63:d, as 63:b; 63:e, slipped: 7.5YR 7/4 (Pink); fig. 63:f, slipped (?): 5YR 7/8 (Reddish Yellow); fig. 63:g, slipped: 2.5YR 6/4; fig. 63:h, plain: 7.5YR 8/6 (Reddish Yellow); fig. 63:i, slipped: 5YR 6/4 (Light Reddish Brown); fig. 63:j, slipped: 10YR 7/4 (Very Pale Brown); fig. 63:k, slipped: 7.5YR 7/4 (Pink); fig. 63:l, plain: 2.5YR 6/6 (Light Red); fig. 63:m, slipped: 2.5YR 6/4 (Light Reddish Brown); fig. 63:n, plain: 2.5YR 5/6 (Red).

61. Preliminary and partial *comparanda* for some of the amphora fragments might include: Handles. Figure 63:a: Chios, Anderson 1954, p. 181, fig. 19:353 (identified as Coan); Athenian Agora, Robinson 1959, p. 43 and Pls. 8 and 42 (G198) with reference to M 54 of similar date (p. 89). Figure 63:b and c, a pinched form common in the assemblage, Ayia Irini, Quilichi 1971, p. 131 and fig. 83:40. Necks. Figure 63:d, pinched handle as figure 63:b. Toes. Figure 63:f: Ayios Philon, du Plat Taylor and Megaw 1981, p. 248 and fig. 61:484. Figure 63:g Ayios Philon, du Plat Taylor 1980, p. 177 and fig. 12:100, du Plat Taylor and Megaw 1981, p. 221 and fig. 42:366; Ayia Irini, Quilichi 1971, p. 103 fig. 44:78 and p. 135, fig. 83:96; and Chois: Anderson 1954, p. 170 and fig. 10:m. Figure 63:h: Ayios Philon: du Plat Taylor and Megaw 1981, p. 248, fig. 61:480 (and 479?); Ayia Irini Quilichi 1971, p. 131 and fig. 83:89 Chois, Anderson 1954, p. 170 and fig. 10:i; Figure 63:j: Ayios Philon, du Plat Taylor 1980, p. 193 and fig. 23.219, p. 203 and fig. 29.257.

62. The author would like to thank his colleague Dr. Kathleen Slane (University of Missouri--Columbia) for her valuable assistance in preparing this review of the fine wares from the survey. Obviously any errors are the fault of the present author.

63. Hayes 1967.

64. Hayes 1977.

65. Hayes 1972, pp. 371-386.

66. Cf., Catling 1972, p. 25 where a similar rim (fig. 16:P475) is included with a group of *lekanai* in "miscellaneous plain ware" from late Hellenistic and Early Roman deposits at Dhiorios.

67. Cf., also Schäfer 1962:fig. 1:9.

68. Cf., also Schäfer 1962: fig. 1:17.

69. Robinson 1959, G 25, p. 25 and Pl. 61.

70. Hayes 1972, pp. 100-107, and fig. 16.

71. Hayes 1972, pp. 323-370; and Hayes 1980, pp. 525-527.

72. See article on roof tiles by John Huffstot in this volume.

73. Last 1975, pp. 39-72.

NOTES: Chapter 6

1. Robert Scranton 1967. I wish to thank Dr. Vassos Karageorghis and the Cypriote Department of Antiquities for allowing our work within the cella of the temple. I also thank Dr. Robert Scranton for returning to Kourion after seventeen years and providing invaluable suggestions and continuity between our work and his own. For a preliminary form of the present article, see "Some New Ideas on Dating and Rebuilding the Temple of Apollo Hylates at Kourion", *RDAC* 1983, pp. 232-244.

2. For the Cesnola letters, see in this volume the addendum to the introductory article by David Soren. The first letter shows Cesnola worked at Kourion as early as 1874 instead of 1876 as George McFadden wrote in the *University of Pennsylvania Museum Bulletin* for 1938 (page 10).

3. Cesnola 1877 p. 343.

4. Writing his letter about his discovery of the famous treasure of Kourion, he said on October 7, 1875: ". . . your friend Cesnola has just made the discovery of *many gold* things beneath a Temple here, the quantity and quality of which throws into shade Schliemann's so-called "Treasure of Priam!" This was apparently not the Temple of Apollo.

5. For this reference I thank Andrew Oliver. The Pease diary was located by him in the Union Theological Seminary in New York City.

6. For warriors with shields, see John and Suzanne Young, 1955, pls. 32 (2134-2147), 33 (2214) 39 (1977).

7. Jeffery 1928 pp. 37-60.

8. George McFadden excavation diary (unpublished, 1935-1953) p. 15 and plan p. 16. The excavation of this area was conducted 11-11-35. The rock-cut channel will be discussed in a separate article. (R.D.A.C. 1984) The site plan was developed in grid form by McFadden and should be read by placing vertical coordinates (A through Q) first and horizontal coordinates (a through q) second; thus the Temple of Apollo is roughly located at Ic.

9. George McFadden 1983, p. 11-13.

10. McFadden diary p. 22. He added: "Wall separating naos from pronaos about 0.15 m under surface."

11. McFadden diary p. 23: date of excavation was 11-19-35.

12. McFadden 1938 pp. 13-15.

13. McFadden 1940, p. 22.

14. Scranton 1967 p. 21.

15. McFadden 1938, p. 13.

16. McFadden diary, p. 618.

17. Scranton 1967, p. 21.

18. McFadden diary p. 311 (4-23-36) and see plan p. 294. See here Fig. 2.

19. Scranton 1967 p. 23. For the capitals at Salamis see Karageorghis *Salamis* 1969 p. 114. They are dated tentatively to the Augustan period by Scranton. The Salamis capital is discussed as Nabataean in origin in G.R.H. Wright, pp. 175-178. I thank Stephen Glover for this reference.

20. Scranton 1967 pp. 21-22; See also Mitford 1971 pp. 199f. The dedicatory inscription (1157) was found 10-29-47 on the east area of the stairs just in front of the temple, probably the very spot where it fell in the earthquake. McFadden described the extraordinary discovery in his diary (p. 684): "17 men. Began levelling off St(reet) from Temple B (the temple) end where there is no paving . . . Mr. (Bert Hodge) Hill removing large fallen stones at south end of St. 1 and placing them with Christo (foreman) and a team of men on the side walls. Also removed large

stones on the east side of Temple B stairway. One found to be inscribed in good large formal lettering which may well prove to be Hellenistic . . . He believes it may be one of the orthostates of the temple in its first period."

21. Scranton 1967 p. 24

22. These ratios are determined by comparing the rise of the roof to twice the run. For example, a roof slope or pitch of one to four could be dervied by examining a pediment. Placing a meter stick vertically on top of the pediment we measure up ten centimeters and at this point we measure twenty centimeters horizontally before we run into the sloping roof. Doubling the twenty centimenters, the result is ten to forty centimeters for the slope ratio, or one to four. A convenient source-book for such problems is Alred S. Gaskell 1969 p. 17-6.

23. The reconstruction was drawn initially by Alexandra Corn after consultation with John Rutherford and Robert Scranton. It was revised by John Huffstot and the rebuilding began in 1980 under the direction of Rutherford.

24. McFadden diary p. 28. For a preliminary report on the dating of the temple, see Soren 1979 pp. 321-327. The date I proposed for the second temple of 50 A.D. to early second century turns out now to be perhaps 65-66 A.D. or at least 50-75 A.D. But my original assignment of a foundation trench to the first temple was in error. The soil 006 believed to be fill in a foundation trench proved to be soil discolored by calicheation from the rocks of the adjacent temple foundations and 006 was not different from the fill around it associated with the second temple, including loci 020 and 003. Thus, my Augustan date for the foundations of the first temple in my preliminary report is now supplemented by my further work and a date of the mid to late sixth century B.C. is the new *terminus post quem* based on finds in the cella.

25. For the Cesnola pieces see L. Cesnola 1885-1903 Volume 2, pl. CXLIII (1065) and Volume 3 pl. CL supplement I; J. L. Myres 1914 pp. 320, 549 (1908). The McFadden sherds were found in 1935, not in 1936 as he says in UMB 1938 p. 11. I wish to thank Dr. Jane Biers of the University of Missouri Museum of Art and Archaeology for her efforts in sorting out the pithos sources. See also Mitford, pp. 238-240.

26. McFadden diary p. 7 (11-6-35). Mitford describes the find spot of the three sherds (his letter d) as "presumably in surface soil, over or in the close vicinity of Section 5 of the West Complex, but McFadden's account would put the discovery further west, perhaps in grid areas Ao-p or Bo-p at the southwest limit of the sanctuary.

27. McFadden 1938 p. 11, p. 17 (photo).

28. The last pithos fragment (Mitford's e) is given by him the grid area I 9-10 J 1-2, F 9-10. The McFadden diary (12-5-35) on page 62 says: "Sherds of large water jar inscribed. Apollo Street 1 k- Λ first stratum. Dec. 5". This is the same as Mitford's location.

29. Mitford 1971 p. 238; Scranton p. 25.

30. Scranton 1967 p. 25.

31. Mitford 1971 p. 240 (with photo). "The pithos was found 11-19-35 and McFadden reported in his diary (p. 23) . . . found large water jar preserved to neck upright in southwest (note: this should be southeast and may be an error in the typed transcript by Dr. Roger Edwards from McFadden's notes) corner of building in loose soft soil . . ."

32. Mitford 1971 p. 240. He speculated that Cesnola's pithos might have been set "into the pavement" of the second temple with the inscribed upper wall and rim rising above pavement level, a normal setting for a *pithos*, so that it might serve as a container or storage vessel within the *naos* of the Temple." Scranton is more explicit about a possible join between the Cesnola jar and that which McFadden found in the cella. He says (p. 25): ". . . the base of a pithos bedded in the fill below the floor of the Temple of a later period in the Southeast corner of the cella, still *in situ*, may actually be part of the same vessel." An added note of interest is the fact that Scranton saw the McFadden pithos or most of it *in situ* in 1962, yet Mitford, who published in 1971, found it gone. Thus we have dates between which the jar was removed, dates which suggest McFadden had saved it despite Mitford's belief that he had not.

33. E. Sjöqvist 1933 p. 311.

34. Sjöqvist 1933 p. 311.

35. Sjöqvist 1933 pp. 316-322 (for olive pits), p. 347 (for anointing). Among the parallels with Kourion shown by Aijia Irini and indeed many cult sites on Cyprus are the open air temenos with major cult house, bull deities, charioteer dedications, sacred pithoi, aniconic worship changing later to anthropomorphism, animal sacrifice, *favissae*, terra cotta votives, snake representations, sacred trees and ritual dancing.

36. For Amathus, see Stillwell 1976 p. 48 and A. S. Murray p. 90 for discussion and bibliography.

37. McFadden Diary (p. 22). He also noted three distinct strata associated with the pronaos of the temple during his 1935 excavations. First was the surface soil "reddish brown and loose," then came "a hard light soil with some gypsum and many stones, fifty centimeters thick." Third was "a layer without stones but slightly darker earth, softer than that of the second stratum."

38. Mitford 1971 p. 201.

39. Ibid p. 204.

40. Ibid p. 153.

41. Ibid p. 156.

42. Scranton 1967 p. 21.

43. For detailed discussions of the rock-cut channels, see Soren and Sanders 1984 pp. 285-293.

NOTES: Chapter 6, Appendix Two

1. Brünnow and Domascewski 1909, vol. 1, passim.

2. Jaussen and Savignac 1909, vol. 1, passim (hereafter Mission).

3. P.C. Hammond 1959, pp.40-48.

4. N. Glueck 1965, pp. 64-69. Goods carried across the Arabian desert arrive at the Nabataean (or Arabian) port of Leuce Come on the northeast side of the Red Sea. From Leuce Come, they travelled by ship to Aila (Aelana) on the Gulf of Aqabah, the northeast extension of the Red Sea, and finally on to Petra. An alternate route was wholly by caravan to Medain Saleh and directly on to Petra.

5. Strabo XVI.4.18.

6. Brünnow and Domascewski 1909; Jaussen and Savignac 1909, vol. 1, p. 388 ff.

7. Boethius and Ward Perkins 1970, p. 432.

8. Jaussen and Savignac 1909, p. 368.

9. Brünnow and Domascewski 1909, p. 157.

10. *Ibid.*, p. 146 ff; and Boethius and Ward Perkins 1970 (n. 7), p. 433. A. Negev 1974, p. 154 does not agree that the typological division has any chronological significance since few tombs are actually dated. In fact, one of the latest dated tombs at Hegra, E16, is of the typologically earliest type (Negev 1974, p. 153, n. 5).

11. Brünnow and Domascewski 1909, pp. 147-148.

12. A. Negev 1974, p. 159.

13. H. Kohl 1910, p. 26.

14. G.R.H. Wright 1961, pp. 124-135.

15. D. Schlumberger 1933, pl. xxxiv.l.

16. *Ibid.*, pl. xxxiv.3 & pl. 2, from the temple.

17. H.C. Butler 1916, p. 388, Illustration 336.

18. G.R.H. Wright 1972, p. 176.

19. L. Borchardt 1903, p. 5.

20. K. Ronczewski 1927, p. 8, fig. 4; p. 9, fig. 5b from Dendera; p. 20, fig. 15; p. 28, fig. 21 from the Sieglin Collection; pl. I; and pl. II.2.

21. Negev 1974, p. 153.

22. Wright 1972, pp. 176-178.

23. Vermeule 1979, pp. 189-193.

24. Borchardt 1903, p. 81.

25. Boethius and Ward Perkins 1970, p. 439; Butler 1910, pp. 371-372.

26. Butler 1910, suggests a date between 33 and 50 A.D. whereas Boethius and Ward Perkins 1970, p. 439 suggest a date toward the end of Nabataean independence, i.e. ca. 100 A.D.

27. D.S. Robertson 1974, p. 382; s.v. cymatium, Vitruvius generally means a cyma reversa moulding.

28. Earthquakes may have done further damage and late Roman squatters might have reused some of the temple blocks. Also, the quality of the local stone is such that it wears quickly and any mouldings are difficult to restore.

29. C.H. Krencker and W. Zschietzschmann 1938, Kasr Naus, p. 9; Hössn Sfiri, p. 25; Nebi Safa, p. 205; and Hibbariye, p. 214.

30. Temple B at Niha, ca. ten kilometers south of Baalbek; H.C. Butler 1910, p. 117. three small distyle *in antis* temples situated between Tyre and Damascus at Ain Libnaye (Butler, p. 176) at Ain Hersha, (Butler, p. 248) and at Akrabe (Butler, p. 265).

31. R. Scranton 1967, p. 73, fig. 67.c shows a simplified version of an attic type base from the central court.

32. Unpublished.

33. This particular combination of mouldings suggested for the missing members of the Temple of Apollo is quite regular. All of them appear in Gerash on the Triumphal Arch near the Hippodrome, the Tetrapylon and the North Gate. C.H. Kraeling 1938. Triumphal Arch, pl. IV and V; Tetrapylon, pl. XIV and XV; North Gate, pl. XIX, XX, and plate XXII.

34. O. Vessberg and A. Westholm 1956, p. 11.

35. *Ibid.*, p. 43.

36. *Ibid.*, p. 34.

37. A small temple with a tripartite cella on the acropolis at Soli has only fragmentary remains, Gjerstad 1937, vol. III, p. 412. There is no evidence for the entrance and therefore it remains unclear as to whether it should be viewed as a Roman temple with an entrance on the short side or as a Cypriote court temple with an entrance on the long side. A French archaelogical team has recently been restoring the first century temple on the Acropolis of Amathus.

38. Argout 1975, pp. 122-141.

39. Karageorghis 1971, p. 399.

40. Karageorghis 1975, p. 840.

41. G. Argout 1975, p. 139.

42. The Temple of Zeus at Salamis was also the focal point, in this case of the Agora. It approach was flanked by two colonnades, each 217 meters long.

43. H.C. Butler 1910, pp. 336 ff.

44. L. Borchardt 1903, p. 74, Abb. 2.

45. C.H. Krencker and W. Zschietzschmann 1938, p. 9.

46. R. Scranton 1967, p. 23.

47. Some 33% of the Roman temples in Syria are distyle in antis.

48. Some 75% of the temples in the Roman east with published plans which indicate the position of the temple within a specific area show prostyle rather than distyle in antis.

NOTES: Chapter 8

1. These descriptions are drawn from the forthcoming typology of the Eastern Fine Wares by Dr. John Hayes of the Royal Ontario Museum. They are currently in press as part of the *Enciclopedia dell' Arte Antica*. Further discussion and bibliography will be found there. We thank Dr. Hayes for providing this information before publication; it has immeasurably increase the clarity and value of the present report.

2. See for example Johns 1971.

3. For this cistern see Robert Scranton 1967, pp. 20, 62: called Cistern 2.

4. For a discussion and analysis of the local Kourion clay, see Young and Young, 1955, pp. 155-186.

5. The two fragments are nos. G12 and G13, to be published by Oliver. Further studies are now being conducted at the Universtiy of Arizona anthropology laboratories. Young and Young cite aluminum silicate clay "stained with ferric oxide" and "probably derived from the weathering of basic igneous rocks such as those of the gabbro clan."

6. On the dedicatory inscription see Lane 1983, pp. 242-244.

NOTES: Chapter 9

1. For an illustration and discussion of Laconian, Sicilian and Corinthian tiles see Lawrence 1967, Fig. 58, p. 108. My thanks to Dr. Eugene Lane of the Department of Classical Studies University of Missouri-Columbia, for generously providing me with epigraphical assistance, and to Dr. Barbara Barletta for her welcome advice in preparing the manuscript. My special gratitude goes to Dr. David Soren for his continued assistance.

2. Scranton 1967, pp. 5-6, pointed out the existence of two types of pan tiles and two types of cover tiles, and a few of their characteristics. He makes no mention of the inscriptions which survive on some of the tiles, nor does Mitford in *The Inscriptions of Kourion.*

3. For a more thorough treatment of this problem see T. Hodge 1960, pp. 60-73.

4. Bechtel 1964.

5. Neumann 1979, p. 214.

6. Gardthausen 1913, pl. 1.

Bibliography

Adelman, C. M.

1976   "Cypro-Geometric Pottery: Refinements in Classification,"
        Studies in Mediterranean Archaeology XLVII, Göteborg.

Adiovasio, J. M. et al

1975   "Prehistoric and Historic Settlement Patterns in Western
        Cyprus," *World Archaeology* V:6, no. 3 pp. 339-364.

1978   "Prehistoric and Historic Settlement Patterns in Western
        Cyprus: an Overview," *Report of the Department of
        Antiquities of Cyprus*, pp. 39-57.

Albright, W.F.

1957   "The High Place in Ancient Palestine," *Vetus Testamentum*
        Supp. 4, pp. 242-258.

Al-Radi

1983   "Philamoudhi Vounari: A Sanctuary Site in Cyprus," *Studies
        in Mediterranean Archaeology* LXV, Göteborg.

Ambraseys, N. N.

1965   *The Seismic History of Cyprus* (University of London).

Anderson, J. K.

1954   "Excavations on the Kofina Ridge, Chios," *Annual of the
        British School at Athens XLIX*, pp. 123-182.

Argout, G.

1975   "Le Temple de Zeus à Salamine," *Report of the
        Department of Antiquities of Cyprus* pp. 122-141.

Barker, Philip

1977   *Techniques of Archaeological Excavation* (New York:
        Universe Books).

321

Bate, D. M. A.

1918   "On a New Genus of Extinct Muscardine Rodent from the Balearic Islands," *Proceedings of the Zoological Society of London.* pp. 209-22.

Bechtel, F.

1964   *Historische•Personennamen des Griechischen bis zur Kaiserzeit* Halle (Nachdruck Hildesheim).

Benson, J. L.

1972   *Bamboula at Kition: The Necropolis and Small Finds.* Philadelphia (University of Pennsylvania Press).

1973   The Necropolis of Kaloriziki," *Studies in Mediterranean Archaeology* XXXVI, Göteborg.

Bikai, Patricia M.

1978   *The Pottery of Tyre.* Warminster (Ares and Phillips).

Birmingham, J.

1963   "The Chronology of some Early and Middle Iron Age Cypriot Sites," *American Journal of Archaeology.* p. 67.

Blakely, Jeffery A. and Toombs, Lawrence E.

1980   *The Tell el Hesi Field Manual.* Cambridge, Mass, (American Schools of Oriental Research).

Boethius, Axel and Ward-Perkins, J. B.

1970   *Etruscan and Roman Architecture.* Baltimore (Pelican).

Borchardt, L.

1903   "Der Augustus Tempel auf Philae," *Jahrbuch der Deutsches Archealogisches Instituts* 18 plate 5.

Brown, B.

1926   "Is this the Earliest Known Fossil Collected by Man?" *Natural History* XXVI/5. p. 535.

Brünnow, R.E. and Domascewski, A.v.,

1904   *Die Provinica Arabia. Erster Band, Die Römerstrasse von Madeba über Petra and Odruh bis El-'Akaba.* Strassburg (Teubner).

Buitron, Diana

1979   "The Archaic Precinct at the Sanctuary of Apollo Hylates, Kourion" *Report of the Department of Antiquities of Cyprus* pp. 316-320.

1980   "The Cult of the God at Kourion" *Walters Art Gallery Bulletin* Vol. 33, No. 3, pp. 1-4.

1981   "Cyprus Excavations" *Walters Art Gallery Bulletin* Vol. 34, No. 3, p. 3.

1982   "The Archaic Precinct at Kourion: 1981 Excavations" *Report of the Department of Antiquities of Cyprus* pp. 144-147.

1982   "Excavations at the Sanctuary of Apollo" *Walters Art Gallery Bulletin* Vol. 35 No. 6, p. 1.

1984   "Terracotta Figurine Deposit Unearthed" *American School of Oriental Research Newsletter* Vol. 35 No. 4, pp. 1-2.

Buitron, Diana and Soren, David

1978   "Excavations at Kourion" *Annual Report of the Director of the Department of Antiquities* p. 41.

1979   "Missouri in Cyprus" *Muse* 13, pp. 22-31.

Butler, H.C.,

1916   *Publications of Princeton University Archaeological Excavations to Syria in 1904-1905 and 1909; Division II, Ancient Architecture in Syria; Section A, Southern Syria;* Part 6: Si (Seeia). Leyden (Brill) p. 388, illustration 336.

Catling, H. W.

1972   "An Early Byzantine Pottery Factory at Dhiorios in Cyprus," *Levant* IV, pp. 1-82.

Catling, H. W. and Dikigoropoulos, A. I.

1970   "The Kornos Cave: An Early Byzantine Site in Cyprus,"
Levant II, pp. 37-62.

Cesnola, L. P. di

1877   *Cyprus: Its Ancient Cities, Tombs and Temples.* London
(John Murray).

1885-1903 *Atlas of the Cesnola Collection in the Metropolitan
Museum of New York.* New York (Metropolitan Museum).

Christensen, A. P., and Johansen, C. F.

1971   *Hama, Fouilles et Recherches 1931-1938, III:2. Les poteries
hellenistiques et les terre sigilles orientales.* Copenhagen
(Nationalmuseets Skrifter, VIII).

Christodoulou, A.

1969   "A Cypro-Classical Tomb at Ayia Marina (Skyllouras)."
Report of the Department of Antiquities of Cyprus pp.
59-64 Figs. 1-3 Pl. XV.

Christou, D.

1978   "Amathus Tomb 151," *Report of the Department of
Antiquities of Cyprus* pp. 132-147.

Cox, Dorothy H.

1959   *Coins from the Excavations at Curium 1932-1953* New York
(American Numismatic Society).

Crowfoot, J.W., Crowfoot, G. M., and Kenyon, K. M.

1957   *The Objects from Samaria*, Vol. 3 of *Samaria-Sebaste.*
London (Palestine Exploration Fund).

Demetropoulos, A.

1970   "Marine Molluscs, Land Snails, etc." Appendix VI in V.
Karageorghis, *Excavations in the Necropolis of Salamis*
4/II pp. 299-305 Figs. 1-2.

1973   "Molluscs and Crustacea from Salamis," Appendix IX in V.
Karageorghis, *Excavations in the Necropolis of Salamis*
5/III. pp. 270-27. Pl. LIII.

1977   "Two Shells from Meniko-'Litharkes.'" Appendix III in V. Karageorghis, *Two Cypriote Sanctuaries of the end of the Cypro-Archaic Period*, p. 81. Pl. XXVIII. Rome (Consiglio Nazionale delle Richerche)

Deneauve, Jean

1969   *Lampes de Carthage*. Paris (Centre National de la recherche scientifique).

Deshayes, J.

1965   "La Necropole de Ktima," *Institut Francais d'archyélogie de Beyrouth, Bibliotheque archeologique et histoire.* Tome LXXV. Paris (Librairie Orientalist Paul Guenther).

de Vaux, R.

1954   "Fouilles au Khirbet Qumrân. Rapport préliminaire sur la Deuxiéme campagne," *Revue Biblique* pp. 206-236.

Dever, William G.

1973   "Two Approaches to Archaeological Method--the Architectural and the Stratigraphic," *Eretz-Israel* 11, pp. 1-8.

Dever, William G. and Lance. H. Darrell

1978   *A Manual of Field Excavation*. New York (Hebrew-Union College-Jewish Institute of Religion).

Diederichs, C.

1980   "Céramiques hellénistiques romaines et byzantines," *Salamine de Chypre* IX Paris (E. de Boccord).

Dietrich, Bernard

1978   "Some Evidence from Cyprus of Apolline Cult," *Rheinisches Museum für Philologie* 121 No. 1 pp. 1-18.

Dray, E., Taylor, B. A. and du Plat, J.

1949   "Tsambres and Aphendrika, Two Classical and Hellenistic Cemeteries in Cyprus" *Report of the Department of Antiquities of Cyprus*, 1937-1939, pp. 24-123.

Gardthausen, V.

1913   *Griechische Palaeographie II.* Leipzig (Von Veit).

Gaskel, Alfred S.

1969   *Architectural Drawing.* Minneapolis (ADG).

Gjerstad, E.

1937   "Finds and Results of the Excavations in Cyprus
       1927-1931" *The Swedish Cyprus Expedition* Vol. III.
       Stockholm (The Swedish Cyprus Expedition).

1948   "The Cypro-Geometric, Cypro-Archaic and Cypro-Classical
       Periods," *The Swedish Cyprus Expedition* Vol. IV Part 2.

1960   "Pottery Types, Cypro-Geometric to Cypro-Classical,"
       Opuscula Atheniensia III< Lund (Svenka Institutet I Athen)
       pp. 102-122.

1977   *Greek Geometric and Archaic Pottery Found in Cyprus.*
       Stockholm (The Swedish Cyprus Expedition).

Glueck, Nelson

1965   *Deities and Dolphins.* New York (Farrar, Strauss and
       Giroux) pp. 64-69.

Goldman, Hetty

1950   *Excavations at Gözlü Kule, Tarsus I The Hellenistic and
       Roman Periods Section VI*: FF Jones "The Pottery",
       Princeton.

Hadidi, A.

1970   "The Pottery from the Roman Forum at Amman," *Annual
       of the Department of Antiquities Jordan* XV, pp. 11-15.

Hadjisavvas, S.

1977   The Archaeological Survey of Paphos," *Report of the
       Department of Antiquities of Cyprus*, pp. 222-231.

1978   "Politiko 'Kouphos'--An Archaic Cemetery," *Report of the
       Department of Antiquities of Cyprus*, pp. 125-131.

Hammond, P.C.

1959   "The Nabataean Bitumen Industry at the Dead Sea," *The Biblical Archaeologist* XXII pp. 40-48.

Harris, Edward C.

1975   "The Stratigraphic Sequence: A Question of Time." *World Archaeology* 7 pp. 109-121.

Hayes, J. W.

1967   "Cypriot Sigillata," *Report of the Department of Antiquities of Cyprus* (Nicosia) pp. 65-77.

1972   *Late Roman Pottery.* London (The British School at Rome).

1976   *Roman Pottery in the Royal Ontario Museum.* Toronto (Royal Ontario Museum).

1977   "Early Roman Wares from the House of Dionysos, Paphos," *Rei Cretariae Romanae Fautorum Acta XVII/XVIII*, pp. 96-108.

1980   *A Supplement to Late Roman Pottery.* London (British School at Rome).

Hellström, P.

1965   *Labraunda II, Part I, Pottery of Classical and Later Date, Terracotta Lamps and Glass.* Lund.

Heywood, H. C.

1982   "The Archaeological Remains of the Akrotiri Peninsula," in Swiny, H. W. 1982: pp. 162-175.

Hill, Sir George

1949   *A History of Cyprus.* Cambridge (University Press).

Hodge, T.

1960   *The Woodwork of Greek Roofs.* Cambridge (University Press).

Hoffmann, Herbert

1973   *Corpus Vasorum Antiquorum*; Fascicule 1, Museum of Fine Arts, Boston *Attic Black Figured Amphorae*. Mainz (Philipp von Zabern).

Jaussen, A.J. and Savignac, M.R.

1909   *Mission Archeologique en Arabie*, 2 Vols. Paris (Leroux).

Jeffery, George

1928   "Notes on the Doric Style of Architecture," *Archaelogia* 78 pp. 37-60.

Johns, Catherine

1971   *Arretine and Samian Pottery*. London (British Museum).

Karageorghis, Vassos

1969   *Salamis*. New York (McGraw-Hill).

1969   *The Ancient Civilization of Cyprus*, Geneva (Nagel).

1971   "Chronique de fouilles et découvertes archéologiques à Chypre en 1970." *Bulletin de correpondance Hellenique* 95 p. 399.

1972   "Two Built Tombs at Patraki, Cyprus," *Report of the Department of Antiquities of Cyprus*, pp. 161-180.

1973   *Excavations in the Necropolis of Salamis*, III. Nicosia.

1975   "Chronique de fouilles et découvertes archéologiques à Chypre en 1974." *Bulletin de correspondance Hellenique* 99 p. 840.

1982   "Black Slip grooved ware from Cyprus," *Report of the Department of Antiquities of Cyprus*.

1983   *Palaepaphos-Skales, An Iron Age Cemetery in Cyprus*. Konstanz.

Kenyon, Kathleen (Dame)

1957   "Pottery: Hellenistic and Later Roman Wares, Stratified Groups," in Crowfoot et al. 1957. pp. 288-306.

1961   *Beginning in Archaeology*. New York (Praeger).

Knipowitsch, F.N.

1929   *Untersuchungen zur Keramik römischer Zeit aus den Griechenstädten an der Nordkuste des Schwarzen Meeres I, Die Keramik römischer Zeit aus Olbia in des Sammlung der Ermitage.* Frankfurt (Materialen zur römisch-germanischen Keramik 4).

Kohl, H.

1910   *Kasr Firaun in Petra.* Leipzig (J.C. Hinrichs).

Kraeling, C.H.

1938   *Gerasa: City of the Decapolis.* Baltimore (J.H. Furst).

Krencker, C.H. and Zschietzschmann, W.

1938   "Römische Tempel in Syrien," *Denkmäler Antikes Architektur*, Band 5 Berlin (Walter de Gruyter) pp. 9, 25, 205, 214.

Lance, H. Darrell

1967   *Excavation Manual for Area Supervisors.* (Privately Circulated).

Lane, Eugene

1983   "A New Fragment of the Dedicatory Inscription of the Temple of Apollo Hylates," *Report of the Department of Antiquities of Cyprus* pp. 242-244.

Lapp, P. W.

1961   *Palestinian Ceramic Chronology: 200 B.C.- A.D. 70.* New Haven (American Schools of Oriental Research).

Last, J. S.

1975   "Kourion: The Ancient Water Supply," *Proceedings of the American Philosophical Society* 119, Philadelphia, (American Philosophical Society), pp. 39-72.

Last, Joseph and Edwards, Roger

1975   "Kourion: The Ancient Water Supply," *Proceedings of the American Philosophical Society*, Vol. 119, No. 1 pp. 39-72.

Lawrence, A.W.

1967   *Greek Architecture.* Baltimore (Penguin).

Loeschcke, S.

1909   "Keramische Funde in Haltern", *Mitteilungen des Altertumskommission für Westfalen.* 5 pp. 101-322.

1912   "Die Arbeiten zu Pergamon 1910-1911, V. Sigillata--Topfereien in Tschandarli," *Mitteilungen des Kaiserlich Deutschen Archäologischen Instituts, Athenische Abteilung* XXXVII, pp. 344-407.

McFadden, Elizabeth

1971   *The Glitter and the Gold.* New York (Dial Press).

McFadden, George H.

1938   "The Sanctuary of Apollo," *University of Pennsylvania Museum Bulletin* 7, 2 pp. 10-17.

1940   "Sanctuary of Apollo at Kourion," *University of Pennsylvania Museum Bulletin* 8, 4 pp. 22-28.

1946   "A Tomb of the Necropolis of Ayios Ermoyenis at Kourion," *American Journal of Archaeology* 50 pp. 449-489.

1950   "Kourion-The Apollo Baths," *University of Pennsylvania Museum Bulletin* 14, 4 pp. 14-26.

1951   "Cyprus," *American Journal of Archaeology* 55 pp. 167-169.

1952   "Cyprus 1950-1951" *American Journal of Archaeology* 56 pp. 128-129.

1952   "1100 Years of the Worship of Apollo of the Woodlands" *Illustrated London News* 1 30 pp. 588-590.

Mitford, Terence

1971   *The Inscriptions of Kourion.* Philadelphia (American Philosophical Society).

Mlynarczyk, Tolanta

1980   "The Paphian Sanctuary of Apollo Hylates," *Report of the Department of Antiquities of Cyprus* pp. 239-252.

Munsell Soil Color Charts

1954   Baltimore (Munsell Color Company).

Murray, A.S.

1900   *Excavation in Cyprus.* London (British Museum).

Myres, John L.

1914   *Handbook of the Cesnola Collection of Antiquities from Cyprus.* New York (Metropolitan Museum of Art.

Negev, A.

1974   "Nabataean Capitals in the Towns of the Negev," *Israel Exploration Journal* p. 153f.

Neumann, G.

1979   "Kyprische Personenamen mit Suffix -U-," *Report of the Department of Antiquities of Cyprus* pp. 214-217.

Nicolaou, I.

1973   Ιερου Αφροδιτης Μορφου *Report of the Department of Antiquities of Cyprus*, pp. 14-28.

1982   "Kourion City: The Epigraphic Evidence," in Swiny, H. W. 1982 pp. 93-97.

Nobis, G.

1977   "Tierreste aus Tamassos auf Zypern," *Acta Praehistorica et Archaeologica* 7/8 (1976/77) pp. 271-300.

Oliver, A., Jr.

1982   "Kourion: Ayios Ermoyenis Cemetery," in Swiny, H. W. 1982 pp. 140-145.

Oswald, F. and Pryce, T. D.

1966   *An Introduction to the Study of Terra Sigillata.* Reprint of the 1920 edition. London (Longmans).

Oxé, August and Comfort, Howard

1968   *Corpus Vasorum Arretinorum.* Bonn (Rudolf Habelt).

Pace, Eric

1984   "Scientists Recast Histories of the Ancient Civilizations,"
    New York Times, p. 20E. August 19.

Purcell, H. D.

1968   *Cyprus.* New York (Praeger).

Quilichi, L.

1971   "Lo scavo all'interno della cinta urbana, prima relazione,"
    in Karageorghis, Vassos et al. *Studi Cypriote e Rapporte*
    di Scavo: I. (Rome Istituto per gli Studi Micenei ed
    Egeo-Anatolici).

Reese, D.S.

    "The Late Bronze and Geometric Shells from Kition,
    Cyprus." In V. Karageorghis, *Excavations at Kition* V,
    forthcoming.

    "Marine Shells from the Sanctuary of Demeter and Kore at
    Corinth, Greece." Unpublished manuscript to appear in
    excavation report by N. Bookidis.

Robertson, D.S

1969   *Greek and Roman Architecture.* Cambridge (University
    Press).

1974   *Greek and Roman Architecture.* Cambridge (University
    Press).

Robinson, H. S.

1959   "Pottery of the Roman Period," *The Athenian Agora* V.
    Princeton (The American School of Classical Studies at
    Athens).

Rocchetti, L.

1978   *Le tombe dei periodi Geometrico ed Arcaico della necropli*
    a mare di Ayia Irini "Paleokastro". Rome (Biblioteca di
    Antichita Cipriote).

Ronczewski, K.

1927   "Les chapiteaux Corinthiens et variés du Musée
        Gréco-Romain d'Alexandrie," *Bulletin de la Societé
        Archeólogique d'Alexandrie*, Supp Fasc. 22 pp.
        8-28.Schafer, J.

1962   "Terra Sigillata aus Pergamon," *Archäologischer Anzeiger*,
        Deutschen Archaologischen Instituts, Spalte 777-802.

Schlumberger, D.

1933   "Les formes anciennes du chapiteau Corinthien en Syrie,
        en Palestine, et en Arabie," *Syria* XIV pls. XIV and
        XXXIV, and p. 307.

Scranton, Robert

1967   "The Sanctuary of Apollo-Hylates at Kourion." *Proceedings
        of the American Philosophical Society* Vol. 57.

Seger, Joe D.

1972   *Handbook for Field Operations*. (Privately Circulated).

Shackleton, N.J.

1969   "Preliminary Observations on the Marine Shells." Appendix
        I in T.W. Jacobsen, "Excavations at Porto Cheli and
        Vicinity, Preliminary Report, II. The Franchthi Cave,
        1967-1968." *Hesperia* 38 pp. 379-80.

Shaw, J.W.

1980   "Excavations at Kommos (Crete) during 1979." *Hesperia* 49
        pp. 207-250.

Sjöqvist, E.

1933   "Die Kultgeschicte einer Cyprischen Temenos," *Archiv Für
        Religionswissenschaft* 30 pp. 308-359.

Soren, David

1979   "The Temple of Apollo at the Sanctuary of Apollo." *Report
        of the Department of Antiquities of Cyprus* pp. 321-327.

1983   "Some New Ideas on Dating and Rebuilding the Temple of
        Apollo Hylates at Kourion." *Report of the Department of
        Antiquities of Cyprus* pp. 232-244.

Soren, David and Lane, Eugene

1981   "New Ideas about the Destruction of Paphos," *Report of the Department of Antiquities of Cyprus.* pp. 178-182.

Soren, David and Sanders, G.

1984   "The Mysterious Rock-cut Channels of Kourion," *Report of the Department of Antiquities of Cyprus.* pp. 285-293.

Sparks, B.A. and Talcott, L.

1970   *The Athenian Agora XII: Black and Plain Pottery of the 6th, 5th, and 4th Centuries B.C..* Princeton (University Press).

Spyridakis, Constantinos

1974   *A Brief History of Cyprus.* Nicosia (Zavallis).

Stillwell, Richard

1961   "Kourion: The Theater," *Proceedings of the American Philosophical Society,* 105, No. 1, pp. 37-78.

1976   "Amathus" et al in the *Princeton Encyclopedia of Classical Sites.* Princeton (University Press).

Strange, James F.

1972   *Khirbet Shema' Manual for Area Supervisors.* (Privately Circulated).

Swiny, H. W., ed.

1982   *An Archaeological Guide to the Ancient Kourion Area and the Akrotiri Peninsula.* Cyprus (Department of Antiquities).

Swiny, S.

1982   "Standing Stones: Perforated Monoliths," in Swiny, H.W. 1982, pp. 151-152.

Taylor, J. du Plat

1951   "An Early Iron Age Tomb-Group from 'Anavrysi' Risokarpaso," *Report of the Department of Antiquities of Cyprus,* 1937- 1939, pp. 14-21.

1958   "Roman Tombs at 'Kambi', Vasa," *Report of the Department of Antiquities of Cyprus*, pp. 10-45.

1959   The Cypriot and Syrian Pottery from Al-Mina, Syria, *Iraq* 21.

1980   "Excavation at Ayios Philon, the Ancient Carpasia. Part I. The Classical to Roman Periods," *Report of the Department of Antiquities of Cyprus* pp. 152-211.

Taylor, J. du Plat and Megaw, A.H.S

1968   *Cyprus.* New York (Praeger).

1981   "Excavations at Ayios Philon, the Ancient Carpasia. Part II. The Early Christian Buildings," *Report of the Department of Antiquities of Cyprus*, pp. 209-250.

Thompson, Homer A.

1934   "Two Centuries of Hellenistic Pottery," *Hesperia* III pp. 311-480.

Tolle-Kastenbein

1974   "Das Kastro Tigani," *Samos* XIV, Bonn (Deutsches Archaologisches Institut).

Toombs, Lawerence E.

        Pella Field Manual. (Privately Circulated).

Vermeule, Cornelius

1979   "An Imperial Commemorative Monument Never Finished: A Possible Memorial of Trajan's Eastern 'Conquests,' at Salamis on Cyprus," *Studies Presented in Memory of Porphyrios Dikaios* Nicosia pp. 189-193.

Vessberg, O., and Westholm, A.

1956   "The Hellenistic and Roman Periods in Cyprus," *The Swedish Cyprus Expedition* Vol. IV Part 3. Stockholm (The Swedish Cyprus Expedition).

Walker, Anita

1971   *Idalion Field Guide.* (Privately Circulated).

Walters, H. B.

1900   "Excavations at Curium," in Murray A. S., Smith, A. H.,
        and Walters, H. B., *Excavations in Cyprus*, London (British
        Museum), pp. 57-86.

Wentworth, C.K.

1922   "A Scale and Class Terms for Clastic Sediments," *Journal
        of Geology* 30. pp. 378-381.

Westholm, A.

1935   "Amathus, the Necropolis," *Swedish Cyprus Expedition.*
        Stockholm (Victor Pettersons) pp. 1-141.

Wheeler, R.E. Mortimer, (Sir)

1954   *Archaeology from the Earth.* Oxford (Oxford University
        Press).

Williams, C. K.

1969   "Excavations at Corinth, 1968," *Hesperia* 38 pp. 36-63.

Williams, C. K., II and Zervos, O. H.

1983   "Corinth 1982: East of the Theater," *Hesperia* 52 pp. 1-47.

Wright, G. Ernest

1965   *Shechem: The Biography of a Biblical City.* London
        (Duckworth).

Wright, G.R.H.

1961   "Petra-The Arched Gate, 1959-60," *Palestine Exploration
        Quarterly* pp. 124-135.

1969   "A Nabataean Capital in the Salamis Gymnasium and its
        Possible Background," *First International Congress of
        Cypriote Studies* Vol. A, 1972 pp. 175-178.

Young, John and Suzanne

1955   *Terracotta Figures from Kourion in Cyprus.* Philadelphia
        (University of Pennsylvania Museum Monographs).

Zayadin, F.

1966   "Early Hellenistic Pottery from the Theater Excavations at Samaria," *Annual of the Department of Antiquities of Jordan* XI, pp. 53-64.

Excavations at Samaria," *Annual of the Department of Antiquities of Jordan* XI, pp. 53-64.

Index